"COMPELLING, HEARTFELT . . . biography."

"FASCINATING . . . allows us to feel the intensity of the fire that ignited Serling." —*Orange County Register*

"WORTHY alone as a volume of cultural history." —*Gannett News Service*

"AN ABSORBING, HONEST, SYMPATHETIC, yet balanced appraisal of one of television's giants." —*The Notebook*

"SHOCKING, FASCINATING . . . Sander gives a sympathetic, informative account of Serling's rise and fall." —*Doylestown Patriot*

"A revealing portrait of an enigmatic man." —*Dayton Daily News*

"Thoroughly researched . . . Sander vividly depicts the heady early days of live TV. . . . The story of Serling's career doubles as a history of the television industry itself." —*Booklist*

"Sympathetic and illuminating." —*Science Fiction Chronicle*

"A fascinating look at a man who was able to use television at its finest as a direct medium to the American consciousness—but who paid the price of his own integrity after passing his prime." —*Anniston Star*

GORDON F. SANDER is a cultural journalist and historian who has written for many publications, including the *New York Times*, *GQ*, and the *International Herald Tribune*. He lives in New York City, where he is a member of the Humanities faculty of Marymount Manhattan College.

SERLING

THE RISE AND TWILIGHT OF TELEVISION'S LAST ANGRY MAN

GORDON F. SANDER

A PLUME BOOK

PLUME
Published by the Penguin Group
Penguin Books USA Inc., 375 Hudson Street,
New York, New York 10014, U.S.A.
Penguin Books Ltd, 27 Wrights Lane,
London W8 5TZ, England
Penguin Books Australia Ltd, Ringwood,
Victoria, Australia
Penguin Books Canada Ltd, 10 Alcorn Avenue,
Toronto, Ontario, Canada M4V 3B2
Penguin Books (N.Z.) Ltd, 182–190 Wairau Road,
Auckland 10, New Zealand

Penguin Books Ltd, Registered Offices:
Harmondsworth, Middlesex, England

Published by Plume, an imprint of Dutton Signet,
a division of Penguin Books USA Inc.
Previously published in a Dutton edition.

First Plume Printing, January, 1994
10 9 8 7 6 5 4 3 2 1

LIBRARY OF CONGRESS CATALOGING-IN-PUBLICATION DATA:
Sander, Gordon F.
    Serling : the rise and twilight of television's last angry man / Gordon F. Sander.
        p. cm.
    Includes bibliographical references and index.
    ISBN 0-452-27038-3
    1. Serling, Rod, 1924–1975—Biography. 2. Authors, American—20th century—Biography.
3. Television personalities—United States—Biography. 4. Twilight Zone (Television program)
I. Title.
[PS3537.E654Z86   1994]
813'.54—dc20
[B]   93-34464
                                                                    CIP

Printed in the United States of America

BOOKS ARE AVAILABLE AT QUANTITY DISCOUNTS WHEN USED TO PROMOTE PRODUCTS OR SERVICES.
FOR INFORMATION PLEASE WRITE TO PREMIUM MARKETING DIVISION, PENGUIN BOOKS USA INC., 375
HUDSON STREET, NEW YORK, NEW YORK 10014.

To my mother, Dorrit,
and to the memory of my father,
Lt. Col. Kurt Sander

CONTENTS

ACKNOWLEDGMENTS

The researching and writing of this biography has been something of an odyssey. I could not have undertaken such a task, nor could I have completed it, without the friendship, support, and assistance of many indeed.

I am grateful first and foremost to Serling himself for having inspired me to write this volume. I met Serling only once, when I was a student at Cornell and he was teaching at Ithaca College; he was well into his premature twilight. I had absolutely no idea then that I would be his biographer. The memory of that encounter is both vivid and warm.

Although I have tried to write this book as if Serling himself were looking over my shoulder—sympathetically, but objectively—this is not an authorized biography, nor would I want it to be. Nevertheless, I have done my best to obtain the approval of the Serling estate, which is presided over by his widow. I met Carol Serling in 1980, when I first contemplated writing this book; then again, in 1986, when I was farther along; and again in 1988. On each occasion she was at once supportive and skittish. By the third meeting, it had become clear that Mrs. Serling would never allow a biography over which she did not exercise creative control, a caveat I found unacceptable; and I decided to forge ahead on my own, with the aid of the leads I had already established. Fortunately, Mrs. Serling's approval was not essential, and the absence of it actually proved a blessing in disguise by catalyzing the bloodhound in me. All told, I located and interviewed over 220 friends, relatives, acquaintances, and associates of Serling in seventeen states—including his former maid, his ex-bookkeeper, and his former Dictaphone repairman. I spent seven months on the road, including extended sojourns in upstate New York, where Serling was raised; southwest Ohio, where Serling attended college and began his TV-writing career; Southern California, where he lived for most of the latter part of his life; and Wisconsin, where his papers are located, and where I and my chief assistant, Jason Davids Scott, examined over ten thousand documents. Fortunately, Serling left an excellent paper trail to follow.

In the course of my research, I interviewed seven of Serling's extant first cousins. Saydelle Agranovitch and Guerson Solomon of New London, Connecticut, and Lou and Leona Kosoff of Pompano Beach, Florida, were especially helpful in drawing a picture of Serling's parents and early family background as well as of the young Rod Serling. I am also obliged to Inez Herr of Syracuse, Claire Phillips of Houston, and the late Frank Hammer of Ithaca for their cooperation.

To the best of my knowledge, Mark Olshaker, a protégé of Serling, now a leading independent filmmaker, is the only person Serling authorized to write his biography. Olshaker himself was too distraught by Serling's untimely death in 1975 to proceed with the project. Instead, he turned over his files to me. I am very grateful for Mark's blessing and cooperation. For the past two years, Mark has been one of my most reliable sounding boards for this project, as well as a dear friend. He is one of the true godfathers of this book. So are the other people whom I consider the country's leading Serling scholars: Marc Scott Zicree, the author of *The Twilight Zone Companion*, the definitive book on *The Twilight Zone*, who plugged up numerous blank spaces; Ron Simon, senior curator for television at the Museum of Television and Radio and curator of the definitive exhibit and catalogue raisonné of Serling, who was my guide to the museum's substantial Serling holdings and who also read the manuscript; William Boddy, adjunct professor of television history in New York University's Department of Cinema Studies, who provided me with both valuable feedback and a copy of his authoritative dissertation on the Serling years in television history; and Arlen Schumer, author and designer of *Visions from the Twilight Zone*, the definitive art book on *The Twilight Zone*, who furnished useful facts, insights, photos, and encouragement, as well as excellent coffee, not necessarily in that order.

Norman Corwin, the great radio dramatist of the 1930s, and Serling's friend and beau ideal, is also high on my own list of patron saints. My conversations with Norman, perhaps the most poetic speaker I have ever encountered, were one of the highlights of this process; they helped me understand why he was such an inspiration to Serling. I would also like to thank Corwin's biographer, Ray Bannerman, for introducing me to Corwin and the lost world he helped to create.

Other witnesses, experts, and organizations were outstandingly helpful at individual stages of my work. I am deeply appreciative of the hospitality and assistance provided by the Binghamton-based Rod Serling Memorial Foundation in retracing Serling's hometown roots during the early stages of my research. Helen Foley, the president of the foundation, and archivists Jules Levitt and Michael Pipher deserve especial praise in this regard.

So do Serling's close hometown friends, Pat Begasse, Herbert Denton, Julius Golden, and Sue Fischer Hirsch; together, they helped me understand why Serling was so attached to, if not obsessed with, his hometown, as well as how he felt about his Judaism. Ann Goodman, of Binghamton, who was a kind of surrogate aunt to Serling throughout his life, was also of immense help. So was Serling's fellow counselor at Camp Oxford, Norman Miller.

I am also thankful to fellow Binghamtonians and paratroopers Vern Hartung and Jerry Shea for their help with reconstructing Serling's service as a combat parachutist in World War II, the source of much of Serling's drama—and "anger"—and for sponsoring my attendance at a thunderous reunion of the 511th Parachute Infantry Regiment in Valley Forge, Pennsylvania. I continue as a dues-paying member of the 511th Parachute Infantry Association. I am especially grateful to Trooper Richard Loughrin, Serling's friend and the 511th's regimental historian, who provided me with a wealth of information and photos about the "Angels'"—and Serling's—progress across the Southwest Pacific, including rare regimental and divisional histories.

The mother lode of Serling archival material—eighty boxes worth—resides at the University of Wisconsin at Madison under the trusty eye of the State Historical Society. Harry Miller is the chief archivist in charge there and was a great help during my and Jason's various sojourns there. He and his staff have my deepest thanks. So do a number of other librarians and archivists: the staff at the University of California at Los Angeles Department of Special Collections, where a smaller collection of Serling material is housed; Catherine Henry at the Broadcast Pioneers Library in Washington;

Acknowledgments

Leslie Slocumb, at the sadly now-defunct Television Information Office in New York City; Jim Poteat at the library annex of the Museum of Television and Radio; and Nina Myatt, the curator of the Antiochiana collection at Serling's alma mater, Antioch College, and the definitive Serling clippings file. I have fond memories of watching a December blizzard from Nina's window in Yellow Springs while perusing Serling's first published short story in an old *Antiochan*.

A number of other individuals were also extremely helpful in illuminating the collegiate Serling: Don Scobel, Serling's freshman roommate; Lillian Blake and Alan Zachary, Serling's supervisor and colleague, respectively, during his first crucial freshman field term at WNYC in New York; Barbara Agranoff, his neighbor in Trailertown; and Arthur and Sara Lithgow, who acted in Serling's Antiochan radio plays, as well as his first televised play in Dayton, before going on to bigger things.

In Cincinnati, where Serling worked as a staff writer at WLW-AM and began his rise as a television writer, I received notable assistance from Serling's colleagues at WLW, Charles Vaughan and Gene Walz, who provided crucial insight into the actual origins of "Patterns," the 1955 teleplay that made Serling a writer-star; Mary Wood, former radio-TV critic of the *Cincinnati Enquirer*; her successor, John Kieswetter, the current media writer for the same paper; Bill Myers, Serling's friend and former TV-writing student at the Cincinnati College of Music; and H. Michael Sanders, media historian and associate professor at the University of Cincinnati, the ultimate authority on Serling's formative Ohio period, who dispensed much-appreciated advice, videographical information, and hospitality.

I would like to offer my most profound thanks to the numerous veterans of New York live television and colleagues of Serling who contributed their mesmerizing recollections of "live" and of Serling. Writers Tad Mosel, Loring Mandel, and Gore Vidal; actors Richard Kiley, Kim Hunter, Leslie Nielsen, and Roddy McDowall; directors Arthur Penn, Delbert Mann, George Roy Hill, Fielder Cook, and Paul Bogart; and producers Felix Jackson and Martin Manulis were especially helpful in helping me conjure up the golden age of television drama. Matt Messina, who used to pound the video beat of the *New York Daily News* before becoming head of entertainment publicity for NBC, also provided key perspective, contacts, and encouragment here. So did then floor manager, now novelist Dominick Dunne, and then agent, now producer Jerome Hellman. Sincere thanks must also go to film director and Serling friend Robert Parrish, whose insight and anecdotes about both Serling and the film industry over the course of two lengthy interviews proved invaluable.

My knowledge of CBS, Serling's home network during the late fifties and early sixties, and of Serling's complicated relationship with the same was considerably furthered by my conversations with a number of top CBS executives, including emeritus CBS president Dr. Frank Stanton and former vice-presidents Mike Dann, Perry Lafferty, and the late Harry Ackerman, and Guy della-Cioppa. John Behrens and Ray Fiola at CBS provided essential videographic information. So did John Collins at NBC.

I was also fortunate to have the assistance of Virginia Cox, Serling's secretary during his *Playhouse 90* years, now a professor of English at the University of Wisconsin, who shed new light on the inner Serling. I am also grateful to Sonny Fox, a neighbor of Serling's during his Westport interregnum, and the producer of the 1982 PBS series *The Golden Age of Television* (and another figure from my own childhood video pantheon) for providing transcripts from the show, as well as a nostalgic and hilarious luncheon in Los Angeles.

My journey through Serling's *Twilight Zone* years was assisted by several score veterans of that landmark show, most of them now living in California. Those to whom I am most grateful in this regard are producer and key collaborator Buck Houghton; associate producer Del Reisman; director of photography George Clemens; casting director Ethel Wynant; directors Allan Reisner, Buzz Kulik, and Douglas Heyes (who between them directed over twenty episodes); writers George Clayton Johnson and Richard Matheson; actors Claude Akins, Martin Landau, William Shatner, Jack Warden, and Cliff Robertson, all of whom made multiple appearances on the show; and publicist Owen Comora. I would also like to thank Jonathan Winters, another actor on the show, for being as funny on the telephone as he is on TV. The same goes for Carol Burnett, another *Zone* voyager. I would also like to thank Lloyd Bridges, star of Serling's short-lived series, *The Loner*, for his time.

Other Serling friends, associates, regimental comrades, acquaintances, employees, and neighbors who graciously allowed me to interview them include, in alphabetical order: Cleveland Amory,

Acknowledgments

Ted Ashley, Dave Barnett, Bill Behan, Buzz Berger, Burt Berman, Dick Bogan, Louis Brandano, Harriet Burns, John Cannon, Marsha Cohen, Ruth Cohen, Peter Cott, Walter Cronkite, Vincent Daddiego, Carson Davidson, Betty Dellavan, Dorothy Dillingham, Lou Dorfman, James Doyle, Chester "Bud" Erion, Holly Falcon, Nancy Falcon, Jane Faulkner, Joseph Feinstein, Don Freeman, Roger Gaskill, Bob Gilbert, Wilma Gilmore, George Githers, Irving Goldman, Len Gorrian, Sybil Goldenberg, Jack Gould, Bert Granet, Constance Griffin, Robert Groh, Richard Grossman, George Grunbok, Ben Gettler, Kenneth Haan, John Haldi, Pat Haley, Esther Hanlon, Dr. Ed Hart, Earl Holliman, Jack Hunter, Judson Jerome, Robert Johnson, Bill Kaiser, Dave Kaufman, Marie Kenny, Lisa Kirk, Herbert Klein, Stanley Klein, Bernard Klionsky, Burton Koffman, Larry Kramer, Col. Edward H. Lahti, David Levy, Frank Lewis, Mrs. William Lindau, Saul and Phyllis Marmer, Bill Nimmo, Bob O'Brien, Maurice O'Brien, Patrick O'Neill, Mel Panett, Joe Pinkston, Anthony Quinn, Robert Redford, Joe Reis, Rudy Ruderman, Janice Rule, Al Schoeman, Barbara Schultz, Marvin Searchinger, Edie Seashore, Joe Short, Penny Singleton, Edward Snyder, Jonathan Spota, Dale Stevens, Lela Swift, Cy and Ilse Tebbets, Harriet Van Horne, Malvin Wald, Carolyn Watts, Max Wilk, Jason Wingreen, Robert Wise, James Woog, and Dean Worth. Several other helpful sources requested that they remain anonymous; they shall.

A number of other kind individuals sent me letters, often with unusual anecdotes or photos I would never have obtained elsewhere, in response to the score of author's queries I placed in publications around the country. This splendid group includes Craig Curtner, Dan Dougherty, Marianne Goldsmith, Benjamin Krepack, Eugene V. Lesner, Jane Pappidas, Von Pittman, Lynn A. Pitts, Bill Pugsley, Sandra Richards, and Wendy Jeanne Murray Zoba.

Portions of the manuscript were researched and written while I was a guest artist at the Risley Residential College of the Arts at Cornell University in 1987 and 1989. I am thankful for the many kindnesses shown me by the Risley staff during my stays there, as well as for the continuing advice and encouragment of my friends and instructors Laurence Moore and Michael Kammen of the Cornell History Department and James McConkey of the Cornell English Department. I am also grateful for the substantial support I have received from the staff of Marymount Manhattan College, which has been my academic home base for the past six years.

Acknowledgments

Marymounters Carol Camper, Bob Vorlicky, Elizabeth Martin, Henry Blanke, Sue Machlin are all on my honor roll.

I am also appreciative of the many kindnesses shown me during the winter and spring of 1989, when I was a guest of Guild Hall in East Hampton, and I finally began to write. Della and Oscar Weinberger, Adam Perle, and other Hamptonites became honorary godparents to this book during those long winter nights. I am also grateful to the staff of Guild Hall for their help. I trust they have closed the treehouse by now.

I am thankful for a small grant-in-aid from PEN.

I was blessed with a first-rate crew on this voyage.

My literary agent, Peter Ginsberg, president of Curtis Brown Associates, has my eternal thanks for getting us out of port, as well as for keeping us afloat. He is not only a devoted representative, but a good friend. The same goes for my stalwart attorney, the brilliant F. Robert Stein, of Pryor, Cashman, Sherman, and Flynn.

Jason Davids Scott was my aide-de-camp and chief research assistant for the last two years of the project. For typing the various drafts of the manuscript; for transcribing my interviews; for his own original insights into Serling's work, many of which are reflected in this book; for giving up his vacation to go to Madison; for helping to organize the videography and filmography; for myriad tasks performed with dispatch and panache, he will always have my deepest thanks.

I am also deeply indebted to Jason's successor, Cecilie Holter, who did outstanding work in completing the videography and other appendices, helping to make this the definitive sourcebook for Serling scholars. Her painstaking attention to detail and original perspectives are woven throughout the book. I am also indebted to the four college students who made a contribution to this work: Gabrielle Berberich, John Carey, Donna Pitterle, and Jennifer Spector. Gabrielle did superb work in tracking down and interviewing several difficult sources. John also has a special place in my hall of fame for hazardous duty—unfortunately I cannot be more specific.

I am indebted, too, to my dear friends and ace editors Jack Huberman and Kent Oswald, who read the entire manuscript through and helped out in numerous ways above and beyond the call of duty. Joe Meisel also has my thanks for his input on the manuscript. And thanks to Jonathan Newhouse for being one of the first to

Acknowledgments

believe. And gratis to Clay Tobias for providing the missing link.

I would like to thank my brother, Lee, for his indispensable interest, encouragement, and advice over the years. And how to thank John Silbersack? I am most fortunate in having found so intelligent and painstaking an editor at NAL/Dutton. There are numerous important points in this book that owe their sharper focus to his insight and perception. Thank you, John. Ditto to Patrice Silverstein for her superlative work on the manuscript itself.

And thank you, too, Jeanne Martinet, for helping bring the work into being. And thanks to Leigh A. Marcous-Devine for her critical care as I neared the finish line.

Another group of friends and relatives furnished me with other forms of welcome assistance, including leads, information, accommodations, meals, and strong sympathy and tea. This noble group includes Maurice Abelson, Diane Becker, Kari Bjelland, Gregory Catsos, Tony Chaskelson, Julianne Cho, Sean Considine, Carol and Jack Dorrian, Jeff Danneman, Don Davis, Steve Fadem, Stephen Farber, Sam Finkel, Mark Gatanas, Mel Green, Vicki and Ken Hoffman, Marc Kaplan, Elaine Kaufman, Jon Keller, Dr. Gary Kelman, Jeff Kroestler, Barbara Langlois, Michael Lindner, James McMamnon, Jane and John Marcham, Dr. George McCormack, Marion Meade, Dr. Martin Meisel, Peter Mikulas, Karen Nazor, James Pullis, Joel Saltzman, Kenny Sander, Hank Schlesinger, Sue Shapiro, Rie Streepy, Ildiko and Jay Trien, Sophia Valenti, Judy and Roger Widmann, Dina and Dr. Marcus Widmann, Barbara and Jay Wittenbaum, and the late, great Peter Berg.

And thanks to the late Mary Martin for that good-luck kiss in the lobby of L'Hermitage.

GFS
New York
August 15, 1991

PREFACE

In 1959, Gerald Green published a novel called *The Last Angry Man*. The novel, which was made into a powerful film starring Paul Muni, was a well-written but sentimental work that survives as a period piece of the late 1950s, when being angry was its own raison d'être—and the British and American theater were well-stocked with bright Angry Young Men.

Green's novel told the at once triumphant and tragic story of Samuel Abelman, a feisty, obstreperous old Jewish doctor who tends his dwindling urban practice with angry devotion, refusing his wife's entreaties to join the exodus to the suburbs, while conducting a one-man campaign against galoots and malefactors—the last angry man of a fast-changing Brooklyn. So unusual is Abelman that a television network decides to devote a television program to him, which he uses with relish to denounce the program's sponsor. Abelman is a doomed creature. Yet throughout, his vigor and bawdy humor remain indestructible, even while the world passes him by and his health deteriorates. In the end, his obstinacy hastens his death.

If Samuel Abelman was the last angry man of Brooklyn, Rod Serling was the last angry man of television. A child of the 1930s, when social concerns and realist aesthetics dominated the arts, Serling was an early devotee of Norman Corwin and the other angry young men who populated the airwaves during the Roosevelt era. Like Corwin, Arch Oboler, and Orson Welles, as well as Clifford Odets and the agitators of the legitimate stage of that era, Serling fervently believed that the theater of the air, like the other literary arts, in addition to being entertaining, should be both relevant and provocative. Serling saw the dramatist's role in American society as that of an agent of change and a spark to controversy. Or, as he put it in a speech to the Library of Congress in 1968: "The writer's role is to menace the public's conscience. He must have a position, a point of view. He must see the arts as a vehicle of social criticism and he must focus on the issues of his time." With television, Serling was able to fulfill the writer's role as he defined it.[1]

And menace the public's conscience he did, during television's golden age, with such powerful plays as "The Strike" and "The Rack," his antiwar diptych; "Patterns," his no-holds-barred look at the corporate jungle; "Requiem for a Heavyweight," his stomach-turning take on the fight game; in both "A Town Has Turned to Dust" and "Noon on Doomsday," his plays on prejudice; and "The Velvet Alley," his semi-autobiographical critique of the television industry itself. And just as Corwin's ethereal masterworks helped to legitimize radio drama as an art form, so did Serling's taut, powerful, and wonderfully visual works, along with those of such fellow video agent provocateurs as Paddy Chayefsky, Gore Vidal, and Robert Alan Aurthur, help make TV one of the lively arts of the 1950s.

While Samuel Beckett and Edward Albee took Broadway on an absurdist, nonrealist track, Serling and his fellow video litterateurs made the television theater of the late 1950s the real spiritual successor of both radio and the legitimate stage of twenty years before. Unfortunately, Serling's Ibsenesque bent did not sit well with the network tastemakers. At the start of the fifties, when TV had only just begun its explosive growth, and was still an accoutrement of the educated classes, there had been room for high populist art like "Marty" and "Patterns" on the airwaves. However, the medium proliferated, and sponsors and network officials began to worry about alienating and losing their audience. As a result, this small window of creative opportunity began to close, and TV playwrights were faced with increasing censorship from timorous ad agencies and broadcasting executives.

Serling, like Samuel Abelman, complained loudest. In 1961, *Television Age* called him the industry's leading critic. As Andrew Sarris has written: "Television was the biggest sociological game in town, and Serling wasn't giving it up without a fight."[2] Unfortunately, it didn't do TV or Serling much good. By the end of the decade, with the exception of *Playhouse 90*, Serling's proscenium and bully pulpit, the dramatic anthology show, had entered extinction, giving way to filmed western and detective shows.

Most of Serling's comrades had long since left television for other less censorious and more "artistic" media, but Serling refused to abandon video: he *believed* in television. And—unquestionably—Serling liked the limelight. Television (contrary to what another biographer has written) was not only the medium best suited to Serling's talents, it was also the one best suited to his intense, quirky personality.

And so Serling continued to badger and probe and moralize—and entertain—as the guiding Aesop of *The Twilight Zone*. As media historian Peter Kaplan recently has written, "On *The Twilight Zone* . . . the nightmare side of American life was opened up. The national soul was the subject, and its real villains were the selfish, the shallow, the rapacious. If there was a real golden age of television, its single commercial offshoot, never to die, was *The Twilight Zone*. It loved wit and had wonderful actors and a patina of writing that is television's answer to the short story."[3]

The Twilight Zone, a remarkable one-man show, ran until 1964. By that time, Serling had added two more Emmys to the three he had already earned for "Patterns," "Requiem," and "The Comedian." (He was to win one more for his 1964 adaptation of the John O'Hara story "It's Mental Work.") Serling had already become a national icon; mentally and physically, he had clearly exhausted himself.

Consumed by the medium he had helped create, he wound up earning most of his money in his later days as a commercial spokesman. Ultimately, he succumbed to the very commercialism he had once decried. This is the tragic part of the Rod Serling tale, and this too must be told.

PROLOGUE

10 P.M. September 1965.
1490 Monaco Drive, Los Angeles.

FADE IN on a MEDIUM SHOT—as the script for this psy-chodrama would say—of *ROD SERLING*, TV writer-host, sitting in the poolside office of his handsome Pacific Palisades estate, purchased in 1958 from former movie star Virginia Bruce, desultorily dictating into his trusty whirring Dictaphone machine. Serling—his dark features recognizable to millions of Americans from his long-running and recently canceled CBS television series *The Twilight Zone*, and from frequent appearances on lesser vehicles like *Match Game* and Budweiser commercials—is half-seated, half-slouching in his favorite working chair, a tall Naugahyde model, with one foot up against the edge of his cluttered wrap-around desk. In his right hand is a microphone, which he clicks on and off, in the left, a sputtering Viceroy, his sixtieth cigarette of the day. Serling is dressed in his usual Hollywood casual-macho style: polo shirt, chino pants, and short leather boots, with lifts to add to his five-foot-four-and-a-half-inch height—and, of course, a tan. On his right wrist is his cherished, triangle-shaped Ventura watch, which had been all the rage in 1957 when Serling bought it after winning his second Emmy. On the left is a silver bracelet with the stenciled parachute-and-wings insignia of his old army unit, the 11th Airborne Division.

At the moment, Serling, now in the second year of his presidency of the National Academy of Television Arts and Sciences, is practicing the short speech he is to make the following night when he co-hosts the 1965 Emmy Awards telecast with comedian Danny

1

Kaye. His words are spoken in quick, smoke-entangled bursts, with the punctuation spelled out for the benefit of his longtime secretary and confidante Marjorie Langsford. Serling, who is about to depart the NATAS after a stormy and depressing tenure as its titular head, has decided to use the occasion to fire off a brief parting statement on the parlous state of the television medium.

Serling pauses, inhales deeply from his Viceroy, and sadly gazes around the cozy, poolside lanai, which he had specially built for himself after purchasing the rambling two-acre estate upon moving to California from Connecticut in 1957, and which he now uses as office, den, occasional pied-à-terre.

On his giant desk, as we share his POINT OF VIEW, are the assorted accoutrements of the busy modern scenarist, and Serling is nothing, if not busy. In addition to Dictaphone and Dictatapes, there is a call directory telephone with buttons for his wife, Carol, his secretary, Langsford, and his agent at Ashley-Steiner, Alden Schwimmer; a portable twelve-inch Sony television set (which, lately, Serling has come to abhor); and a dozen or so thumb-eared scripts from television and film projects either in development or in production, including several upcoming episodes of the writer's new iconoclastic Western series, *The Loner*, Serling's first venture into continuing character television, and the final shooting script of *Assault on a Queen*, a feature film about the hijacking of a cruise liner, which he is writing on order for Frank Sinatra. There is also one conspicuous piece of personal memorabilia, an oak frame containing the Purple Heart with Oak Leaf Cluster, which Serling was awarded after receiving two wounds during the bitter and bloody battle to retake the Japanese-held city of Manila at the close of World War II.

Next Serling's wistful gaze takes in the six gleaming Emmy statuettes he has received over the past decade, arrayed on the wall before him. There is the first, which Serling, then thirty, won for "Patterns," the vitriolic portrait of the carpet-lined corporate jungle, which he wrote for the dramatic anthology show *Kraft Television Theatre*, and which made Serling a media hero after it was broadcast in January 1955. Next to that Emmy is the one that Serling won for "Requiem for a Heavyweight," his acclaimed, searing ringside drama, which confirmed Serling's status as the television writer to watch, and which the author, a former amateur boxer himself, considers his finest writing for the medium. Then there is the next back-to-back Emmy, the one Serling got in 1958 for his wrenching adaptation of Ernest Lehman's story "The Comedian," about a megalomaniacal comedian, which also made a star of its director, John Frankenheimer, when it was shown on *Playhouse 90*. And on the shelf below, the Emmys, from 1960 and 1961, for *The Twilight Zone*; and finally, the sixth and most recent, earned for Serling's pungent adaptation of John O'Hara's classic short story about the weary art of bartending, "It's Mental Work," broadcast in April 1964 on *Bob Hope Presents the Chrysler Theater*, a filmed anthology show and one of the last shows of its kind on the air.

There are other glittering prizes nearby: the prestigious Peabody Award from 1956, the first ever given to a writer; the 1959 *Look* Magazine Annual Television Award; the Golden Globe Award for Best Male Television Star of 1962; the 1956 and 1958 Writers Guild of America Awards.

Beneath these, as we PAN DOWN, is a gallery of still photographs of some of the writer's most prized video moments: the electrifying scene in "The Rack," Serling's 1955 drama about cowardice and men's breaking points, set during the Korean War, in which Wasnik, the defense attorney, played by Keenan Wynn, finally forces out of his client, Captain Hall (Marshall Thompson)—under court-martial for making treasonable statements while a North Korean prisoner of war—a choking description of how he "broke"; the famous night scene in "Patterns," where Fred Staples (Richard Kiley), young executive on the rise at Ramsey and Company, finds Andy Sloane (Ed Begley) alone in their office, after the failing Sloane has taken another pounding from Ramsey, the ruthless, manipulative company president, and tries to persuade Sloane to resign before Ramsey utterly crushes him; the shattering moment in "Requiem" when Jack Palance, playing the battered ex-boxer, Mountain McClintock, looks into the mirror for the first time after his morally bankrupt manager (Keenan Wynn again) has successfully connived to make him a wrestler, and sees himself as a clown.

Finally, our inquiring camera PANS RIGHT to the sliding glass doors leading to the standard Hollywood over-sized, and rarely used, swimming pool, the very same sort of pool that Serling and his friends and fellow video immigrants from the East used to nervously joke about when they "sold out" and left New York for "the land of mink swimming pools" in the late 1950s, and the metaphor that the guiltily successful teledramatist used for spiritual corruption in his autobiographical study of the hazards of Hollywood–style TV writing, "The Velvet Alley." The pool as usual is empty on this night, but its underwater lights cast a strange, slightly surreal glow.

Serling's bittersweet reverie ends. He continues dictating the requiem for the television medium he is to deliver the following evening. Outwardly, one would think, Rod Serling has little to complain about. Clearly, he has the respect and affection of his peers in television—witness his election to the presidency of the National Academy of Television Arts and Sciences, the closest thing the television industry has to a governing body, and the first time the post had gone to a writer; the previous president was Walter Cronkite.

Serling, as his cluttered desk indicates, has never had more work. Only one year after CBS's final cancellation of the five-year-old *Twilight Zone* series—a development that the burned-out writer-creator-host had actually welcomed—he is already back on the air, and seemingly back in business, with the promising *Loner*.

Serling's parallel screenwriting career also appears to be thriving. After years of disappointment in the cinema, the writer had received critical acclaim for his taut screenplay for *Seven Days in May*, a political thriller directed by his old friend John Frankenheimer, helping to drive his fee per script over the $150,000 mark and bringing him to the attention of Frank Sinatra and other film producers. Besides Sinatra's commission for *Assault on a Queen*, he has two other original screenplays or adaptations for major producers in the works. The always articulate and increasingly politically active Serling has also been increasingly in demand as a speaker. In the next month of September 1965, alone, Citizen Serling is scheduled to give a dozen speeches on various issues around the country in his capacity as NATAS president.

The outspoken and successful writer has a beautiful wife, Carol, whom he met and married while they were undergraduates at Antioch College, and two pretty daughters, Jody, fourteen, and Nan, nine. They have two dogs: Beau, an Irish setter, currently resting on the couch at the far end of the studio, and George, a dachshund. They have a full household staff, including a maid and a gardener. They have the huge stone-studded house; a country estate on Cayuga Lake in upstate New York; a thirty-six-foot Chris-Craft tri-cabin on which they spend a large part of the summer cruising the Finger Lakes. An old car buff, Serling also possesses a fourteen-thousand-dollar replica of a classic 1936 Auburn Speedster, which his wife —who drives a black Cadillac Eldorado—despises.

The writer stops dictating and curses, apologizes to his secretary, turns off the machine, lights another Viceroy, looks at the ceiling, and contemplates the nightmare his life has become.

For Rod Serling is not a happy man.

It began in March, when the writer was hospitalized for chest pains while making a speech before the Academy's Washington, D.C., chapter. Initial news reports indicated that Serling had suffered a coronary attack; in fact it was "only" exhaustion, but Serling, whose family has a history of heart trouble, believes it is only a matter of time before he has the real thing. He believes he will die within a year or two, so why, he rationalizes, should he slow down? Within days of leaving the hospital, he is tearing around the country again, like the driven, fatally sick protagonist of the concurrent series *Run for Your Life*, played by Serling's friend Ben Gazzara. By the same skewed logic, the writer rationalizes his suicidal four-pack-a-day smoking habit.

Serling's marriage is also in disrepair. Indeed, although Rod and Carol live on the same grounds, they have become virtual strangers to each other, with the writer essentially moving into the lanai, female visitors and all, while his wife remains in the house a mere 150 feet away.

Prosperous appearances notwithstanding, matters on the business front aren't especially rosy for Serling either. No sooner had he sold CBS the syndication rights to *The Twilight Zone*, thinking that the show would *never* make money in syndication, than he learned that the network was making a fortune from syndication, a fortune he had signed away—a fortune that would have guaranteed his family's economic security.

In fact, Rod Serling doesn't much like being Rod Serling. He doesn't even like being president of the National Academy of Television Arts and Sciences. Already his controversial plan to refine the Academy's Emmy Award system has caused considerable internecine warfare within the organization and made enemies of such former friends as Fred Friendly, the president of CBS News, and others within the television industry.

In fact, Rod Serling doesn't like television. It isn't a serious writer's medium anymore, he feels. Just five years before, in 1960, there had been thirteen dramatic anthology shows on the air, including his own landmark series *The Twilight Zone*. Now, in the fall of 1965, there are none; even *Bob Hope Presents the Chrysler Theater*, Serling's last video proscenium, has been canceled, a victim of ratings.

It is the era of the situation comedy. The hottest program of the new fall season is *Hogan's Heroes*, an inane comedy set in a German prisoner of war camp, a show that Serling, an ethnic Jew, deeply loathes.

Then there is *The Loner*. Serling was initially excited about the show, starring Lloyd Bridges as Civil War veteran William Colton. A "cerebral Western," Serling had optimistically called it. CBS, though, thought it was *too* cerebral. The network, to Serling's dismay, wanted more action, which Serling read as more violence. A bitter feud ensued. Serling, true to his frequent foot-in-the-mouth form, made matters worse by publicizing his dissatisfaction with the network in an interview with the *Philadelphia Inquirer* several weeks before.

The Loner is now in limbo, and Serling, as he recently discovered during a visit to CBS headquarters in New York, has succeeded in making himself persona non grata at the very network, CBS, which had originally spawned him during the golden years of the 1950s. Production of the show has been halted pending a resolution of the writer's and the network's "creative differences," as the Hollywood euphemism goes.

To be sure, if Serling had his druthers now, he would quit Hollywood, return to New York, write plays and novels; at least that's what he tells people. But of course, he won't: too expensive. And too scary.

If this isn't the nadir, it is close to it. Indeed, Serling's life, on this warm September evening in the Pacific Palisades, resembles a page from his own "Velvet Alley" script. "You know how they do it, Ernie?" Eddie, the cynical director, brilliantly played by Leslie Nielsen, had warned in the mordant 1959 *Playhouse 90* drama. "They give you $1000 a week and keep giving you $1000 a week until that's what you need to live on. Then . . . you live in a nightmare for fear that they'll take it away from you."[1]

At the moment, Rod Serling is living that very nightmare. Right now, like his video alter ego Ernie Pandish, he is afraid that the powers that be in "Bubbleland," as he disparagingly calls his adopted hometown, are indeed going to take it all away from him, all the money, all the attention, all the access. Lately, like Pandish, he has begun wondering whether he has "optioned his soul," and so have many of his fans. If not, then how to explain Serling's recent crop of game show appearances, not to mention aspirin and floor wax ads? If that isn't selling out, what is?

But the hour is late for regrets.

Meanwhile, the Emmy Awards, which Serling is hosting the following evening, must go on. And the vestigial "angry young man" in Serling is determined to say his piece before the monster medium that he helped create swallows him whole.

Sitting up in his Naugahyde chair, ready once again for verbal combat, he clicks on his microphone and continues dictating and cursing into the night.

SLOW FADE TO BLACK.

1

BINGHAMTON
(1924 – 35)

And also like all men perhaps there'll be an occasion—maybe a summer night sometime—when he'll look up from what he's doing and listen to the distant music of a calliope, and hear the voices and the laughter of his past. And perhaps across his mind there'll flit a little errant wish, that a man might not have to become old, never outgrow the parks and the merry-go-rounds of his youth. And he'll smile then too because he'll know it is just an errant wish, some wisp of memory not too important, really, some laughing ghosts that cross a man's mind—that are a part of the Twilight Zone.

—closing narration of "Walking Distance," first aired October 30, 1959[1]

"Everybody has a hometown," Rod Serling wrote in 1959, shortly before the launch of *The Twilight Zone*. "In the strangely brittle, terribly sensitive make-up of a human being, there is a need for a place to hang a hat, for a kind of geographic womb to crawl back into. Binghamton's mine."[2] Did everyone in transient, midcentury United States really have such a hometown or even need one? Rod Serling did.

More than most writers, Rod Serling was formed by and preoccupied with his background, particularly by the fact of having grown up in Binghamton, the medium-sized, Middle-American upstate New York city where Serling spent the first eighteen years of his life. On the one hand, it is Binghamton, the cozy, stately, very Gentile "Parlor City of New York," as it used to be called, which accounts for much of the lyricism and sentimentalism of Serling's mature video corpus. On the other hand, it is Binghamton, hide-bound, anti-Semitic Binghamton, which lies at the root of Serling's conflicted feelings about his Jewish heritage, including his eventual decision to convert to Unitarianism. For these and numerous other critical questions regarding Rod Serling's life and career, all roads indeed lead to Binghamton.

Serling himself recognized his nearly umbilical tie to his hometown, reveled in it, agonized over it, was proud of it—and could be quite silly about it. In a sense, the writer, who also lived in Ohio, Connecticut, and California during his television-writing career, never really left Binghamton. In 1953, when the fledgling television playwright was still living in Cincinnati turning out video potboilers for his first anthology television show, *The Storm*, on WKRC-TV, he and his wife, Carol, established a summer residence in Interlaken, on Lake Cayuga, sixty miles away from Binghamton; they moved into a lakeside cottage once owned by Carol's grandfather. From there, Serling drove or flew to his hometown at least a dozen times a year, usually alone. He never actually *moved back* into his hometown—that would have been a bit too surreal, even for Rod Serling, but he came awfully close. Did Binghamton Central need a high school graduation speaker? Rod Serling would be there, even if it meant flying in from Los Angeles. Did Broome County need a celebrity to crown the Broome County Aviation Queen of 1960? Rod Serling, Hollywood celebrity, proud son of the Southern Tier, would be there, gladly, regardless of the expense.

More often than not, the restless playwright returned to his hometown out of pure, obsessive nostalgia. Thus the solo car trips southward, away from Lake Cayuga, back to Binghamton, which would often end with the writer driving in circles around his old neighborhood, occasionally stopping and getting out and staring at his family's old house on Bennett Avenue, or some other monument of his youth—much like the world-weary protagonist of the classic *Twilight Zone* episode "Walking Distance"—before reluctantly returning to the present day.

To be sure, much of *The Twilight Zone*, a show that is far more autobiographical in nature than many viewers realize, is Rod Serling's video testament to the Binghamton of his youth.

"Willoughby! Next stop Willoughby!" cries the conductor in "A Stop at Willoughby," another memorable, Serling-scripted episode about a stressed-out advertising executive, being slowly crushed, as by a vise, between the stresses of office and home; he thirstily dreams of escaping to Willoughby, an Arcadian town of his imagination "where a man can live his life full measure," while snoozing on the New York-to-Westport express. The bedeviled man does, at last, "get off" at Willoughby, sleepwalking off the train, in what he imagines is Willoughby, to his death. Willoughby, of course, is actually Binghamton, as Serling dreamed and daydreamed of it when he was caught in the deadly grip of network success.

And so is Homewood, the hometown of Martin Sloan, the past-possessed protagonist of "Walking Distance" starring the late Gig Young in one of his finest pieces of work. As Sloan, the poignantly convincing homesick actor takes a short walk down the road a piece while having his car repaired and winds up in Serling's Aesopian Twilight Zone on a cautionary trip back in time to the actual mise-en-scène of his 1930s youth. Sloan belatedly realizes that he is revisiting his past when he impulsively chases a twelve-year-old boy whom he recognizes as himself and winds up at the steps of his old house, confronting his long-dead parents, now amazingly alive. This fable ends more happily: the father persuades his son, who has thoughts of staying in the too cozy past, to return to his own day and age, with all of its troubles and cares. "Maybe there are merry-go-rounds there, too. . . . Maybe you haven't been looking in the right place," the elder Sloan advises.[3] In the end, Sloan reluctantly boards the carousel in the park near his home and returns from his rendezvous with the furies with a new mature perspective on life—and one that often eluded Serling himself.

The original white clapboard model for Sloan's house, the house that Rod Serling grew up in and doted on, still stands in Binghamton, as do most of its 1920s-era neighbors. So does the carousel of "Walking Distance" and the Seurat-like gazebo of "A Stop at Willoughby," as well as hundreds of other human and architectural details that made their way into The Twilight Zone.

In fact, most of the millions of fans of The Twilight Zone would readily feel at home in the Binghamton of today. More than thirty years after Serling memorialized his Hopperesque hometown on his hit television series, the city's pastoral character hasn't altered very much, and neither have its people. In fact, it looks very much the way it must have on that hot day in July 1926, when Sam and Esther Serling and their two young sons, Robert and Rodman, moved into town, full of hopes and dreams of their own.

Binghamton, New York, the seat of Broome County, in south-central New York, lies at the confluence of the Chenango and Susquehanna rivers near the Pennsylvania border, seventy-five miles south of Syracuse; with Johnson City and Endicott, it forms the Triple Cities. Settled in 1787 at the site of an Iroquois village, Ochenang, it was first known as Chenango Point and was later named for William Bingham, who owned land tracts on both sides of the Susquehanna. Laid out in 1800, the village prospered after the Chenango and the Erie Canal were linked in 1837 and the Erie Railroad arrived in 1848; by the turn of the century, Binghamton's transportation advantages made it a bustling industrial city with a population of thirty thousand.

Spurring and guiding Binghamton's continued growth was a rare ensemble of inventive and entrepreneurial spirits: men like "General" Edward Jones, stalwart founder of Jones Scale Works and author of the early, nationally known advertising phrase "Jones, he pays the freight"; and Robert Kilmer, the ingenious, slightly diabolical head and chief chemist of Kilmer Laboratories, which issued the renowned "Swamp Root" elixir and an array of other "sovereign remedies" for America's real and imagined aches and pains before the turn of the century; and the enterprising German immigrant brothers Anthony and Lee Scoville, who would turn their Ansco Camera Works into one of the giants of the photographic supply industry.

Then, too, there was the inspired example of Binghamton's greatest capitalistic genius, George F. Johnson. In 1899, Johnson, an ambitious superintendent in Henry B. Endicott's shoe factory, had purchased a half-interest in the firm for $150,000. Endicott loaned Johnson, who had little or no money, the entire amount on the strength of a personal note. This proved to be a fortunate investment; the dynamic Johnson was soon able to repay the principal with interest and to forge the company into one of the largest of its kind, as well as one of the most generous to its employees in the United States. By the eve of World War I, more than twenty thousand busy factory workers, many of them Eastern European and Italian immigrants, were on the "E-J" payroll, and George Johnson and his brother Howard did their best to keep them there, providing them (and Binghamton) with such amenities as comfortable and attractive housing, inexpensive trolley-car transportation, free libraries, verdant parks filled with gazebos and carousels, spanking new secondary schools, and up-to-date medical care, including the first hospital in the country to treat alcoholism as a disease. Not surprisingly, "Which way to Eee-Jay?" was a question often heard on Ellis Island during the early 1900s.

Newcomers who weren't interested in the industrial and mechanical arts could try their hand at the soil. There was plenty of good farmland amidst the rolling hills beyond the steeples and chimneys of the Triple Cities.

To be sure, early twentieth-century Binghamton wasn't a particularly sophisticated city, in Eastern terms. Movies and band concerts were perhaps its most popular advanced form of culture. The city didn't have any stage theaters; and it lacked any institutions of education higher than a vocational school. Indeed, in many respects, Binghamton resembled the relentlessly plain and complacent Middle American cities Sinclair Lewis and H. L. Mencken sent up in their writings. Babbit would have felt at home in the Binghamton of the 1920s. It was the sort of place where the mayor could boast of presiding over the longest parabolic bridge in all of New York State and the finest operating set of fully water-powered elevators in the country, where the wealthiest menfolk spent their Saturdays on one of the eight golf courses around town, or tinkered with their new noiseless refrigerators while their wives admired the advertisements in *The Saturday Evening Post*.

However, if the Binghamton that the Serlings moved to in 1926 was culturally unsophisticated, its fifty thousand previously established residents didn't seem to know it, or mind terribly. To them, it was home, and a good one.

If there was any aspect of their lives in the Binghamton Valley that Binghamtonians *would* change if they could, it was the damp Southern Tier weather. Still, one could get used to it, even love it.

Better yet, according to the words inscribed on the stone archway lovingly erected by boosterish Endicott-Johnson workers, under which Sam Serling and his expectant family probably passed as they motored to their handsome new home on the city's genteel West Side, it was HOME OF THE SQUARE DEAL.

Jews like the Serlings could also get a fair deal in the conservative and prejudice-bound Triple Cities, albeit somewhat grudgingly. Although never a major center of Jewish settlement, Binghamton had a thriving community of approximately fifteen hundred Jews by 1920, complete with its own synagogue and community center; by the time the Serlings decided to move there from Syracuse six years later, the number was steadily increasing. Before World War I, most of the city's Jews had been concentrated in a relatively small enclave in the city's gray downtown district. Now, as the city's Jewish community—like many other similar ones across the country—underwent a period of "Americanization," Jews began to ride the so-called "ethnic escalator" up to suburban, middle-class neighborhoods, like Binghamton's West Side. At the same time, Binghamton's Jews began moving out of retailing, their previous principal mode of economic activity, and into the professions.

The movement toward even greater acculturation was checked by the unfortunate rise of anti-Semitism among the older upper class of Binghamton society, a phenomenon that also corresponded with a fearsome recrudescence of anti-Semitism nationwide. These were the days when men like Henry Ford engaged in public Jew-baiting and Ku Klux Klan membership soared into the millions.

The Southern Tier itself was a stronghold for the Klan during the interwar years. State Klan headquarters were located in Oneida in adjoining Onondaga County, and Klansmen, both in and out of uniform, operated openly in Broome County. The Jewish community's consternation grew to paranoiac proportions in 1925, when a Klan-backed candidate won the Binghamton Republican mayoral primary and came close to winning the general election. Doubtless, if the Klan had managed to capture City Hall, as it did in some of Binghamton's nativistic sister cities in the Midwest, there would have been a mass exodus, and Sam Serling would have picked someplace else to go into the grocery business.

After the scare of 1925, however, overt anti-Semitism quickly diminished. As elsewhere, Jew- and Catholic-bashing tended to go underground, taking the form of hiring bars at certain corporations and membership bars at private clubs. Jews were free to move to the West Side, or any other neighborhood of the Triple Cities—they just couldn't join the Binghamton Club (indeed, they couldn't do so until the 1960s). Perhaps, too, their children might have to put up with a certain amount of harassment at school, like having to take examinations that were deliberately scheduled for the Jewish High Holy Days. These widely known and accepted strictures were annoying, perhaps even worrisome, but not enough to offset Binghamton's economic and other advantages, and certainly not enough to put off a doughty Jewish emigrant like Sam Serling, who was already inured to the vicissitudes of life beyond the Catskills.

Indeed, the Klan notwithstanding, Binghamton's Jewish community increased by two-thirds during the first seven years of the 1920s, more than double the national rate of American Jewry.[4] Adapting the requisite civic camouflage, the Binghamton area's Jewish population, 5 percent of the whole, acquired a sort of Rotarian attitude toward their Jewishness: it became a club, with its own insignia and baseball team (the Millville Sluggers) and community center, and less of a religion. Inevitably, many Jewish families of Binghamton wound up abandoning their faith altogether and converting from Judaism to its next closest Christian cousin, Unitarianism, even though most would retain their ethnic Jewish pride.

A second-generation American Jew, Sam Serling was born in 1890 in Detroit, the son of poor Lithuanian-Jewish immigrants. His father tried to eke out a living as a peddler, but it wasn't enough to support his family. To add to the family purse, Sam dropped out of school in the tenth grade and worked at various odd jobs before taking to the road and working his way east as a freelance male secretary.

Sam Serling's strongest suit, aside from the tough hide he acquired from living on the road, was his mechanical aptitude. He was a whiz with machines, all kinds of machines. A blindingly fast typist, he could type up to 120 words per minute. And he could fix anything. The bespectacled Michigan native was also a perennial inventor. Sam was endlessly spinning off ideas for things like the "frankburger" machine, a gadget for making hamburger-shaped frankfurters, and other sometimes odd devices for the common good. Indeed, he probably would have been happiest working as a laboratory engineer someplace; unfortunately, Sam's lack of advanced education made that an unrealistic option—as did his Jewishness. Otherwise, Sam was eminently assimilable. He spoke extremely clearly, almost typing out his speech, a trait that he passed on to his son Rod. He dressed impeccably. Although introspective by nature, his manner with company was warm and ingratiating. He made friends easily.

In 1914, Sam Serling's eastward peregrinations led him to Auburn, New York, a small industrial town in north-central New York State. There he met his future wife, Esther Cooper, the radiant and becoming daughter of a well-to-do Jewish grocery-chain owner. Although he was of modest means, Sam's impeccable manners, good intentions, and evident love for Esther won over his skeptical future in-laws, and after a brief courtship, Sam and Esther were married.

To a large degree, the union was a pairing of opposites. Where Sam was reserved and introverted, Esther was outgoing. Sam tended to be impractical and not interested in money matters; Esther, as befitting the daughter of a man of means, was much more hard-headed. Politically, Sam tended to be conservative. Esther, on the other hand, was a fervent Democrat, who brandished her liberal views and was given to writing fiery letters to the editors of the generally reactionary upper New York State newspapers. The two often argued about politics, say friends and relatives, but on domestic matters there was generally harmony. Sam unfailingly addressed his wife as "Dearest." He meant it. Theirs was a strong marriage, lasting thirty years.

To be sure, the Serlings had a slight conflict of plans at the start of their life together. Esther hoped that Sam would settle down and go into the family's grocery business, especially after their first son, Robert, was born. Instead, her husband prevailed on Esther to join him for a spell in the Canal Zone, of all places. Sam had applied for and obtained a clerical position with "General" George C. Goethals, the supervisor of the construction of the canal and one of the most illustrious engineers of the day. The position with Goethals, Sam evidently thought, would also be his ticket to engineering success.

It wasn't. When Sam, Esther, and young Robert returned to the United States two years later, Sam Serling was merely a secretary with a colorful résumé. Still, Sam would always remember the legendary Goethals and think of his minor role in the most momentous engineering project of the modern era as his finest moment.

More ominously, Esther had contracted yellow fever and, in spite of a successful recovery, had been informed that she could not have any more children. Hence the couple's joy when, shortly after their return to New York State, Esther became pregnant again.

Now, with a wife and young son, and another child on the way, Sam was ready to surrender to more mundane concerns, like making a steady living. Unfortunately, that proved difficult to accomplish as a secretary. Sam had no intention of moving back with his in-laws. One of the reasons was that the Coopers were Orthodox Jews; he was Reformed, very Reformed. Nor did he especially want to go into his father-in-law's business.

Leaving Auburn, the couple next set up residence in Syracuse. There, on Christmas Day in 1924, their second child, Rodman Edward, was born. The Serlings were now four. It was time for

Sam to get *praktisch* (Yiddish for "practical"). Finally, the next year, Sam succumbed to his wife's arguments and moved to Binghamton to set up a new outpost of the Cooper grocery chain. Serling's Sanitary Grocery, it was to be called.

"I can see his name in lights: ROD SERLING!" an exuberant and very pregnant Esther Serling dramatically exclaimed at a family get-together in Syracuse, by way of explaining why she hadn't followed the traditional Jewish custom of naming her soon-to-be-born son after a male relative.[5]

Whether that's how it actually happened, Rodman Edward Serling acted and talked as if he *was* a star, or at least the star of the Serling family, from almost the moment he was born, and he was. Often, in families with more than one child, it is the firstborn who receives the most attention; but in the Serling family it was definitely the secondborn, Rod—or Roddie, as he was called in his early youth—who got the star treatment. This was partly because, with Sam's grocery doing well (at least at first), both Sam and Esther had more attention to give than they had when their firstborn, Robert, was born. Partly, no doubt, this was because of the child's killer grin—the first thing that his friends generally remember about him—and his intensely alive dark brown eyes.

Partly, too, Rod received much more attention than Robert because, unlike his older brother, he was more obviously a mixture of Sam and Esther, reflecting what could be considered the best qualities of both parents. As they never could with Robert, each parent could say he was "their boy." From his father, Rod inherited a love of language; from his mother, he received his sunny disposition and his fierce intelligence. Finally, there was something about the frenetic—many would say "hyper"—child, some innate insecurity that demanded extra special attention.

And he got it. Whether the setting was a long-distance car drive to visit relatives in Syracuse or a family party at the Serlings' elegantly cozy home, Rod Serling was indeed star of the show, talking, singing, acting out dialogue for hours on end, and oftentimes exhausting his bemused auditors. As one cousin, Saydelle Agranovitch, put it, "He was always on and on stage."[6] The precocious tot derived most of his material from the radio; Agranovitch remembers Rod humming "The Girl I Marry," a broadcast favorite of the early thirties, at family gatherings.

To further accommodate Rod's continuous need to perform, Sam built a small stage for his son in the basement of the Serling house. There Rod and his elementary-school friends would stage their own musicals. Sometimes they would even charge admission, according to Herbie Denton, a childhood acquaintance. Sam also gave Rod his own Speedo minibike, with which the young whirling dervish would tear up and down Bennett Avenue. In fact, Sam and Esther gave Rod just about everything he wanted.

Still, Sam's indulgence did have its limits: when Rod asked his father for a Christmas tree because of peer pressure at his mostly Gentile elementary school, Sam balked. Sam was still at least officially committed to practicing his religion, and in fact became vice-president of his temple. This did not include eating kosher; when his in-laws paid one of their sudden visits, Sam stationed Esther at the front door while he guiltily hid all of the nonkosher food.

Robert naturally resented his parents' obvious favoritism toward their second son, although he tried not to let it show. If anything, Rod's boisterousness caused Robert to become even more withdrawn, according to his cousins. The two were reasonably close while they were growing up under the same roof. Sometimes the two oddly disparate brothers attended movies together, where the child mimic found additional inspiration. *Dr. Jekyll and Mr. Hyde* was an early Serling inspiration. After attending one performance of the film with his older brother, Rod launched into his own maniacally accurate rendition of the doctor-psychopath, complete with laboratory sound effects. He also learned all of the roles in *Stagecoach*, and would gladly perform the same on demand. Indeed, such were the young Serling's thespian gifts that many of his early acquaintances are still surprised that he didn't become an actor or a comedian. Serling's bag of impressions also included a hilarious imitation of King Kong, and a highly effective Franklin D. Roosevelt, both of which became Serling perennials.

Rod doesn't seem to have found much in his older brother he wanted to emulate: if anything, while loving Robert, he seems to have used him more as an exemplar of what not to be. Indeed, it is difficult to think of two brothers who were as different from each other in character and temperament as Robert and Rod Serling. Where Robert was quiet and withdrawn, Rod was loud and boisterous. Robert avoided sports; Rod loved them. Robert, like his father, was conservative; Rod, like his mother, would become an outspoken liberal.

One side of Robert that did rub off on Rod was his keen interest in model planes. Under his proud supervision, Rod became a model plane fanatic. The childhood hobby would remain an obsession for the rest of Serling's life. The most junior Serling was also a born prankster, given to sometimes dangerous stunts, like jumping off of houses, or slier ones like inviting his brother to a bogus meeting with the family rabbi by perfectly mimicking the latter's voice on the phone.

Serling also imitated his father's brisk, stenographic speech pattern. And, like Sam, he took to calling Esther "Dearest." From childhood on, his mother would always be "Dearest" to him.

Young Rod Serling's star qualities, such as they were, took somewhat longer to evince themselves at school. His teachers at Alexander Hamilton Elementary School generally marked him off as a cute, if overly garrulous child whose mouth was more of an annoyance than anything else. He and his equally talkative friend and classmate Herbie Denton were often asked to sit at the back of the room.

Serling's teachers at his next school, West Junior High School, tended to have the same opinion of their irrepressible charge, with one notable exception. Helen Foley, Rod's seventh-grade English teacher—and the one who, according to local legend, "discovered" Rod Serling—was perspicacious enough to discern that the gabby youth possessed real oratorical talent and encouraged him to develop it by engaging in open public-speaking activities. Thanks to Foley's encouragement, as well as the winsome youth's popularity among his peers, Rod was selected to give the graduation speech for his class at West. Foley recalled that it included a quotation from Goethe that duly impressed his teachers and classmates; the future parablist had already become an avid collector of proverbs and famous quotations.

Rod also used his increasing repertoire of verbal skills, including his outsized vocabulary, to good effect when he wrote for the West Falls school newspaper. Taking a cue from his mother, he established an early reputation as a social activist, writing flaming editorials for the school newspaper, as well as becoming active in various school charitable organizations. Nevertheless, the future television playwright could hardly be described as an intellectual, nor even as an especially good student. Indeed, in nonverbal subjects like science and math, where he had no interest whatsoever, he did abysmally and often required tutoring from his more practical friends.

One person who apparently did engage the impetuous youth's interest was Isidore Friedlander, the director of the Binghamton Jewish Community Center and teacher of its Sunday school, where Serling was enrolled from the age of eight to twelve. Fluent in Hebrew and Yiddish, the center's gifted resident was a poet, musician, translator, and playwright. He and his wife, Esther, were the spiritual mentors to hundreds of Binghamton's Jewish children from 1931, when they arrived at the center, until his retirement twenty-six years later. It was the kindly, philosophical Friedlander who helped inculcate Serling with his fierce moralism even while the Serling family was in some ways straying from the actual Jewish faith. Still, the young Rod Serling could hardly be described as spiritually inclined.

Yet, even though his mother and Helen Foley, and perhaps several others, continued to see stars for him, Rod Serling was pretty much an average kid, which is precisely what he wanted to be. He was very athletic, showing talent and a lot of aggressiveness at Ping-Pong and tennis, although not enough to play competitively. And, like his close cinematic contemporary, Andy Hardy, he showed a lot of talent with girls.

It would be these wonderfully ordinary and relatively trouble-free years, Serling's early teens, that he would later romanticize as a writer—the years when Sam was prospering, or at least doing well enough to keep up with his Babbittish neighbors on Bennett Avenue, and the years immediately after Robert had left for college, leaving Rod with no competition for his already over-indulgent parents' affection and attention. These, for Serling, would be the best years, the time that Serling's *Twilight Zone* alter ego, Martin Sloan, would frantically try to recapture when he returned to his hometown of Homewood.

Of course, these, the mid-1930s, were also the Depression years; however, because of the continued health of Endicott-Johnson and Binghamton's other main industries, the Depression largely bypassed the Triple Cities. Binghamton's teenagers, like Rod, weren't uninformed or insensitive. They knew a Depression was going on —Rod certainly had to know from the political arguments his parents had; it was just going on somewhere else—like Buffalo, perhaps. Doubtless it concerned the socially conscious youth, but probably not as much as did the fortunes of the town baseball team, the Triplets, or those of Joe Matesi, one of the Southern Tier's numerous ranking heavyweights (and the boxer upon whom Serling would partly model Mountain McClintock, the battered centerpiece of "Requiem for a Heavyweight").

To an outsider looking in, Binghamton may have seemed a fairly boring place, but to young Rod Serling, it was, well, Willoughby. On a spring afternoon he could hook up with some of his neighborhood friends and watch the Triplets play. Or he could bicycle over to Ross Park to pick up a game of tennis; later, as the weather grew warmer, he and his friends might cool off in the afternoon with a swim in Lily Lake.

Binghamton could also be romantic. On Friday and Saturday evenings in the late thirties, Rod could escort one of his many readily available dates to see Gable and Lombard or March and Garbo at the Lyric Theater or the plusher State. Afterward, he and his date often stopped at Dinty's drugstore and soda fountain for coffee and hamburgers, where, as was his wont, he smothered his meal with ketchup. Afterward, there might be a deliberately long walk home over the invitingly moonlit Washington Street Bridge. The rollatorium on Water Street was another popular meeting place for Binghamton teens. If he was lucky enough to get Sam's car, Rod could drive out to Barbara's Coffee Den on Route 17 and take in a round of miniature golf on the trip back.

If he didn't have a date—apparently rarely a problem for Serling, who is alleged to have dated half the girls in his class at Binghamton Central High School—he could whip up a game of pool or Ping-Pong at the community center. Or, weather permitting, he might hang out in the courthouse square and just shoot the breeze, like Jerry Whipple and his friends did in the radio show *County Seat*. Or he could stay at home and watch his father tinkering with his latest contraption, like the wonderful mechanism that allowed the Serlings to buzz in Antoinette, the family terrier, from upstairs.

This was the Binghamton that Rod Serling would remember and dote upon and mythologize. This, in the words of Martin Sloan, as he urged his perplexed, twelve-year-old self to squeeze the most out of 1936, this, indeed, was "the wonderful time."

Reality in some of its harsher forms began to puncture Rod Serling's dreamy world in high school.

First, in early 1941, his sophomore year at BCHS, Rod discovered the hurtful aspect of being short when he tried out for quarterback of the Bulldogs, the redoubtable varsity football team. The problem was, as the coach of the football team, Henry Merz, tried to tell the teary five-foot-four sixteen-year-old, he was ten pounds too light. "He found it difficult to reconcile a quarterback who weighed less than the team mascot," is the way Serling joked about the matter twenty years later—nevertheless, the memory still hurt.[7]

If anything, however, Serling's failure to make the football team spurred him on even more. "Because he was short," said Sybil Goldenberg, a classmate from Central, "he felt he had to prove himself doubly."[8]

Chagrined at his failure to make varsity, Serling compensated by joining and playing aggressively—sometimes overly aggressively—for the intramural football and tennis teams. He also enlisted in Central's debating team, where he savored the opportunity to box it out with his peers from around the state on the verbal playing field. Lloyd Hartman, the debating club's faculty advisor, recalled that the quick-witted Serling's forte as a debater was the humorous rebuttal.[9]

Serling used his gift for verbal jabbing to good effect in the election for General Organization president, as his unsuccessful competitor for the post, Maurice O'Brien, ruefully recalled. O'Brien, who happened to have had a skiing accident a short time before the election, gave his final campaign speech on crutches, winning the sympathy of most of the hundreds of assembled student voters. Or so he thought. Then a self-assured Rod Serling stepped up. "Rod comes on, takes a pause, flashes that grin of his, and says really quickly, 'I would like to apologize for the fact that I don't have a cast, too, but I hope that I have your sympathy nevertheless,' or words to that effect—and won them back. I felt that he had knocked the crutches out from under me!" A mischievously grinning Serling won the consequent vote by a resounding margin.[10]

Dimly, some aspects of the latter-day Serling persona—the humor, the ken for verbal one-upmanship—were coming to the fore.

In addition to debating and school politics, Serling threw himself into a number of other competitive and noncompetitive school activities. Once again, he joined the school newspaper, the *Panorama*, rising to its editorship, where he wrote flaming and occasionally verbose editorials that reminded some of the letters Esther wrote to the editors of the local papers. He tried out for and won a small role as the male half of "an old Jewish couple" in the senior high school play. He joined the Junior Red Cross. Much of this constructive activity can be traced to Serling's need to compensate for his size, along with his pre-existing desire to be the center of things.

If his short stature was a spur, it was also an onus. Cousin Leona Serling called it "the bane of his existence. He felt if he were taller he could have done anything in the world. I remember one time before he became such an important person, I was visiting with him at the Cooper family residence, and he came down the stairs to greet me, but he stayed on the first step, so he was taller than me, and said, 'See, I'm taller. This is the way I would like to be.'" As an adult, the perennially size-conscious Serling, who would level off at five-foot-four-and-a-half inches as an adult, would wear elevator shoes and refuse to be filmed full-frame in the lead-ins to *The Twilight Zone*. Serling had to face it: he was short. And he didn't like it.[11]

Meanwhile, another blow fell when Serling was voted out of Phi Lambda Chi, the school's Jewish fraternity, for dating Gentile girls. The experience, apparently a traumatic one, increased his already conflicted feelings about being a Jew. Still, it didn't douse his enthusiasm for dating girls of all religions.

Norman Miller, who befriended Serling at Camp Oxford, a well-heeled Jewish camp in Guildford, New York, where the teenaged Serling spent several summers, recalled that Serling was "very much a ladies' man. The girls were crazy about him." Miller also remembered that the parents of Serling's girlfriend that summer "didn't like him because he wasn't Jewish enough."[12]

To add insult to injury, Serling was *also* banned from a non-Jewish fraternity at BCHS. "It was the first time in my life I became aware of religious differences," he said, still stung by the incident, thirty years later. Isidore Friedlander's devoted Rod Serling was still deeply proud of being a Jew, and would continue to be; but from high school on, he would have a jaded view of all organized religion. In time, he too, like many assimilated Jews of his era, would convert to Unitarianism.[13]

In Rod's sophomore year at Central, came another shock: Serling's Sanitary Grocery failed. Sam quickly picked up the pieces and went back into business as a wholesale butcher. But the illusion of economic security he had given his family had been jarred, an illusion that was finally shattered when Sam was forced to sell the family's house in order to pay for Robert's tuition at Antioch. After the sale, a chagrined Sam Serling moved his wife and teenage son to an apartment in another, less-refined part of town. Even then, the Serlings continued to be hard-strapped. One high school classmate, Vernon Hartung, who would later enlist with Rod in the paratroops, recalled his friend going without lunch for lack of funds on several occasions. Hard times had reached the Serling household.

Hurt, probably confused, Rod reacted the same way that many of his Depression-age peers did: by resolving to make a lot of money some day, as he would.

In the meantime, there were adjustments to be made, and Rod made them willingly enough. Previously, Sam had been able to send Rod away to summer camp at Camp Oxford. Now, if he wanted to go, Rod would have to work his way. Before there had been money for movies and miniature golf. Now, Rod turned to more solitary, less expensive leisure activities, like reading books and listening to the radio.

And so, with his trademark grin, young Rod Serling gamely rolled with the punches—the rejection by the Bulldogs and the social clubs, the move to smaller quarters, Sam's financial straits—and came out a better, if slightly more cynical man for it.

Outwardly, he was still the chipper, happy-go-lucky "Roddie" of yore, but inwardly, he had begun to change, to harden.

Serling still loved Binghamton. But now, as he approached manhood, he knew its limitations as well. He had experienced intolerance there, and rejection, and he would never forget it.

2
RADIO LAND
(1936 – 41)

Assume it is morning
You know what mornings are
You have seen thousands of them:
They rise out of the East, huge as the universe
And stand in the sky till noon.
Oh, you've seen all kinds of them . . .
   —*They Fly through the Air with the Greatest of Ease*, a radio play
   by Norman Corwin broadcast February 19, 1939, over CBS[1]

A wave of mass hysteria seized thousands of radio listeners throughout
the nation between 8:15 and 9:30 o'clock last night when a broadcast
of a dramatization of H. G. Wells's fantasy, *The War of the Worlds*,
led thousands to believe that an interplanetary conflict had started
with invading Martians spreading wide death and destruction in New
Jersey and New York . . .
   —*The New York Times*, October 31, 1938

(Rat-tat-tat of machine guns)
(Police sirens)
(Rat-tat-tat of machine guns)
(Shuffle of prisoners in prison yard)
ANNOUNCER: "Gang Busters!"
   —opening to *Gang Busters*, popular radio crime serial of the 1930s

The major formative influence on Rod Serling's imagination and
world view, besides Binghamton, was radio. The creator of
"Requiem for a Heavyweight" and *The Twilight Zone* would eventually blossom into "the golden boy of television," as he was called
at the apex of his video career, but first and foremost, he was the

devoted child of radio. Indeed, the antecedents for most of Serling's mature video oeuvre—as well as for his dynamic, highly political idea of what a dramatist ought to be—can be found in radio—or Big Radio as it was called during his wonder years in upstate New York.

And radio *was* big in the 1930s. Ten short years after its "birth," network radio had become nothing less than a new national religion, commanding an almost irrational loyalty among its estimated 15 million regular listeners, especially the hard-core poor and unemployed, who, huddled together at night in Hoovervilles and migrant labor camps, were often more willing to go without food than without their daily ration of *Amos 'n' Andy* or *One Man's Family*. The individual radio set had become for Americans a kind of portable shaman, magically summoning voices out of the ambient void, voices offering amusement, suspense, information, and succor. Voices like that of torch singer Ruth Etting, belting out the lachrymose lyrics of "Love Me or Leave Me" and "No, No, a Thousand Times No," or CBS discovery Bing Crosby crooning "When We Find That Long Lost Gold Mine in the Sky"; or the scary voice of radio priest Father Charles F. Coughlin, spreading the seeds of American fascism as he blamed the Depression on Jews and money changers; or the five-alarm voice, punctuated with blaring sirens and spitting machine guns, which announced the newest episode of *Gang Busters*. Or the voice of Orson Welles, as the insidious laugh of the radio mystery show *The Shadow*, wondering, "Who knows what evil lurks in the hearts of men?!" And soaring through the ether, somehow making sense of the chaotic times, was the avuncular, supremely confident voice of the pope of the new radio nation, Franklin Delano Roosevelt, soothingly explaining to his friends, as he called his millions of rapt listeners, the compelling need for a bank holiday or a National Recovery Act, appealing directly to his vast constituency as they listened to their sets.

Like most Americans, the Triple Cities had embraced radio, as they had embraced the automobile and mah-jongg. By the mid-thirties, the Binghamton area boasted not one, but two radio stations of its own, NBC affiliate WBNF and CBS affiliate WINR, where Serling would work briefly as an announcer after World War II. Radio broadcasting was a central feature of everyday life. Binghamton was radio land, too. And the Serlings loved the friendly new medium as much as anyone. So many choices! There was such euphonious network-produced musical fare as Paul Whiteman and Benny Goodman and Ruth Etting and Jessica Dragonette, for when the Serlings were in a jazzy mood. Then there were the Ipana Troubadours and the Vicks VapoRub Quartet—or Rod's early favorite, the locally produced variety show *The Weeks and Dickinson Hour.* And the sound was better than anything you could get off a phonograph. And it was free!

Radio wasn't only getting bigger by the late 1930s, when Rod Serling and his teenage peers were tuning in; it was also becoming a much more stimulating, even intriguing medium. During its first decade, radio had been primarily a derivative medium—and to many, a boring one—parroting the newspaper, the stage, the pulpit, and the concert hall. Educated listeners had difficulty taking the medium seriously; yes, Roosevelt's "fireside chats" could be uplifting, but there were still too many ukulele trios and singing mouse contests, and the like.

Then, in 1936, when Serling turned twelve, radio began to get serious. In that landmark year, CBS correspondent H. V. Kaltenborn astonished American audiences with the first live newscast from a war in progress, reporting on the Spanish Civil War from the dubious sanctuary of a haystack located directly between Loyalist and Republican lines. Over the next few years, as war clouds gathered over the rest of the Continent, Kaltenborn, Edward R. Murrow, William Shirer, Charles Collingwood, and the rest of Murrow's "gang" of brash young foreign correspondents would forge the remote broadcast into a veritable art. They also helped make CBS News "must" listening for the nation's elite, as well as for young audiophiles like Rod Serling, who had vivid, word-intoxicated imaginations of their own.

At about the same time, interesting things were happening at CBS in radio drama. Witness the auspicious birth, in July 1936, of the *Columbia Experimental Workshop.* The first network program devoted to original radio drama, and one that would develop into a kind of Group Theater of the Air, the *Workshop* was the brainchild of CBS's gifted, sound-obsessed engineer-artist Irving Reis. Startled first-time listeners to the novel program found themselves at the mercy of eerily realistic-sounding bombing planes about to unleash their deadly loads, or angry, trapped bees ready for the kill.

27

Next poet Archibald MacLeish, one of the growing number of writers who were beginning to take radio seriously, seized the moment and weighed in with "The Fall of the City." The first play dealing with an adult theme—fascism—that was written directly for the microphone, "The Fall of the City" was an instant sensation when it was staged by Reis's players in 1937. According to a laudatory article in *Theater Arts* at the time by Merrill Denison, the play tells of "the coming of a dictator to a free city":

> . . . In a beleaguered town, unidentified as to time or space, a dead woman speaks from the tomb warning of the coming of a Conqueror. An Announcer tells of the panic that seized the milling crowd below him and communicates the news brought by the messengers of the Conqueror's landing on a distant shore. Speakers harangue the murmuring throng. A statesman, an old general and a priest each has his say as the Conqueror draws nearer to the gates.
>
> Between these contradictory speeches, the Announcer describes the arrival of other messengers with the news of the Conqueror's approach. But as doom draws nearer, the crowd can do nothing but vacillate and argue, unable to agree on a course of action. When the Conqueror at last enters the gates—a great martial figure as broad as a brass door walking with a thunderous clang of metal on the paving stones—the crowd casts away its weapons and grovels face down on the ground. Only the Announcer sees that there is no Conqueror. Only he knows that there is nothing inside the armor, that the brass mantelpiece is empty, that the crowd has been vanquished by its own fears. The prophecy of the dead woman has been made good: "Masterless men must take a master."[2]

In an inspired move, MacLeish's parable was staged in New York's Park Avenue Regiment Armory, the better to create the hollow, reverberating sound Reis felt was necessary. Denison enthused: "One had the sense of actuality and importance which is conveyed by broadcasts of contemporaneous events." "The Fall of the City" had legitimized radio drama, much as Paddy Chayefsky's ground-breaking television drama, "Marty," and Serling's "Patterns" would help to legitimize television drama two decades later.[3] Further, *The Twilight Zone* was clearly heir to the tradition of parable that, in terms of broadcasting media, began with "The Fall of the City."

After the galvanic success of "The Fall of the City," Reis's successor as director of the *Columbia Experimental Workshop*, William Robson, found himself fielding calls from some of the most famous poets and dramatists of the day, all anxious to follow MacLeish's lead. Robson obliged as many of them as he could, commissioning plays from W. H. Auden, Stephen Vincent Benet, and Maxwell Anderson, among others.

As the prestigiousness of the *Workshop* grew, so did its audience, so much so that in 1938 William Paley, President of CBS, decided to make it a regular Sunday night feature, even though it was an unsponsored or non-income-producing show. This was one of those periods in Paley's conflicted career when he was willing to carry a show like the *Workshop* for the sake of prestige alone. Another powerful incentive was an enlightened Federal Communications Commission edict ordering both CBS and NBC to broadcast more intelligent fare. Ten years later, when the FCC was in a more laissez-faire mood, Paley decided he could no longer afford to be as magnanimous, but for now he was happy to play along.

The play was the thing at the *Workshop*'s cramped studio headquarters at 485 Madison Avenue. In addition to adding new luster to the reputation and careers of established poets and dramatists, CBS helped launch a second generation of radio auteurs who took up the horizons of radio drama.

Of course, Orson Welles's infamous contribution to radio drama is well known, if to no one else than the residents of Grover's Mill, New Jersey. Welles, then in his early twenties, was already a radio veteran when CBS vice-president William Lewis gave the theatrical wunderkind from Wisconsin his own show, in the summer of 1938. He had been the insidious Shadow. He had played the pivotal role of the omniscient Announcer in "The Fall of the City." He was ready for new things, although Lewis didn't realize *how* new until the fateful Halloween night, when—as his own "radio version of dressing up in a sheet and jumping out of a bush and saying 'Boo!' " as Welles put it the night before—the Mercury Theater players staged a modern-day, original adaptation of H. G. Wells's *War of the Worlds*. By the time the impish writer, producer, and director wearily signed off after finishing his broadcast tour de force, "The War of the Worlds" had conveyed all too well "the actuality of contemporaneous events" (in Merrill Denison's words), especially the recent broadcasts of the fall of Vienna and the dismemberment of Czechoslovakia—tapping into the American public's mounting anxiety about events abroad. When a mortified Welles, confronted with the mob of police reporters who converged on the CBS studios that evening, suddenly realized what havoc he had wrought, he assumed that his career was finished. Of course, it had only begun.

Another rambunctious, talented, and somewhat perverse young man who left his fingerprints on the radio medium—and on young Rod Serling's prankish consciousness—was the late Arch Oboler. A short, dark, raffish man from Chicago with a strong interest in fantasy and sound effects, Oboler was an early contributor to the *Columbia Workshop*.

However, it was on the NBC show *Lights Out* that the horror master left his signature on millions of adolescent nightmares. *"This is the witching hour,"* Oboler's Grand Guignol of the air began. *"It is the hour when dogs howl and evil is let loose on the sleeping world. Want to hear about it? Then turn off your lights!"* Only on *Lights Out*, to cite a few memorable, gruesome examples, could a man be turned inside-out by a demonic fog or a woman metamorphose into a human-sized cat with convincingly macabre sound effects.

Oboler ultimately tired of operating in the aural netherworld and turned his skills to didactic psychodramas like his famed radio version of Dalton Trumbo's antiwar melodrama *Johnny Got His Gun*, about a blind, deaf, quadruple-amputee World War I veteran. Thirty years later, a still-impressed Rod Serling also commissioned Oboler to write an episode of *The Twilight Zone* for the series' final season.

Of all the newfangled radio bards, none was more influential or more beloved by the listening public of the late 1930s and early 1940s than Norman Corwin, also known as "Mr. Radio." And none was more idolized by the young Rod Serling.

There are numerous parallels between Corwin's career and Serling's. Corwin, originally a newspaperman from Massachusetts, began writing for radio in 1936 at WLW, the powerful CBS affiliate that dominated the Midwest located in Cincinnati—the same place where Serling would get his start in broadcasting in 1950.

A fervent liberal, Corwin didn't last very long at the conservative station, quitting after WLW refused to cover several labor strikes in the area. Then he set off for New York, where he briefly found happiness at WQXR, "the station for people who hate radio," writing a poetry program—for Corwin was and is essentially a poet—before being invited by William Lewis to contribute to the *Columbia Workshop.*

The impressive results were two back-to-back and highly disparate aural masterpieces that are still vividly etched into the word-excited imaginations of listeners of that day: "The Plot to Overthrow Christmas," a rhyming comic fantasy about a satanic plot to steal Christmas, which immediately became a holiday favorite; and the even more sensational antiwar play "They Fly Through the Air with the Greatest of Ease," a kind of radio Guernica that was inspired by the barbaric remarks of Vittorio Mussolini (the dictator's son) in the press, likening the sight of Italian bombs dropping on Ethiopians to the unfolding of the petals of a rose. The incensed writer mordantly dedicated the screeching aural drama "to all aviators who have bombed defenseless civilian populations and machine-gunned hapless refugees."[4]

In the fifty-year-old piece, which still retains its frightening immediacy when listened to today, the crew of a bomber, nationality unstated, blithely set out for their day's destruction, exchanging small talk along the way. Shortly, they sight their objective, "regiments of tenements arrayed beneath the banner of their wet wash." We listen, horrified, to the unsuspecting apartment dwellers below, just before the bombs drop: in one apartment, a family argues over breakfast; in another, someone idly plays a piano étude; in another, a baby cries.[5]

The bombs drop, but Corwin doesn't let us hear them. Instead, we listen to the aviators congratulate themselves, à la Mussolini. "This work always reminds me of mowing wheat," the bombardier chortles. "Nice symmetrical pattern," his copilot agrees.[6]

But there is justice yet in Corwin's vitriolic parable: a plane from the country under attack catches the bomber and sends it down in flames, while a narrator adds, "Be calm, sit back, there is still time to see a final symmetry—a corkscrew in the sky." With "They Fly Through the Air," Corwin proved his mastery of the medium. *Time* called him the "golden boy" of radio. CBS had its first writer-star.[7]

And the hit scripts kept coming. In 1938, Corwin began writing for *County Seat,* a series about the whimsical doings of "Doc" Will Hackett, the crackerbarrel philosopher from the fictional hamlet of

Northbury, and the adventures and misadventures of Doc's nephew, Jerry Whipple. Next, Corwin brought his vernacular-based verse and bravura directing skills to *The Pursuit of Happiness*, a series featuring the actor Burgess Meredith and dedicated to the uplifting, if somewhat vague, proposition that "democracy is a good thing." It featured dramatic and musical adaptations by various writers, including a rousing radio opera about the Magna Carta by the illustrious team of Maxwell Anderson and Kurt Weill.

Then, in 1940, came *26 by Corwin*, a biweekly tour de force written entirely by Corwin and featuring everything from farce, like "My Client Curley," a Broadway agent's "memoir" of his "client," a multi-talented caterpillar, to political fables like "The Oracle of Philadelphia" with Corwinesque sound effects to boot. And, two hundred miles away in Binghamton, an impressionable young teen-ager named Rod Serling was eagerly listening on his bedside Philco.

Many years later, after he had abandoned radio for television and Serling and Corwin had become friends, Serling readily acknowledged Corwin's great influence on him. Upon inspection, the connections are clear enough: Serling's mordant *Twilight Zone* lead-ins, his love for the common man, the parablelike quality of much of his later writing, the sophisticated sound effects, the occasionally purple prose, the cautiously optimistic world view—all these aspects of Serling's work have their antecedents in the works of Corwin. One crucial difference: Corwin disliked controversy. Serling thrived on it. Corwin himself would be typically gracious in comparing his golden moment with Serling's. "Rod's achievement was much more striking than mine. He was operating during the McCarthy period. He was swimming against the tide. I had the freedom. I had the creativity. I had the ambience. He didn't."[8]

Of course, Serling didn't listen to *only* radio drama. He also loved to listen to sports. "The sportscaster I listened to was Tom McMahon, and later on Jack Hand," he recalled in a nostalgic article he wrote for the *Binghamton Sun* in 1955. "And on the radio, it was Harry Trenner, Ralph Carroll, Dee Finch, and the quavering voice of an old man named Weeks who used to sing, 'How do you do everybody, how do you do, this is *The Weeks and Dickinson Hour* we bring to you.' What ever happened to *The Weeks and Dickinson Hour*?"[9]

Corwin, Serling's dramaturgical hero, reached the pinnacle of his prewar fame on December 1, 1941, when, just six days before Pearl

Harbor, his radio drama celebrating the 150th anniversary of the Bill of Rights, "We Hold These Truths," was broadcast on all four networks. With a star-studded cast, the play, earnestly narrated by Jimmy Stewart, was heard by approximately sixty million listeners, by far the largest audience in history for any kind of dramatic performance. Even Serling would never match those numbers. No writer would, really. Afterward, director Corwin nimbly cut to the Oval Office for some fighting words from the Commander-in-Chief.

Radio was on the march. Now it was about to go to war.

3

THE PURPLE TESTAMENT (1941 – 45)

Infantry platoon, U.S. Army, Philippine Islands, 1945. These are the faces of the young men who fight. . . . For this is the province of combat, and these are the faces of war.
—from "The Purple Testament," first aired February 12, 1960[1]

It took about six months for the full impact of World War II to reach Binghamton. Serling found a grimmer, more resolute town when he returned from Camp Oxford to complete his last term at Binghamton Central in the fall of 1942. The reflexive patriotism that had followed Pearl Harbor had now given way to the sobering, collective realization that most of the area men who were already in uniform wouldn't be home by Christmas, and probably not the next either. Some Central graduates overseas, their names somberly intoned at morning assembly that grim fall, had already been killed. Almost every Triple Cities family had already had a son or daughter in uniform—including the Serlings of 67 Bennett Avenue, who had already given Bob up to the army—and still, every week, the local draft board sent out orders for more.

High school life itself had also taken on a more subdued tone. The school's noxious air raid signal—four short blasts from the hallway buzzers—which had once prompted smug smiles from students, now sent them scrambling; the rules for emergency first aid were posted in every homeroom and eagerly memorized. After classes, students gathered for sodas at the patriotically renamed "V" spa on Front Street to dissect the latest war bulletin from the fronts;

34

en route home, like other dutiful students, they grimly scoured the streets of Binghamton for metal scrap.

Of course, certain things about Binghamton hadn't changed, would never change, war or no war. The Triplets still played baseball for their loyal fans, and the Saturday afternoon matinee at the State Theater was still packed, and the *Binghamton Press* was still faithfully delivered, boomerang-style, every morning, and the *Bulletin* in the afternoon, but now their once comfortingly familiar front pages were splashed with the names of strange foreign places like Guadalcanal and Wake Island and Kasserine Pass, bloody places where Americans were fighting and dying and not always winning, and the relentlessly upbeat Movietone newsreels of the expanding war that were shown before features now included more and more shots of American casualties.

Families still gathered around their living room consoles every Sunday evening to listen to Jack Benny, but now, after one of his hilarious pauses, Benny was apt to end his popular show with an earnest pitch for war bonds. There was still music and dancing every Saturday night over at the George F. Johnson Pavilion, too, but now the big bands that played there usually began their sets with "The Star-Spangled Banner" or a rousing singalong like "Remember Pearl Harbor," before segueing to more languorous fare. Binghamton's innocence was ending, and Rod Serling's was about to as well.

As the new editor of *Panorama*, Rod Serling, like hundreds of other high school editors across the country, used the editorial page to urge his fellow students to do Their Part for the war effort. A typically earnest and slightly melodramatic Serling opinion, about an imminent war stamp sale, appeared in the October 22, 1942, issue: "When a doctor despairs of curing a patient and when the last vestige of hope for recovery is gone," the archly worded leading editorial article entitled "Prognosis-Negative" began, "his case report may confine itself to two brief words—prognosis-negative. Two weeks ago we were ready to indicate our school's chances for a decent war stamp sale were practically nil and a prognosis-negative would be the appropriate mask of hopelessness. Let's make the prognosis of our stamp sale not negative, but positive; make it a fat, healthy sale, make it an assurance that America's younger generation realizes its obligations and wants to go 'all out' for final, complete, unstipulated victory!"[2]

But Serling wanted to do more than cheerlead. He wanted to fight; specifically, he wanted to be an Army Air Force tailgunner, the entry under his picture in the 1943 Binghamton Central yearbook notes. "He had heard that tailgunners had the highest mortality rate," says Norman Miller. Indeed, Serling was so eager to get into the thick of the fray that he almost quit school early, and would have, by his own account, if he hadn't been dissuaded by Gus Youngstrom, a civics and history teacher from Central, who told the impatient senior, "War is a temporal thing. It ends. An education doesn't. Without your degree, where will you be *after* the war?" The would-be aerial sharpshooter reluctantly conceded that he had a point.[3]

On January 15, 1943, three weeks after his eighteenth birthday, Rod Serling graduated from Binghamton Central. His class rank was 35th out of 185. The next morning, he enlisted in the United States Army. The gung-ho teenager may still have wanted to become a tailgunner; probably his eyesight wasn't sharp enough. Instead, he wound up in the paratroopers. According to his friend Vernon Hartung, who reported for induction at the same time and wound up in the same outfit, the 511th Parachute Infantry Regiment, the two Binghamtonians got the idea of becoming paratroopers after seeing a newsreel about the recent Allied landings in French North Africa, while awaiting processing into the infantry at Fort Niagara. The film gave considerable credit to the American airborne troops who participated in the successful Allied operation. "All I know is that when Roddie and I got out of that theater, he was kind of chanting to himself, 'I want to be a paratrooper, I want to be a paratrooper,' " recalls Hartung.[4]

Of course, there remained one all-too-familiar problem—Serling's size. According to army regulations, he was at least an inch too short to be a skytrooper, as paratroopers were then called.

But Serling didn't let that stand in his way. Within days, he jumped on a train for Georgia—paratrooper training country; and brazened his way past the reception officer for the newly formed 511th Parachute Infantry Regiment, part of the brand new 11th Airborne Division.

Like most of his propagandized fellows, Private Serling was still living in a dream world when he first fell out for roll call amidst the sun-baked confines of Camp Toccoa, Georgia, home of the 11th Airborne Division under the hawk eyes of General Raymond Swing, the division commander. The jaunty American "skytroopers" whom Serling and Hartung had first seen leaping out of army transport planes over French-held North Africa might have looked formidable in the newsreels. However, many of the unevenly trained men had actually misjumped and been killed. Indeed, the airborne "concept"—i.e., the notion of lifting entire divisions of heavily armed parachutists over long distances and dropping them over an entrenched enemy—had largely been a washout, at least for the United States, thus far in the war. The samurailike Swing was determined to turn that situation around with the hapless if eager men assembled before him. Whether Swing took note that one or two of the men like Serling were a shade under the minimum regulation height is not recorded. Doubtless, Swing, who didn't miss much, did. However, at the moment, the general was more interested in seeing whether a man had the right stuff to prove the legitimacy of the airborne "concept." An early airborne devotee, and one of the army's first generals to make the five jumps needed to earn "the silver badge of courage," Swing had witnessed previous American airborne debacles in North Africa and Sicily (where planeloads of troopers were shot up by friendly fire) and was determined not to see their likes again. *His* division, the 11th, would prove the worthiness of Army Airborne, or it would die trying.

One of those listening approvingly to Swing's grim welcoming speech was Colonel Oren "Hard Rock" Haugen, commander of Serling's regiment and one of the division's two full-fledged regiments, the 511th. An airborne fanatic like Swing, Haugen had earned his nickname well, as Serling and his fellow recruits would soon learn. A favorite Haugen technique was leading his cursing, breathless green troops on forced, sometimes barefooted, runs up and down mile-high Curahee Mountain. Assigned to regimental headquarters company as part of its S2, or intelligence, platoon, Serling would get to know Haugen especially well before the war was over; eventually the Colonel would metamorphose into a major character in Serling's first hit teleplay, "Patterns."

"Toccoa was a hellhole," says Jack Warden, the actor and *Zone* player, who belonged to the 511th's brother regiment, the 503rd, and whose common divisional bond with Serling brought the two closer, seventeen years later, when Warden was asked to appear in Serling's show. "You'd get up every morning at five o'clock and run the hill in full field pack. The hill was about seven miles, almost a forty-five-degree angle. And the ones that fell out were sent back to the infantry. I remember one colonel said at the beginning, 'Look around now. In three months, you won't see either the person to your left or to your right.' That sounds like Haugen."[5]

Four months and hundreds of grueling runs, forced marches, obstacle course challenges, and surprise duffel bag inspections later, Serling, Hartung, Warden, and the other jump-conditioned men who survived thus far entrained for the army's first primitive jump school, at Fort Benning, Georgia.

Lasting two months, jump school was divided into four progressively grueling parts: Parachute Packing, wherein the still nervous para-trainees were painstakingly instructed on the rigorous art of packing, inspecting, folding, and adjusting their silken lifejackets; Jump Training, where the men were inculcated in the proper technique for jumping *and* landing—knees flexed, hips *slightly* flexed, body upright, landing with equal force on the *balls* of the feet—by having them jump off a seven-foot platform over and over to the beat of braying para-sergeants; Tower Training, in which the remaining, beaten and bruised "paraguys" (Serling's macho expression) were slowly hauled up to the top of a 250-foot parachute tower and dropped onto the ground; and finally, Jump Qualification, or "D" stage, in which the soldiers had to make five actual jumps, including two mass jumps of twelve men each, from C-47 skytrains.

This is where the paratroopers were separated from the mere soldiers. The men of "D" stage were generally full of bluff talk as they boarded the plane from which they would make the first jump, and as it took off. However, a hush would fall over the men as they sat in their bucket seats, facing each other as their plane approached the "DZ" or drop zone, the point of no return. A few chutists would capitulate to the pressure and refuse to go on; their orders were that they didn't have to. Then, almost mercifully, the green light would go on and the jumpmaster would give the order for the men to STAND UP AND HOOK UP their static lines, the cables that would open their chutes after deplaning. Then, in a whoosh, the men were filing out the open door of the plane—too late for second thoughts now. And then, as the chutes ripped open and the canopies billowed open in the prop blast, WHAM! They were airborne—and generally in shock. No matter how well-trained or self-confident a man was, nothing could quite prepare him for the mighty jerk when his chute flew open—or for the weird feeling of stasis right after jumping, followed by that of having the earth rush up at him. A man's first jump was always a spiritual watershed: proof positive that he was a man. After that, the other jumps were easy. Now they could shout with proud finality that they were airborne—or, rather, Airborne!

So much for jump training. Now it was time to progress from discrete to unit technique. Confident in themselves as individual paratroopers, the men and their officers learned how to think and act as larger elements of the dynamic divisional whole. There were dozens of jumps: squad jumps, company jumps, regimental jumps, day jumps, night jumps, twilight jumps. Down on the ground, the troops were subject to platoon proficiency tests, infiltration course tests, close combat tests—all under the eyes of Swing, Haugen, and the other top officers. All that plus advanced weapons training, topography, meteorology, communication, and demolition assault training, everything that Swing felt was necessary to make his men complete paratroopers and to prove the airborne concept once the men of the 11th got to the battlefield—which, to Swing's and the men's disgust, would take another two years. And so, as General Swing proudly wrote in the division's 1943 college-style yearbook, the troopers were "pared down in number and physique until only the steel and whalebone remained"—the American samurai.[6]

Meanwhile, the division faced its first great test as an airborne unit in November 1943, when the troopers made practice jumps for distinguished visitors—including Secretary of War Henry Stimson, who was sufficiently impressed by the division's performance to give the go-ahead for another airborne division.

The men followed the war's progress on their barracks radio sets. But, while forced to wait for the war, they didn't wait long to use their fists. And Private First Class Rod Serling was as eager to mix it up as the rest of his fellow troopers—perhaps even more so—to prove that he was as rough and tough as his taller comrades. "He used to write me about going into pubs in Columbus [Georgia] with other troopers, hunting down Air Force and Armored guys," said Norman Miller. "I knew he was locked up at least once for getting into fights."[7]

Fortunately, thanks to the encouragement of General Swing, the division also held legal, if not necessarily less bloody, boxing tournaments. Serling, competing as a flyweight, participated with seemingly masochistic glee. Ken Haan, another regimental mate, remembered Serling's kamikaze boxing style from the time the regiment was bivouacked at Camp Polk, Louisiana, during the famous mass army maneuvers there in 1943. In one bout, Serling was inexplicably matched with a heavyweight named Kelly. "Kelly was two hundred pounds, six-two maybe," Haan remembered. "And they put on the boxing gloves, and he said to Rod, 'Okay, hit me.' And he kept parrying Rod's blows, and every once in a while, when he'd see an opening, he'd go 'BOOM' and down Serling would go. I don't think Serling ever did lay a glove on him!"[8]

The scrappy kid from Binghamton ultimately entered sixteen fights, advancing as far as the second round of the division finals before being knocked out decisively in his seventeenth and what would turn out to be the last fight of his career, with splintered nose and a badly cut right eye. One of those rushing to assist the bloodied berserker was Private Vern Hartung, who hadn't seen his hometown buddy since being inducted together at Fort Niagara, or known he was in the same unit. There wasn't much time to get reacquainted. According to Hartung, "All he said was 'Where you been, old buddy?' and he passed out."[9]

Requiem for a flyweight: From then on Serling would do his fighting in his own imagination, and on paper—or in network boardrooms. "No question about it, he had a boxer's eyes—that way of looking at you that good boxers have," said Richard Grossman, a former college boxer who served as Serling's editor at Simon and Schuster for the book version of "Patterns." "When he got you in one of those eyelocks of his you *knew* you were in trouble," said former CBS programmer Mike Dann, who often had to play the network heavy versus Serling's outraged Angry Man.[10]

Another highlight of Serling's stateside training period, besides his last bout, was a brief visit from Sam Serling. A picture of the occasion shows a smiling if tired-looking Sam and his beaming son. Rod is flaunting his "silver wings." Unbeknownst to either, it was the last time they would see each other.

No doubt, like many of the division's concupiscent "paraguys," he also chased barracks town women during his fifteen months in the South. And he honed his increasingly blue sense of humor.

Finally, on April 25, 1944, the eight thousand troopers of the 11th Airborne Division got their marching orders. All they knew was that they were headed west. That meant California, and the

South Pacific—and the Japanese. As a Jew anxious to fight Hitler, Serling was disappointed. Of course, he hated the Japanese, but he despised the Nazis even more.

Two weeks later, on May 5, the division embarked for points west aboard the U.S.S. *Sea Pike*, nervously uncertain of their ultimate destination. Where were they actually going? the men wondered. China? Burma? Australia? Few guessed New Guinea.

Ever the cutup, Serling helped keep his comrades entertained during the long, nerve-racking voyage, with his ready supply of jokes and impressions, blue and otherwise. He was also master of ceremonies during the 511th's raucous equator-crossing ceremony, when his penchant for risqué jokes finally brought down the wrath of the regimental chaplain, the Reverend Gerald Walker, who had the comic's microphone unceremoniously cut off in the midst of his spiel.

And then the men learned where they were going. New Guinea. A year before, Serling might have known from the newsreels, the northern coast of the thirteen-hundred-mile-long island had been a Japanese fortress and the scene of some of the heaviest fighting in the Southwest Pacific Theater as General Douglas MacArthur had jumped from one Japanese stronghold to another.

However, by the time the *Sea Pike* sailed up Oro Bay on the southern coast of the bird-shaped island in July 1944, the main pockets of Japanese resistance on the island had been eliminated. General Swing assured his disappointed men that the 11th would soon be employed in a large operation, possibly even the retaking of the Philippines; MacArthur had told him so. In the meantime, they were to undergo jungle training—whatever that meant. In practice, it meant a lot of speeches and marches, and jumps, and weapons instruction, and a lot of watching after-dinner movies in the rain. And a lot of waiting.

And listening to a lot of radio. Thanks to the long reach of Armed Forces Radio's "mosquito network," New Guinea was part of radio land, too. Serling and his fellow troopers could listen to all their favorite radio friends as they waited for their jumping orders: Ma Perkins, FDR, Fibber McGee—the whole crew; even Serling's beau ideal, Norman Corwin, who had been conscripted to write "service dramas" about a GI's first encounter with the Brits. And there was the *Command Performance* series, "written to the specifications of homesick fighting men," which carried such heart-tuggingly familiar sounds as the sizzle of Betty Hutton frying a steak, with commentary by Bob Hope, followed by a rousing orchestral chaser by Major Glenn Miller and band.

Nevertheless, despite the best efforts of Swing and his commanders to keep their men entertained and combat-ready, the division's morale sunk to its lowest level during its strange, five-month New Guinean interlude. It is not a period about which 11th veterans, who tend to be militantly nostalgic about their wartime experiences, are fond of talking. A number of men suffered breakdowns. At one point the idle men of Serling's regiment grew so restless that they took to shooting bats for amusement, leading an enraged Colonel Haugen to send them on a long forced march, which resulted in more casualties.

Serling himself appears to have borne up relatively well during this arduous period, putting up with the new, seemingly gratuitous cycle of practice and training with his usual rough humor. He wrote a lot of letters home. He tried his hand at writing poetry. "He'd write a couple of verses and he'd say, 'What do you think of this?' " a regimental comrade recalled. "I can remember a tiny bit of it . . . 'We're tough and we know it. We're good and we'll show it. There's paraguys fighting this war.' And he sent it to his brother. And after a time he got a letter from his brother, and he [Robert] said: 'Forget about poetry, Rod.' "[11]

He got similar advice from Leo Kosoff, then an editor at the *Syracuse Journal*, via Sam, who had also received a copy of his son's ode to para-manhood. Did Rod have potential? Sam eagerly asked. "Better the boy should be a butcher," Kosoff told Sam to tell Rod. The would-be Siegfried Sassoon was stung. Twenty years later, the overly sensitive Serling, who never forgot a negative review, was able to pull Kosoff's letter out of his files and show it to his mortified cousin-in-law. No doubt he did the same with Robert's nugatory notice.[12]

The aspiring writer had somewhat better success when he tried his hand at radio, serving as the continuity writer of and bit player in a morbid, if well-received, propaganda skit about Japanese treachery during comedian Jack Benny's visit to the 511th's "Amphitheater in the Jungle," which in turn was sent by shortwave to other stations of the AFR's "mosquito network."

ANNOUNCER: The playlet that you've just heard was sent to you via shortwave by the S2 section of the 511th Parachute

Infantry. If it has given you insight into modern war, we feel that we've accomplished our mission. (MUSIC. . . . SOFT).[13]

It wasn't much, but the skit gave Serling a taste of writing for the air, and he liked it. He had also gotten a chance to act and to meet Jack Benny. (In 1962, Benny surprised Serling by remembering the encounter when he once again invited the former private to appear on *The Jack Benny Show.*)

The crusader of the air was also an active participant in the freewheeling discussions of the whimsically named "Dobadura Chapter of the New Guinea Literary, Metaphysical, and Philosophical Discussion Society of Old Men of the Five One One," a kind of bull session society for the intellectuals of the regiment. Reverend Walker, with whom Serling had since become reconciled, recalls that Serling was very affected by the news of how the Nazis were treating the Jews.

And, like most of his fellow "paraguys," he daydreamed about his hometown. And certain women. And, he wondered, would he ever see combat, and how would he handle it when and if he did?

On November 20, 1944, the eight thousand men of the 11th Airborne Division, including the eighteen hundred men of Serling's 511th Parachute Infantry Regiment, broke camp at Dobadura and boarded a flotilla of amphibious landing crafts bound for the embattled Filipino island of Leyte, some five hundred miles away. After their nearly two years of training, General MacArthur had finally made good on his promise: the 11th had been assigned to a major operation, the reduction of Leyte Island, perhaps the most important stop on the road to Japan and to the end of the war in the Pacific. Because of the lack of drop-carrier planes in the Pacific, as well as the peculiar nature of the war on Leyte, the somewhat disappointed men of the 11th learned they would be fighting not as an airborne division but as light infantry, mopping up after the other six divisions of the 6th Army had gone ashore at Bito Beach ahead of them. But at least they were under way.

To be sure, the battle for Leyte Island *had* been won, for all intents and purposes, by the time the 11th hit the sands of the island and began pushing inland; but the Japanese commander of the occupied archipelago, General Tomoyuki Yamashita—who had called the battle for Leyte the decisive battle of the Philippines campaign—didn't think so, and neither did the sixty thousand die-hards dug in around the island.

Over the next few weeks, the 11th would feel the full brunt of Yamashita's obstinacy. The division's mission, as the men learned at Bito, was twofold: they were to relieve the battered 7th Division—one of the divisions involved in the initial assault—along the Burauen-La Paz-Rugho line, a jungle-infested ten-mile perpendicular extending down the middle of the fig-shaped isle, and destroy the Japanese forces in that sector; then, according to 6th Army orders, they were to make a forbiddingly difficult overland attack across the Mahonag Mountains and break out on the west coast, a trip of roughly five hundred miles.[14]

The first assignment proved deceptively easy. Fortunately, there were relatively few of Yamashita's men left, and after a few minor firefights the Burauen-La Paz-Rugho line was quickly "disinfected."

The overland attack, though, proved much more difficult than expected. There were, to be sure, *three* enemies on Leyte. There were, first and foremost, the Japanese troops themselves. Specially trained and equipped for night fighting, one or two would suddenly materialize out of the dark on the regiment's perimeter, cut a sentry's throat, and silently disappear, leaving their terrifying handiwork to be discovered at dawn; or they would rain terror en masse in crazed, sake-fortified banzai charges that frequently ended with one of the attackers obliterating himself by detonating a land mine attached to his waist, taking the unlucky occupants of the nearest 511th foxhole with him.

The second enemy was Leyte's terrifying—and stupefying—topography. The men of the 511th PIR were shocked. There had been mountains and jungles back in New Guinea, but none like the steep, dense entanglements the troopers encountered here. And the hot, sticky, ninety-degree weather coupled with the frequent monsoons made things worse. Together, these elements made the 511th's five-hundred-mile trek across the Mahonags a solid continuum of horror and misery.

By day, the regiment, slogging single-file through the warm rain and root-entangled mud, might advance a mile around and through the razor-backed mountains, sometimes not even a mile, before setting up a defensive perimeter for the night. Then, after dark, the Japanese would come. The next day and night would be the same.

Further hindering the 511th's antlike progress was the lack of even basic military intelligence, forcing the regiment to march blind—and often directly into Japanese positions. The easily ambushed trail also made it hard to maintain an adequate train of supplies, no less for the 511th to remain a coherent fighting unit. About halfway through this march, the befogged 511th found itself besieged atop one of the foothills of the Mahonags. They would not come down for two weeks. Those two weeks in December 1944 would be the regiment's—and Serling's—Golgotha.

By this time, Serling, slogging along with the rest of his troopers-turned-grunts, had been transferred out of the S2 platoon to the 511th's demolition platoon. Surely the move was not a voluntary one. Serling may have been gung-ho, but he didn't want to die, and the demo platoon had the highest rate of casualties. "He screwed up somewhere along the line," said Sergeant Frank Lewis, leader of the regiment's "death squad." "Apparently he got on somebody's nerves or something. He tended to make too many jokes." The assignment may have been the result of the dreamy-headed private's decision to go exploring on his own one day, and getting lost. At any rate, Lewis recalled, Private Serling failed to obey a vital order during this mountaintop siege. "We were in a pretty good firefight," Lewis explained, "and we were all beat to shit, and we got into the foxhole, sitting there waiting, and it starts to get dark and here I find out he didn't reload any of the magazines. And I said, 'Dammit, you can't do this . . .'" Serling's no doubt abashed reaction is unrecorded. According to Lewis, Serling was a good garrison soldier, "but he didn't have the wits or aggressiveness required for combat."[15] Perhaps he didn't have the stomach for it either.

One incident in particular that occurred during the siege, during a close-in food drop by army cargo planes, traumatized the once gung-ho "paraguy." A friend in the outfit, an equally loquacious Jewish corporal from Brooklyn by the name of Melvin Levy, had a refreshing habit of mock-directing the "biscuit bombers" during the intense, unchuted food drops. Then, during one of the drops, while Levy, Serling, and the rest of the platoon were taking cover under a palm tree and Levy was doing his monologue, one of the huge crates came crashing through the leaves and decapitated him. Afterward, Serling, still in shock, led the services for Levy and arranged a Star of David on his makeshift grave.

Death was a close companion during those two weeks of hell in Leyte. Today it was Levy, killed by a food crate. Who would it be tomorrow—and how would *he* die? By a "friendly" food crate? Or by an enemy jungle knife or bayonet? Was there, perhaps, something about a man's face that indicated his number was up? If only they could tell, the battered and beleaguered men wished, as they hunkered down in their foxholes. Years later, that idea, taken to its supernatural conclusion, would animate "The Purple Testament," one of Serling's grimmest and most haunting episodes of *Twilight Zone*, and one of several war stories with a Filipino setting.

To add to Serling's and the other besieged troopers' sense of hopelessness, news came through of a surprise paratroop attack on the division's rear echelon headquarters at Bito Beach. The attack, a rare instance of airborne troops jumping against other airborne troops, and an especially rare one for the Japanese, was beaten off with only minimal casualties, thanks to General Swing, who quickly grabbed a pistol and organized a successful counterattack. But the shock effect on the entire division, including forward elements like the 511th, was considerable. If Division wasn't safe, who was?

Mercifully, on December 22, Haugen's eighteen hundred tattered and benumbed men finally broke through the jungle-and-Japanese chain surrounding them and achieved their objective by linking up with American forces at Ormoc, on Leyte's west coast.

Two weeks later, on Christmas Day, 1944—Rod Serling's twentieth birthday—the troopers were relieved and ordered back to Bito, concluding what had been the longest month of their short lives. Later Serling would write about that miraculous day for an anthology of Christmas stories and articles collected by Chaplain Walker:

> It was a gray morning carved out of gray clay and shadowed by fog. It was not just a time—it was a mood—the kind of mood that is part of the province of combat and never conveyed vicariously to the human being who has not lived physically with the tension, the violence, the anguish of protracted war.[16]

Of course, from the moment he left the army and decided to take up writing—like James Jones and Norman Mailer—Serling would attempt to do just that—convey the anguish and horror of modern, protracted war:

. . . A nineteen-year-old Second Looie got up to his feet and spoke through the first beard he'd ever worn.

"All right—on your feet. Let's move out."

We rose—the packs, the ammo belts, weaponry, all fused to us like extensions of our bodies, the weight so constant that it was all part of us—and we started to plod slowly through the ankle-deep mud . . . a long line of dirty, bearded sameness.

And then somebody far up the line stopped dead, and there was a whispered message that went down past the ranks . . . the whispered voice of the man in front of me said, "It's Christmas."[17]

All in all, a nice birthday present: Private Serling had survived. He hadn't won any medals, but he had survived. Somewhere, possibly during the siege, Serling had also received two injuries, including one in the kneecap that would perpetually plague him, giving out at unexpected moments and causing him to limp and sometimes to fall. Like many veterans, Serling would rarely if ever discuss his war injuries, and their exact origin and nature are difficult to affix. Perhaps after what he had seen happen to Levy and some of his other unlucky comrades—the 511th took two hundred casualties on Leyte, one hundred and twenty killed in action—Serling may have been abashed to discuss his relatively light wounds.

The regiment as a whole had nothing to be ashamed of. Clearly, the 511th had helped defeat the Japanese on Leyte. Although pockets of Yamashita's men would hold out for months, by the time Haugen's exhausted expeditioners recamped at Bito, Japanese resistance had essentially been broken. However, the 511th's dirty work was far from done. MacArthur was anxious to take the archipelago's main prize, Luzon, site of the Filipino capital of Manila, and the Bataan Peninsula, site of Corregidor Island, where, in early 1942, his outnumbered U.S. and Filipino forces had fought a long delaying action before being overwhelmed and death-marched into captivity. MacArthur, who had barely escaped before the American capitulation, had vowed to return. And, he told General Swing, the 11th Airborne would help lead the way. Furthermore, he informed his airborne commander, this time he intended to use the 11th as originally intended, as an airborne assault division; this time he would make sure that his troopers got the carrier planes they needed to complete their mission.

The 511th's specific mission, as MacArthur explained to Swing, and Swing explained to Haugen, centered around a mass jump by the core of the 511th onto Tagaytay Ridge, one of the most important tactical positions near Manila; the 511th's sister regiment, the 503rd, was given the hazardous assignment of retaking Corregidor Island from the air. After that, Haugen's storm troops were to link up with other elements of the division that had been landed twenty miles southwest at Nasugbu Bay two weeks before. They then were to spread from the north into Manila along with the 9th Infantry and rescue the beleaguered city. The jump would be made in three waves, with "Rock" Haugen and regimental headquarters company, including Serling, going in with the first drop, deep in enemy territory.

And so, on the morning of February 3, 1945, a day that would be forever etched into Trooper Serling's excellent memory, the twenty-year-old private found himself boarding a C-47 cargo plane on Mindoro Island (the island that had been taken after Leyte), along with the twenty-three other combat-loaded men of his "stick," en route to his first authentic combat jump. Like most of the other men, Serling was a zombie.

The jump was a mess. One of the jumpmasters in the first drop "jumped" his men prematurely, leading them into the wrong drop zone—causing the other jumpmasters, including Serling's, to misdrop *their* sticks, and sending Haugen into a fury. Haugen was yet more livid when jumpmasters in the following two drops also misdropped their men.

Fortunately, although there were numerous injuries, no one was killed as a result of the error. What if several dozen *had* been killed as a result of a jumpmaster's error, as they had been during similar mishaps in North Africa? How would those men live with themselves? That excruciating question, and how one guilt-torn ex-jumpmaster dealt with it, would be at the core of one of Serling's most riveting postwar, *anti*war videos, "24 Men to a Plane." Serling would file this unforgettable situation away for future dramatization.

As it was, there were only negligible Japanese forces in the area along Tagaytay Ridge where Serling and the other fifteen hundred parachutists landed. After the botched but nonlethal jump the 511th had little trouble assembling and linking up with the rest of the division for the drive on Manila, forming a speedy "flying column" of men and equipment that moved sixty miles in four days. Resistance was slight. Indeed, the major obstacles to the division's progress were the hundreds of overjoyed Filipinos who overwhelmed the caravan with kisses, hugs, and armfuls of bananas. The carnival-like atmosphere stopped quickly, however, once the division reached the heavily fortified outskirts of Manila proper. General Yamashita, a realist who had been resigned to eventual defeat after the loss of Leyte, had wisely and humanely declared the Filipino capital an open city and ordered his forces to retreat to the east. However, Admiral Iwabuchi, the diehard commander of the local Imperial Marines detachment, had disregarded Yamashita's orders and turned the city into a mammoth fort surrounded by a forbiddingly thick band of pillboxes, anti-aircraft guns depressed for point-blank fire, and hidden aerial bombs. He gave his seventeen thousand men burrowed throughout the city orders to fight to the death, and they did. The subsequent battle raged through the city's streets for an entire month as the 11th and the 9th divisions retook the capital block by blazing block, suffering hundreds of casualties. The 511th, which had been lucky with casualties on Leyte, suffered particularly hard.

The regiment's newest ordeal started at the Paranque River, the widest of the concentrically arranged waterways surrounding the occupied city, while the men were being feted by a group of Filipino entertainers. Suddenly, the entire perimeter came under intense Japanese artillery fire from the other side of the river, creating bedlam and numerous civilian casualties.

Serling gave an excellent account of himself here, according to Frank Lewis, at least as a humanitarian, exposing himself to the incoming fire to carry one of the wounded female performers to safety. "He cradled her like a baby," Lewis said. Serling, still a private after three years in the services, may not have been a great soldier, his former sergeant admitted, "but that took guts."[18]

The next few weeks were a protracted ordeal for Serling and everyone else in the 511th, as they advanced through the huge death trap Iwabuchi and his determined men had prepared for them. No quarter was given; no quarter was asked. Not even the city's baseball stadium, Rizal Stadium, where Serling shot a Japanese soldier standing on third base, was safe from the inferno. At another point, in an incident which would haunt him for the rest of his life, Serling found himself staring at a nearby Japanese soldier who had lined him up in his rifle sights and was about to shoot him—couldn't miss him. Certain that he was about to die, Serling continued to watch until a fellow G.I. came up over his shoulder and beat the enemy soldier to the draw. Significantly, few newsreels of the actual fighting for Manila exist today because most of the cameramen were killed. The regiment itself wound up suffering 50-percent casualties, including four hundred killed. One of the fallen was Colonel Haugen. The "Rock" was cut down by a Japanese artillery shell while leading a patrol at one particularly hazardous intersection. There was no time to grieve, even for Haugen. His men, or what was left of them, were too busy trying to survive the apocalypse themselves.

While walking in a demolition platoon "termite patrol," Serling was again injured, this time by shrapnel from one of the anti-aircraft guns that the Japanese were firing point-blank down the street. Serling was lucky. Three of the other men in his "termite patrol" were killed.

Serling was sent to a rehabilitation camp in New Guinea to recover from his wounds. Although badly injured, he was mobile enough to have a torrid affair with one of the camp nurses, according to Norman Miller, with whom he had kept up a running correspondence.

Serling returned to the 511th in May 1945, spending another four months in the line helping to "clean out" the eastern portion of the island of enemy resistance and seeing numerous of his other friends killed and maimed in what struck him as an increasingly pointless war. The dropping of the A-bomb on Hiroshima and Nagasaki brought the carnage, at least on the American side, thankfully to a halt. When informed of the full effects of the weapon, Serling would be horrified; ultimately, he would become an antinuclear activist. But for now, like millions of other G.I.s in the Pacific theater, he was relieved.

By the time Japan finally sued for peace on August 6, 1945, only 30 percent of the original members of the regiment from Camp Toccoa were still alive.

Then, on that same day, came the telegram informing Serling of the death of his father, of a heart attack, at the age of fifty-five.

4
YELLOW SPRINGS
(1946 – 48)

Be ashamed to die until you have won some victory for humanity.
  —Horace Mann, founder of Antioch College

One of the most fascinating and neglected periods of Rod Serling's pre-*Twilight Zone* life and work is the eight years, nearly a decade, that he spent in Ohio, first as an undergraduate at Antioch College, then as a novice TV staff writer and freelance scriptwriter based in Cincinnati.

Interestingly, and significantly, those eight years parallel the time when the greater Cincinnati-Dayton area was a feeder area for the networks, supplying such future talents as actor-comedian Jonathan Winters, a native of Dayton; singers Rosemary Clooney and the Mills Brothers, who first rose to prominence at "the nation's station," WLW, where Serling would get his start as a continuity writer after graduating from Antioch; Earl Hamner, Jr., creator of *The Waltons* (and contributor to *The Twilight Zone*) and a fellow staff writer of Serling's at WLW; and Serling himself.

Rod Serling had little notion of the fine future in broadcasting that lay ahead for him when he disembarked from the train that had taken him from New York to Yellow Springs, home of Antioch, in September 1946. The year following Sam Serling's sudden death had been a troubling one for his younger son. Following the armistice, Private Serling and his regiment, plus the rest of the 11th Airborne, had flown directly to Japan from the Philippines to serve as part of the first American occupation forces there. Serling had put in a request for emergency home leave in order to be able to attend his father's funeral in Syracuse, only to have it turned down by division command, deepening his already strong distaste for the military and sending him into a deep depression. This psychologically—and physically—bruised veteran nonetheless remained proud of his service with the airborne and acquired a bracelet with the parachute-and-wings insignia, which he would wear on his left wrist for the rest of his life.

Serling's homecoming to Binghamton in January 1946 was one of joy mixed with grief. As happy as Serling was to see his mother again, he was distraught by her withered appearance. It seemed that she had aged ten years in three—and she had. Her weight had shrunk to ninety-five pounds. Sam's sudden death had devastated her in every way, leaving her helpless and dependent on Rod and Robert. At first, she moved in with Robert, who had spent the war working as a UPI correspondent in Washington; later, she was persuaded to move in with relatives in Syracuse.[1]

Meanwhile, Serling continued to be haunted by his memories of the war. Norman Miller recalled meeting Serling in New York City in 1946 to view *Back to Bataan*, a John Wayne flag-waver putatively based on the Filipino campaign, with guerrilla Wayne and his native friends leading the way to the archipelago's liberation. If only it had been so easy in real life. "He came to test himself," Miller explained, "but he wanted me there in case he cracked up." Miller hardly recognized the sinewy, unsmiling ex-serviceman he encountered in Times Square before the film. "He wasn't a boy anymore, he was a man." The film itself bore little resemblance to the real thing, as Serling repeatedly pointed out to Miller, who had been stateside during the war and had not seen combat himself. "They never came at us like that," he whispered matter-of-factly to Miller in the middle of one of the movie's show-stopping banzai charges. "They came at us in twos and threes."

Nevertheless, the effect on Serling, who may have been suffering from what today would be described as posttraumatic stress disorder, was sufficiently authentic to make this ex-jungle fighter break a sweat. "He didn't crack up," Miller remembered years later, "but I'm telling you he must have smoked two packs of cigarettes right there in the balcony of the movie theater."[2]

Spooked by his memories of the war, Serling had difficulty thinking about the future. After a few desultory months at home, he decided, almost by default, to matriculate at Antioch College, his brother's alma mater, where he had applied and been accepted for admission before the war. "I was kind of mixed up and restless, and I kind of liked their work-for-a-term, go-to-school-for-a-term set-up," he later explained.[3]

Serling had chosen a good time to come to Antioch. Founded by educator Horace Mann in 1853, this small liberal arts college had recently undergone a renaissance under Anthony Morgan, becoming an important laboratory for progressive higher education and one of the most talked-about colleges in the nation. The centerpiece of Morgan's reforms was the school's four-year work-study plan, which required Antiochans to divide their time between the Yellow Springs campus—where they took traditional academic courses—and the outside world, where they were gainfully employed in work designed to bring them face to face with "practical realities in all their stubborn complexity" (to quote Morgan).[4]

Back on the rolling, hundred-acre, tree-lined campus, there were few class meetings, attendance was not required, and each student had an individual, self-directed plan of study. A democratic community government, composed of students and faculty, made and carried out decisions normally left to governing boards and administrators in traditional colleges. It made for an institution that was about as radical in form and temperament as one could then find in American higher education, as well as one that well-suited Serling's rebellious mood and temperament.

Yellow Springs itself had had a history of nurturing visionaries and radicals going back to the Owenites, who had first set up their utopian, nonsectarian commune there in 1825. There was something about the secluded southwestern Ohio town and spa, with its lush glens and yellow springs and tinglingly clear air that seemed to stimulate unorthodox thinking. "Yellow Springs [was] a great place for 'cults' to take root and flourish," one longtime resident recalled in 1939. "It reminded me of old Athens, in those elder days of the Greek philosophers, who would meet in forums and issue propaganda of their various doctrines and theories." Under the Morgan plan, that Athenian modality took hold and flourished. By the time Serling arrived, twenty years after the Morgan reforms, the "new Antioch" had established itself as a thriving, if occasionally besieged, outpost of liberalism in the conservative Midwest, as well as one of the best-regarded small liberal arts colleges in the nation.

Antiochans were conscious of being on the cutting edge of higher education and proud of it.

Visitors from mainstream institutions were scandalized by Antioch's unorthodox curriculum and campus mores. It was difficult to know what to make of a school where attendance was optional and vital decisions were made by students, not to mention one where women openly smoked cigarettes and wore pants. Antiochans had as little respect for organized religion as for organized academics. The relatively few students of various denominations who felt they needed a faith often followed in the anti-establishmentarian footsteps of Horace Mann and became Unitarians. All this suited Serling just fine.

Like many of the other veterans in the class who flooded Yellow Springs that first postwar autumn, Serling truly felt he had arrived in Shangri-la. "The year he [Serling] got there was a very interesting year," said John Kittross, a member of the previous class. "During the war, there were very few males. It had been about four hundred and fifty women and fifty men, mostly four-F. Then the end of the war came, and all of a sudden came these hundreds of deactivated veterans. These were fellows who had [had] pretty strong experiences, and who wanted to learn. They really made the campus get up and do things. Many of the [few existing] rules disappeared. It was quite a place."[5]

It even had sports of a kind. It would have been out of character for non-traditional Antioch to have an organized system of varsity sports. The prevailing attitude toward such things was fairly well summed up by a college "anti-yell," which was popular at the time.

> Boomalack, boomalack, boomalack a-beam,
> Riff-raff, riff-raff, riff-raff ream,
> Ip skidy iki wahoo wah,
> Antioch, Antioch, RAH-RAH-RAH!

However, Serling was pleased to discover that the college did have an intense, if somewhat disorganized, intramural program that included touch football, and he threw himself into the fray with abandon. Cheering this leathery quarterback were a reliable claque of female Serling-watchers. "You know, the girls used to come around and watch the football games. They came for Rod because

he just threw himself, *and I mean threw himself*, into the game,"
Don Scobel, his freshman roommate, recalled.

"He was just absolutely reckless. And sometimes, he would just
lie there and we thought he was dead . . . and then someone would
go over and pick him up by the belt and carry him back to the
huddle. That was the way he played."[6] Serling's wounded knee,
giving out at unexpected moments, did not deter him from playing.
It helped him garner more sympathy from the co-eds.

Classes were definitely a secondary concern for Serling. The war
apparently had leveled his nascent literary ambitions. Mysteriously,
he declared physical education as his first major; however, a first-
year required course in language and literature taught by Antioch's
writer-in-residence, Nolan Miller, helped Serling rejuvenate his old
prewar dreams of artistic fame. Under Miller's guiding hand, the
psychologically bruised veteran dabbled in various fiction and non-
fiction forms, including the short story, the playlet, and the long
memoir. He also took a lot of courses in psychology and philosophy.
At first, Serling saw Miller's writing assignments primarily as an
outlet for his war experiences. Thus, most of his initial stories and
essays were about the war, including a vivid, thinly disguised account of the 511th's bloody progress across the Pacific. Like many
combat veterans who also became writers, Serling would never quite
purge himself of the war and what the war did, good and bad, to
its participants. It was to be his dominant literary concern for the
next decade.

There were also a lot of boxing stories, including one about
Danny, a down-and-out heavyweight whose career is threatened by
a ring injury. Miller thought the piece, entitled "The Good Right
Hand," worthy of publication in the Antioch literary magazine, *The
Antiochan*. The story, published in March 1948, illustrates Serling's
flair for creating memorable, if somewhat sentimentalized characters
and writing taut dialogue. A good example is the following passage
in which Danny's manager, Googy, tries to convince his damaged
charge that there is life after the boxing ring—suggesting that Serling
may have been privately trying to convince himself that there was
life after paratrooping:

"This is the only racket I know, Googy," Danny said. "It's
the only one I care anything about. Some guys don't care how

they make a living, just as long as they do. Me . . . I'm different. I gotta fight, Googy. If I can't fight, well, hell, I don't care much about living."

"Now you listen to me you snotty nosed kid," Googy screamed in tearful desperation. "All right, you got a bum break . . . you got a busted up hand. All right, so you can't push gloves no more. So what? That damned ring post made mincemeat out of your hand . . . but I didn't think it'd screw up your guts, too. You ain't no quitter . . . I know that. Dammit, Danny, get wise. Just cause you're washed up in the ring ain't no sign you're washed up in everything . . ."

Eight years later, Serling would transpose and enlarge many of the elements of "The Good Right Hand" into "Requiem for a Heavyweight."[7] The pungent, almost willfully obtuse dialogue clearly showed the influence of Ernest Hemingway. "At first, everything I wrote began with the line 'It was hot,' " Serling once said in deference to his novelistic mentor.[8] Indeed, the shell-shocked veterans, over-the-hill fighters, and cynical bartenders who inhabit Serling's college writings sometimes seem to have been taken whole from Hemingway's short fiction.

The tough-talking ex-paratrooper may have flirted with the idea of becoming a novelist himself. However, radio continued to be his preferred medium, as it would for the next four years. Secretly, Serling still wanted to be the next Norman Corwin.

Serling got his first experience as a scriptwriter when he worked at New York public radio station WNYC in the fall of 1946 as an Antioch intern. "There's no question about [it], as soon as he got that job at WNYC," remembered John Kittross, "he was in seventh heaven, particularly since he was allowed to write scripts."[9] (Playwright Edward Albee, another Antioch product, followed in Serling's steps at WNYC ten years later.)

Fittingly, Serling's first scriptwriting assignment was to conjure up a fifteen-minute squib to commemorate the nation's first Veterans Day. The assignment gave the injured veteran an opportunity to provide his own posttraumatic definition of courage:

Not all battles are fought, not all victories are won on a battlefield. And not all courage is found only in actual combat.

As an aftermath to this war, there are many men fighting new battles . . . personal struggles that must be fought and won . . . and these need as much if not more courage. They are conflicts which thousands of disabled veterans are facing with themselves . . . veterans come back confronted with readjustments to a life without an arm or a leg. . . . It's a tough fight which requires a certain requisite of courage.

As a municipal employee, the fledgling radio writer also dutifully wrote public service announcements to order for the New York City Department of Corrections and other city government departments. The job at WNYC gave Serling the essential experience of learning "time"—writing for a medium that is measured in seconds. The experience also reinforced his desire to enter broadcasting himself upon graduation. He would use subsequent field terms to work at other radio stations around the country, including a stint at Binghamton's CBS affiliate, WINR.

Serling, like most Americans, had as yet given little thought to television, no less a career in television. TV was yet in its infancy in 1946, at least in terms of commercial development; the exigencies of war had cut short its development. Most of the few prewar sets had been confiscated by the Government and used to train air-raid wardens, or had become museum pieces. CBS and NBC had experimented fitfully with TV drama with not especially intriguing results. By the time Serling came to New York—the capital of the broadcasting industry—to start his internship, there were merely one hundred thousand sets in the entire country. A handful of stations transmitted a highly mixed grab bag of programming fare.

The new medium's strong suit, if it could be said to have one, was sports. An avid sports fan and a fair drinker, it is more than likely Serling watched *Gillette's Cavalcade of Sports*, a live sports spectator's program and one of the most popular programs of the day, at one of the many bars near the WNYC studio close by City Hall. He may even have visited the live TV studio that the DuMont network had built in Wanamaker's department store in midtown. But TV had yet to impact on his consciousness, or America's.

Unfortunately, Serling's internship at WNYC didn't pay enough to meet his expenses, so he decided to look for outside work. According to his former broadcast colleagues, the freshman from Binghamton hit upon a novel—outlandish and considerably dangerous—means of supplementing his income: testing parachutes for the Army Air Force. Lillian Blake, his supervisor at WNYC, found out about her subaltern's somewhat bizarre part-time job when he staggered into the newsroom one winter's day with a major gash across his cheek. Serling sheepishly explained that the parachute he was testing proved impossible to control, and the wind had blown him into a barbed-wire fence. "You wouldn't know it to look at him, though," said Blake. "He was very modestly behaved, not at all the swashbuckling type."[10]

Other strange details of Serling's parachute-testing career were furnished years later by his still amazed co-worker Alan Zachary. According to Zachary, Serling received fifty dollars for every successful jump he made; once, he was allegedly paid five hundred dollars for testing a particularly hazardous chute—half beforehand, half after the jump—providing he survived. The impecunious veteran also hitched an Army Air Force flight back to Ohio, from which he is said to have parachuted onto campus, apparently to impress his girlfriend of the moment.

Upon his return to Antioch, a recharged Serling began applying himself to writing in a monomaniacal way, as he would more or less for the rest of his life. At this point, as his roommate Don Scobel recalled, he still used a typewriter—and did he.

> Glenn [Serling's other roommate] and I were evicted from the room, not just for a few hours, but for the whole night. Rodman was creating a radio script. He pecked away at his typewriter, using only the goose finger of his right hand to find the keys while his left hand held an endless parade of deeply puffed cigarettes. . . . Rodman and his infernal machine fused into one, banging and puffing away, chigging out his wild creations at a rate of fifty words a minute. Along about dawn, he would emerge from the room, red-eyed, unkempt, creaking at every bending point. But under his arm was a neatly typed manuscript.

Like many of Serling's early acquaintances, Scobel was still inclined to see the voluble wordsmith more as a performer than as a writer. "He was a marvelous storyteller. We all thought if Rod ever made it, he'd make it as a performer, as a kind of a stand-up comic."[11]

Serling was further encouraged in his dream of becoming a radio writer by Pearl Bentel, a visiting scriptwriter who taught a course at Antioch in 1947. Bentel would become accustomed to the sight of her eager student waiting for her with a batch of fresh scripts. She was so impressed by Serling's talent and drive that she gave him a freelance job writing dialogue for her station, WCAE in Pittsburgh, at two dollars per page. She also encouraged him by predicting that he would be making five thousand dollars within his first year of graduation. Fifteen years later, the scriptwriter and her protégé would reverse roles somewhat when Serling, weary of the fame and success of his career, returned to Antioch to teach and Bentel became *his* adoring student.

Serling's rakish charm and super-masculine antics helped him parachute into the hearts of numerous Antioch coeds, including that of his future wife, Carolyn Kramer. He had "the reputation of being quite a ladies' man," Carol Serling recalled years later. "He had dated about every other girl in the school before he got to me," she said, exaggerating only slightly. But she would be the first woman with whom he formed an intimate bond.

At first, she admitted, she was as overwhelmed by the leather-jacketed kamikaze as the rest of the distaff Antiochans Serling had brought to ground. "He struck me as being very intelligent, with a wonderful sense of humor. And there was something about him that fascinated me. I had never met anyone . . . so self-assured before."[12]

To be sure, as the nineteen-year-old education major was soon to discover, that blustery layer of self-assurance was a thin one. Beneath was a war-scarred young man with a mass of psychological wounds and insecurities.

From Rod's point of view, the stunning-looking brunette—who bore a distinct resemblance to the then popular actress Teresa Wright—had just about everything Serling could have consciously or subconsciously desired in a woman, including great intelligence and a self-possessed, almost regal air, both of which fascinated him. "She's a strong person, very literate, the descendant of college presidents and professors," he said in 1959, in a rare dual interview devoted to his wife. In a word, she was so different.

Indeed, Carol Kramer was the ultimate *shiksa*. The strength, the literacy, and the Waspish lineage that drew him to his future wife were the legacy of Carol's estimable maternal grandparents and surrogate parents, Louise Taft Orton Caldwell, a scion of the Taft dynasty and daughter of the first president of Ohio State University, and Frank Caldwell, a wealthy engineering professor and inventor. Carol had been placed in the Caldwells' care when she was a young child, after her mother died. Her dowager grandmother, with whom she remained close throughout life, had effectively taught Carol to keep an emotional distance from people, endowing her with a sweet but distant, and somewhat disingenuous, air. For beneath the veneer of refinement was a willful, determined, and highly opinionated woman. "Her taste is excellent, and she has an unerring instinct about whether my work is good or bad," her husband would later boast to a reporter. This was the woman who would be Rod Serling's anchor and his cheerleader, as well as his emotional governess, for the following twenty-seven years. Within several months of meeting, the couple was engaged.[13]

Both sets of in-laws balked at the union. Like most Jewish mothers, Esther had hoped that Rod would marry a Jewish girl, Taft or no Taft, and had not hesitated to say so. Eventually, she gave her blessing, as did Robert.

Carol's father, for his part, was vehemently opposed to the marriage. "Her father abandoned her because he didn't want her marrying a Jew," said Ann Goodman. "He was very anti-Semitic."[14] Carol's sister also opposed the union and would eventually stop speaking to her as a result. Indeed, with the notable exception of her grandmother, who liked and approved of Rod, the Kramers would essentially disown Carol because of her love for the Jew from Binghamton.

It was a heavy price to pay for love, and Carol, who was as much in love with her betrothed as vice versa, gladly paid it, but she never let Rod forget that she had paid it. In return she demanded total control over the emotional life of her man-child husband—and she got it.

And she never let Rod's family forget that she was, after all, a Taft. "I don't think she ever accepted our family," said Leona Serling. "She seemed to look down her nose at all of us."[15] Inevitably Carol also all but totally eclipsed Esther Serling in Rod's heart. She wanted to be the dominant and dominating woman in Rod Serling's life—and she became just that.

Carol's prissy relations would have probably been even more

opposed to her marriage if they had known that their future in-law was the sort of man who earned money by testing experimental parachutes for the army. According to Don Scobel, Serling took one final harrowing turn as a human fly in the spring of 1948. The pay was reportedly higher than before—one thousand dollars—but so were the risks. Instead of parachutes, this time Serling agreed to test one of the Army Air Force's new jet ejection seats.

Scobel became understandably nervous when Serling was late in returning from his dangerous rendezvous.

"We drove to the station to meet the train, and no Rod," Scobel remembered.

> And we started getting nervous—it was several hours before the next train was supposed to arrive, so we went and met it, and the next, and the next, and the next. I don't know how many trains we met—we'd sort of given up hope.
>
> Sure enough, later that night, a train came in, sort of a milk train, from New York via Atlanta or someplace like that. And right at the very end where people are getting off, these two conductors are carrying a sack, and they put it down by one of the benches. And it's Rod, sort of wrapped up like a mummy. He had scratches and wounds all over.[16]

As Serling later told his amazed friends, three other volunteers involved in the "experiment" were killed before Serling succeeded.

Their respective families' reservations and ejection-seat injuries notwithstanding, Carol Kramer and Rod Serling were wed on June 30, 1948, in a simple ecumenical ceremony at Rockford Chapel at Antioch before a small group of friends, including several of Rod's buddies from the 511th regiment.

When the newlyweds returned for the fall term, after honeymooning at Carol's grandparents' lakeside cottage in Interlaken, New York, they set up their first household in Trailertown—as the married student housing area of Antioch was called—moving their few worldly goods into a crude, kerosene-heated 16-foot surplus government aluminum trailer. The Serlings performed their toilet in a communal bathroom. For richer or for poorer? Life in Trailertown was decidedly poorer. The Serlings didn't care. They were married, in love, and at Antioch.

Antioch itself was never cozier—nor more out of touch with the times. In Eastern Europe, the Iron Curtain had descended; at home another Red Scare had begun. But at Antioch, Utopia was still in style. Emotionalism, as all extemporaneous displays of emotion were called, was out—a stricture that the tempestuous Serling had difficulty adhering to; Rationalism was in. Antioch's pipe-smoking president, Douglas McGregor, amiably presided over an idealistic attempt to run the campus according to the principles of "Group Dynamics." Socialist presidential candidate Henry Wallace, who would be trounced in the November 1948 elections, came to speak and was greeted like a hero. Pacifist student Robert Summers was arrested by the Federal Bureau of Investigation that fall for refusing to register for the draft. Other liberal-minded campus denizens were determinedly integrating Yellow Springs' last outpost of racial prejudice—the town movie theater. The progressive ideals for which most Antiochans stood might be taking a beating elsewhere, but at Antioch, all were sure, the humanistic millennium was very near. While they waited for the promised time, Antiochans dined on "Snacks of Social Significance," as they were billed, at the Antioch cafeteria, relaxed by singing along to Paul Robeson.

There was a particularly intense feeling of camaraderie among the residents of Trailertown, according to Barbara Agranoff, Trailertown resident and neighbor of the Serlings. "We were all poor," the Antiochan recalled. "And we were all living on the GI Bill. Really, in a sense, I've never been able to recreate that level of community in all my life since. Everybody was able to discuss their thoughts and ideas without worrying about whether it was going to interfere with their social life and promotions. We could make friends and everyone was equal. I've always missed the quality of that time."[17] Rod Serling would never forget that time, either, or Antioch. In many ways, he would always be an Antiochan: passionate, committed, intent on winning victories for humanity. *"Be ashamed to die until you have won some victory for humanity,"* the campus statue of founder Horace Mann still adjures students and visitors. That imposing statue and its commandment would reappear in an episode of *The Twilight Zone* about a private-school teacher haunted by his failure to live up to the founder's dictum.

Liberal actor and folksinger Theodore Bikel, who befriended the ex-Antiochan in the 1950s (and later appeared in a memorable *Twilight Zone* episode about blacklisting), traced Serling's "unabashed intellectuality" to his offbeat alma mater. "He was the product of a very eclectic education," said Bikel. "Antioch is like a smorgasbord from which people partake as they feel the need, rather than being forced into a straitjacket of learning, with distinctive hours and curricula. It showed that he came [from] an education that allowed him to wander and roam at will."[18]

In November 1948, Serling was appointed to the newly created position of manager of the campus radio station—the augustly named (but in fact quite modest) Antioch Broadcasting System. As the primitively equipped station's first paid manager, Serling earned the then sizable salary of five hundred dollars a month and administered a thirty-five-person staff. It was, without doubt, the best job he had ever had.

Serling wore many hats in his ABS job. As chief programmer, he attempted to cater to every shade of Antiochan radiogenic taste. He filled the ether with everything from news and sports, which Serling himself helped announce, and "long hair" music (jazz), and "platter stuff" (swing), to such already golden broadcast oldies as Norman Corwin's pre-Pearl Harbor broadcast of "We Hold These Truths" and FDR's still stirring declaration of war speech.

Ultimately, the resourceful junior was able to forge his own dramatic anthology show. Each week, he would write an original dramatic script or adaptation, direct it, and often act in it himself— sort of a *26 by Serling* after the Corwin mode. Thus, Serling got a taste, on a small scale, of the sort of creative freedom that Corwin and Welles had had in the heady prewar days of Big Radio—and he liked it. "There was a lot of Orson Welles in Rod," said Rudy Ruderman, one of Serling's troupe of on-air players. "He knew how to grab an idea and see its potential to provoke an audience . . . given the limited tools at that time, which was [sic] merely a microphone, limited sound effects, and a small station in a small town. And he communicated a sense of excitement in the show."[19]

Heard today, most of Serling's ABS scripts were sometimes too derivative of Corwin, Welles, et al. In order to keep his marathon series going, Serling seemingly devoured—and regurgitated, often barely digested—everything he had ever written, heard, or seen. Often he did so without acknowledging the source, or he conveniently forgot that the story was from another source. Don Scobel recalled his amusement upon hearing a story he had told Serling one night broadcast across campus the next. Future, unwitting Serling "contributors" would not be as amused. Indeed, Serling's tendency to consciously or unconsciously appropriate stories and story material would one day be the cause of serious controversy and real lawsuits during the making of *The Twilight Zone*.

Nevertheless, no one denied that the main engine behind his remarkable series, which ran from November 1948 through February 1949, was Serling himself. One of Serling's more intriguing and original efforts was "The Button Pushers," a parable about the self-destruction of civilization, as bemusedly monitored by a coven of cruel, unseen gods. Years later, Serling would employ this script as the basis for the classic *Twilight Zone* episode "Monsters Are Due on Maple Street." There were also a number of *radio noir* pieces, including an Oboleresque tour-de-force, "Concerto," written and performed by Serling, about a pianist in the process of killing himself with gas while composing his one and final masterpiece. At ABS, Serling was star of his own one-man show, as he would be years later with *The Twilight Zone*, and he loved it. But eventually, the manifold responsibilities of running his own radio station and his own dramatic series while continuing his education, trying to pursue his outside scriptwriting career, and spending time with his bride proved too much, even for the seemingly indefatigable Rod Serling. In March 1949, he quit the manager's job, much to the dismay of his campuswide listenership, and focused on developing his own freelance work for network radio, as Pearl Bentel and others had urged.

Carol, too, was four-square behind her husband's flourishing writing career. At ABS, she served as his girl Friday, typing his scripts and correcting his horrendous spelling. And it was she who gave Rod the idea and the push to enter one of his ABS scripts in the weekly script competition for *The Dr. Christian Show*, "the show where the audience writes the show!" Auspiciously, Serling's old hero Arch Oboler was one of the judges on the CBS show.

Shortly, the telegram arrived in Trailer #10 informing Serling that his script "To Live a Dream" had won third prize, complete with five hundred dollars and an expenses-paid trip to New York City. Serling's dream of becoming the next golden boy of the airwaves, it seemed, was that much closer to being realized.

5

WLW-AM IN CINCINNATI (1949–52)

If the [television] craze continues . . . we are destined to have a nation of morons.
   —Daniel L. Marsh, president of Boston University, in a graduation day speech, June 1950[1]

Rod Serling got his first euphoric taste of national fame on the evening of May 18, 1949, when he appeared at the New York studios of *The Dr. Christian Show* to accept his third-prize script-writing check for five hundred dollars from Jean Hersholt, the program's genial Danish host.

Serling's and Hersholt's ceremonial words had been written out on cards for them. "Well, I've always been fond of boxing," a nervous Serling piped on cue. Yes, he intended to follow writing as a profession; his wife, who dutifully stood for a bow and applause from the studio audience at the right moment, did also. The couple's other pressing joint ambition, the prizewinner announced, was "to buy a big house, live in the suburb of a large city, and have two dogs!!!"[2]

There was nothing contrived about Serling's joy at garnering the coveted prize and seemingly huge check. Sharing the Serlings' joy was another prizewinner from Ohio, Earl Hamner, Jr., future creator of *The Waltons* and contributor to *The Twilight Zone*, who, like Serling, would soon begin work at WLW-AM in Cincinnati. "I felt like Norman Corwin!" Serling later said of that ecstatic moment.[3]

*   *   *

Actually, the golden boy of prewar radio drama wasn't feeling all too well himself in the spring of 1949. With the end of the conflagration, radio had lost its sense of purpose, and so had radio drama. Moreover, Corwin's patron, William Paley, had lost his appetite for noncommercial, highbrow programming. In keeping with the getting-back-to-business mood of the country, the recently deactivated colonel and broadcast mogul was anxious to make up for lost time, and lost money, and Corwin and his kind of radio didn't fit into the picture.

Corwin's former home, the *Columbia Experimental Workshop*, was canceled, leaving only soap opera and suspense as the principal forms of "serious" radio entertainment. In November 1948, Paley let the writer know that his time, and his career at CBS, were over, when the two happened to meet on a transcontinental train speeding back to New York. "You know," the broadcast baron told his dispirited passenger over dinner, "you've done big things that are appreciated by us and by a special audience. But couldn't you write for a broader public?" Of course, Paley knew that the scrupulously high-minded Corwin couldn't. "We've simply got to face up to the fact that we're in a commercial business," Paley concluded.[4]

"A different Paley," Corwin thought to himself. "War and the competition of NBC had apparently changed his thinking."

Television was a major factor in Paley's new strategic thinking, too. It was the coming medium, he smugly intoned. Corwin got the essential message: get with it, or get out. "I [felt] uninspired, sorry for myself, certain of the death of my medium, dull from Scotch, and unnecessary."[5]

Corwin decided to get the gist of Paley's message and to depart network broadcasting. He chose not to stick around for the coming millennium of "air-pic entertainment," as TV had been dubbed; radio was still "his" medium. He would live by it and fade away with it. By the spring of 1949, when Rod Serling won his *Dr. Christian* award, his hero had left CBS's employ and was working as a part-time radio producer for the special projects division of the United Nations. His last work for CBS, "Citizen of the World," an idealistic documentary about the new world organization, narrated by actor Lee J. Cobb (one of the numerous actors who would perform in both Corwin's and Serling's work), was broadcast in July 1949.

In the meantime, partly because of his UN work, the avowedly liberal writer had become the focus of new, unwanted attention after it was publicly disclosed that his name was on the FBI's latest list of notable Communist sympathizers and "fellow travelers." A year later, Corwin's name was also included in the first "official" broadcasting blacklist compiled by the witchhunting circular, *Counterattack*. Serling's other prewar radio mentors, Orson Welles and Arch Oboler, weren't faring too well either. Welles, who had leaped from radio to the movies, topping himself in that medium with *Citizen Kane*, had effectively been banished by Hollywood and was living in limbo abroad. Oboler, too, had become an old name.[6]

In New York, the Hollywood Ten went on trial. And in Wisconsin, Senator Joseph McCarthy, sensing his moment had arrived, was about to go on the attack.

Serling's scriptwriting award was major news back in Ohio. The *Cleveland Plain-Dealer* ran a photo of the twenty-four-year-old writer and his wife-cum-girl Friday in the ABS studio. In the picture, a weary but earnest Serling is standing before a microphone holding a script, looking tired and unshaven. A stern-faced Carol is standing next to the Great Man, helping him hold the golden script.

The *Dr. Christian* award made Serling a big man at Antioch—insofar as it was possible for the obsessively egalitarian college to have such a thing. SERLING GOES TO CHRISTIAN REWARD! wagged the *Daily Record*.

A newly confident Serling took the hoopla in stride. "He was not a braggart about it," said Carson Davidson, a campus friend. "The times when I was in his presence, he was always a little self-effacing. His ability spoke for itself, he didn't have to broadcast it or point it out to anybody. Other people bragged about him, but he didn't brag about himself."[7]

It was at this fateful moment that Serling decided to switch horses and take on television. The perspicacious Antioch senior sensed that his future was with the newer medium, and he was ready and willing to do what he had to do to master it. By late 1949, he had signed with the Dayton Trailer Association to pen his first television script, a "comedy" about trailer life. The script for the resulting teleplay, "The Bad Penny," is nowhere to be found in the Serling archives.

This is probably no great loss. One can reasonably assume that it made use of the Serlings' own comical domestic experiences in their cramped, kerosene-smelling aluminum trailer, without putting them or their trailer in too laughable a light.

To be sure, during the three years Serling had been incubating at Antioch, so had TV. Now it was beginning to explode: the number of television stations, divided among the four networks (CBS, NBC, ABC and DuMont), had jumped from six to fifty, and there would have been more if not for a freeze on new stations imposed by a still cautious FCC. Meanwhile, the demand for television sets in those areas that could be reached by TV had caused their numbers to jump from eight thousand in 1946 to nearly a million. Nineteen forty-nine was the first year Sears, Roebuck included TV sets in its authoritative consumer catalog. The advertised sets had tiny screens and resembled the first radio consoles in their cumbersome dimensions. But they sold. RCA manufactured that year alone 2.5 million new sets to keep up with the galloping demand.

Like the radio boom of the 1930s, "The TV boom" or "TV craze," as it was coming to be called, was fed as much by the *idea* of television as anything else; bored with radio, with money to spend and a booming number of children to entertain, Americans were ready for a new medium by 1949. The radio and film industries, both based in California, were more cautious. Film people particularly looked down on television—just as they had looked down on radio. So television had to create its own talent.

By 1949 it had begun to do just that. Witness the phenomenal success of comedian Milton Berle, whose vaudevillian comedy-variety show, *Texaco Star Theater*, telecast from New York, had quickly become the country's most watched show. "Mr. Television," Berle was called; it was said he "owned" the country on Tuesday nights.

Meanwhile, TV had also begun to create more serious fare. *Kraft Television Theatre*, the first major dramatic anthology show, had been on the air since 1947. By the fall of 1949, there were half a dozen more. The ingredients for what would come to be called the "golden age of television" were falling into place.

Like most Antiochans, Rod and Carol couldn't afford their own black-and-white set, so they shared the one communal TV set that the college had installed. This added to the fun and experience of witnessing TV's merry, static-charged birth.

Quick to sense the new market for television, the management of radio station WLW in Cincinnati took out a license that covered the entire tristate area. The FCC approved it, making Cincinnati one of the country's pioneer "television cities," as they were called during those prefreeze days. Though conservative in many ways, residents of the greater Cincinnati area proved partial to the new medium. "Television came in and there was this total explosion," said Mary Wood, longtime radio and television critic of the *Cincinnati Enquirer*. "This town is mostly populated by Germans, and the Germans do not like to leave home. And when they could get entertainment in their home, for free, my God, they had it made."[8]

One could literally see the impact that television was having on the region from one's car by 1949. "Hey," the exuberant writer nudged his wife as they drove back from the broadcast of "The Bad Penny," pointing out the antennae that were sprouting all over the Queen City's landscape, "that's for us."[9]

Carol was more cautious. Like many, she looked down on television as an inferior medium, just as many had looked down on radio in its early days. "Carol thought that TV was trash for the mind," said Charles Vaughan, who later worked with Serling at WLW.[10] So, for that matter, did most writers for other media (*and* their wives), as well as most college-educated people.

For his part, Rod Serling had become dismayed—and angered—with what he saw as the increasing trashiness of radio. "Radio drama, after 20-odd years as king, left no lasting imprint of any importance," he wrote, still bitter six years later. "It produced very few talents who could be remembered uniquely for their contributions to radio drama. Beyond Norman Corwin and Arch Oboler go back for a known name among radio writers. Radio, in terms of . . . drama, dug its own grave. It had aimed downward, had become cheap and unbelievable, and had willingly settled for second best."[11]

Still, Serling had not entirely given up on radio. Aside from testing parachutes and jet-ejection seats, radio writing remained his only reasonably surefire way of earning money. Besides, Serling did not feel secure enough of his television-writing talents, or the market for such, to assay the life of a full-time TV scripter just yet. Although quick to sense an opportunity, Serling was not a strategically career-minded thinker, a deficiency that would later hurt him. All he *really* wanted as he approached his graduation from Antioch was a job.[12]

Hence the alacrity with which Serling accepted an offer to work as a staff writer for WLW-AM as well as to pen occasional scripts for the newly formed WLW-T, the sister television station. In addition to being a paying job, it promised to give him an opportunity to freelance both radio and television scripts at night. And working at WLW seemed certain to bring him good luck. WLW was "the Nation's Station,"—as the large midwestern mega-station roosterishly called itself—and the alma mater of such diverse broadcasting luminaries as Rosemary Clooney, the McGuire Sisters, the Mills Brothers, not to mention Norman Corwin. It was "The Cradle of the Stars!" And it was the only place that had offered Serling a job. So WLW and Cincinnati it was, at least for a while.

On a hot day in July, Rod and Carol Serling evacuated Trailer #10 and drove to Cincinnati, in much the same spirit that had moved Sam and Esther Serling when they had motored from Syracuse to Binghamton in pursuit of *their* American dream a quarter of a century before.

First, the Serlings moved into a small but comfortable one-bedroom apartment at 2822 Victoria Avenue. Several days later, Serling showed up for work at the bustling fifth-floor offices of WLW at Crosby Square in downtown Cincinnati.

The Serlings' boosterish mood was reinforced by Serling's sale of a script to *Stars Over Hollywood*, a Hollywood-based filmed drama anthology. The script, "Grady Everett for the People," a political drama with a Huey Long–style villain at its center, was clearly derivative of *All the King's Men*, the sensational recently published novel by Robert Penn Warren. Indeed, it was so imitative of it that it could be said to have been an adaptation and an uncredited one, as Serling's friends Saul and Phyllis Marmer recalled. When they pointed out the resemblance to Serling, he shrugged it off. What mattered to him was that he had broken into television.[13] Surely the house with two dogs wasn't far off.

But the Serlings' video millennium was slow in coming. Serling soon found that he liked WLW about as much as his predecessor and mentor Corwin had—that is, hardly at all. Just as Corwin had taken umbrage at the station's far right-wing politics and censorious news practices, so did Serling, although the latter was less inclined to do anything about it. As a resident of the area, Serling probably had a better idea of what to expect from the ultraconservative AVCO Corporation, which owned WLW, than had Corwin. But the young scriptwriter, though full of indignation at life's injustices, was not an Angry Man yet. That role would come later.

What irked Serling more was the sheer, inescapable, all-consuming tedium of his work and the programs he had to write for. Stuck in a hot, airless cubicle, Serling had to turn out two scripts a week for shows like *Leave It to Kathy*, a fatuous situation-comedy about a shop girl who works at the complaint counter of Goober's Department Store; *We'll Print That*, ". . . a show which spotlights the daily and weekly presses of the Midwest . . ."; and *Melody Showcase*, a program that essentially required, as Serling witheringly put it years later, ". . . two elements. A hayseed emcee who strummed a guitar and said 'Shucks, friends,' and a girl yodeler whose falsetto could break a beer mug at twenty paces."[14]

In addition to everything else, the job paid only seventy-five dollars a week, $50 a week less than Serling had earned as manager of ABS, his college radio station, and not really enough to make ends meet. "Rod was starving," Charles Vaughan, one of the fellow occupants of WLW's staff-writing "bullpen" recalled. In fact, the Serlings were eating, but there wasn't much variety in their diet: ten years later, the then successful television writer joked about the number of tuna casseroles he was forced to eat during this lean period (a reference that annoyed his wife, who was present and who had had to cook those casseroles).[15] The writer-cum-entertainer jumped at the chance to supplement his modest seventy-five-dollar-a-week salary by doing walk-ons on various WLW-T shows.

The working environment at the "Nation's Station" also left something to be desired. Serling was particularly horrified at the way the station treated its top executives, including one program executive who was apparently driven to a heart attack by the station manager's machinations. "M [the station manager] was an evil man who liked to play his executives off each other," said Gene Walz, a Cincinnati colleague of Serling's. "There was a guy called Jack Z. who worked at WLW, who actually died of a heart attack because of the pressure. And there was another guy who helped put the screws to him by the name of Fred G. All of them wanted Z out. The trick they used was to write memos that they had in corporate meetings, put his name on the list of those to receive the memo— but never actually give him a copy."

Several years later, Serling would use this distressing situation, including the memo stratagem used to "kill" Jack Z., as the basis for the acidulous portrait of the corporate life in "Patterns," his breakthrough teleplay. For the moment, though, Serling simply wanted out—not out of television necessarily, but certainly out of WLW.[16]

Serling's desperation to break out of WLW was poignantly manifest to Paul Bogart, a novice CBS director, who was part of a delegation from CBS headquarters that visited WLW in Cincinnati in late 1950 to help the affiliate commemorate its twenty-fifth anniversary.

"I was approached by a writer on a local show," Bogart recalled. "I think it was called *Midwest Hayride*. It was Serling. He didn't know that I had just started myself. He told me he had some scripts he was writing and that he wanted to get into Big Television [sic], and asked me what I could do for him. . . . He was desperate. He thought he had outgrown WLW, and that it was time for him to move on to the big time. He wanted to get out of that hayride show."

Bogart, who went on to direct *The Adams Chronicles* on public television and the film *Torch Song Trilogy*, promised to see what he could do, taking some of the scripts Serling foisted on him and passing them to another network functionary, who passed them on to someone else.[17]

Serling would remain mired at WLW-AM/T for yet another year and a half. He couldn't simply quit in disgust and take off for New York as Norman Corwin had done in 1936 after he had sickened of the WLW milieu. Unlike Corwin, Serling had a wife to support—by the end of 1951, a pregnant wife. Moreover, as much as Serling was anxious to break into "Big Television," the Ohio resident was still viscerally frightened of New York and all it represented.

For all of his desperation, Serling was still the life of the party, when the Serlings did party, cracking jokes, performing his gorilla imitation, going through his duffel bag of dirty limericks. At the same time, it was clear to observers, sometimes disturbingly so, who really ran the Rod Serling Show. "I remember the time they were at my home," said Charlie Vaughan, "and Carol snapped her fingers and pointed at her feet for Rod to come over. And he came over and sat at her feet. I was amazed."

Many others of the Serlings' early acquaintances were also surprised at the power that Carol exercised over her husband. "She was really the controlling one," Mary Wood remembered. "If she said, 'Rod, you can't spend that much money,' he didn't argue. That was surprising to us because he was so strong in other areas." The couple frequently bickered, according to neighbors.[18]

Trapped in his work and frustrated by his lack of success in freelancing and not particularly happy with his home life, Rod often retreated into his own fantasy world. It is probably no coincidence that one of the favorite themes of Serling's early video oeuvre was of entrapment. Hence an early effort like "The Air Is Free," a video script about a man trapped at the bottom of a mineshaft.

Still very much the man-child, Serling especially enjoyed hanging out with his neighbors' children, spinning stories and playing. He also returned to one of his own childhood hobbies, making and flying model airplanes. Numerous of his adult acquaintances from this strange, transitional period recall him as remote and introspective.

Serling's professional horizons began to expand toward the end of 1951 as a result of two significant developments, one commercial, the other artistic.

First, he found a reputable New York agent who was willing to represent him to the networks. Her name was Blanche Gaines, and she was to play a key role in Serling's career as well as his theatrical imagination. "Blanche Gaines was a lovely, charming woman who had a small agency where she was representing writers exclusively," recalled film producer Jerome Hellman. "It was a very small, very personalized, hands-on business, and Blanche was one of those people who did a lot of hands-on nurturing. She could find a young writer and devote a lot of time and attention and concern in a way that might not have been economically practical from the perspective of a larger agency. And Rod was one of those early people she worked with."[19] "She kept me on for a year before I made my first TV sale to *Lux Video Theatre*," Serling gratefully noted in an article in *Writer's Digest* in 1953. "I doubt that Blanche will add any writers to her present 18-man stable," Serling cautioned readers who might be interested in her services. "But if I die, look her up. She's number one in the field."[20]

Thanks to Gaines, Serling was able to sell a half dozen of his radio and television scripts to various New York and Hollywood shows during his first year at WLW—although none would actually

73

be produced until the following year. His freelance income—$650 for 1950, $3,000 for 1951—was still far below the $5,000 mark that his mentor Pearl Bentel had predicted for him back at Antioch, but he seemed to be making progress. And Gaines's motherly encouragement helped to take the sting out of the many rejections he continued to receive.

Meanwhile, Serling had signed on as a contributing writer to a brand-new anthology show, *The Storm*, on Cincinnati station WKRC that was directed and produced by a talented young Cincinnatian by the name of Robert Huber. For $125 a week, Serling turned out a script a week for Huber and WKRC-TV. In effect, Serling had his second anthology show—and his first on television.

Looking back on the few remaining kinescopes of *The Storm* today, it is hard to believe that *this* was television. Broadcast from WKRC's primitive studio in the old *Times-Star* building downtown on Tuesday evenings at ten, *The Storm* wasn't really television so much as radio drama with pictures—and not very good radio drama at that.

"The WKRC studios had these low ceilings," Charles Vaughan recalled. "Rod had to write something that could be shot in close-up."[21] And without much movement on the part of the cast. After all, they might bump their heads on the ceiling. Partly, and understandably, the generally hokey and inhibited quality of these programs was also a result of Serling's own rather limited dramatic—and teledramatic—skills. Most of the characters in Serling's early teleplays tend to be cliché-ridden stick figures. Also, they are almost always men; Serling hadn't learned the knack of writing about women, and, some argue, never did. When Serling's characters speak, they tend to speak too much, or orate. Like most writers who were attempting to make the transition from radio to television, Serling still wrote for the ear rather than the eye. He had yet to master the quick character development and punchy dialogue that TV required. Occasionally, a particularly pungent line would stick, but generally it would be drowned out by a flood of rhetoric.

Thematically, the early Serling was also somewhat inhibited, generally confining himself to crude military morality plays, in which he transposed many of his scarifying experiences in the Filipino campaign to the setting of the Korean War, which had just broken out. For example, "No Gods to Serve," the first script for *The Storm* and later produced for NBC's *The Doctor*, was about a young

Jewish soldier and a wounded army chaplain who undergo a crisis of faith and courage in a besieged Korean farmhouse. "We all have a God to serve," says the young Serling-like figure—"an intelligent, sensitive man," according to the stage directions—to the chaplain in the play's key scene. Another early Serling effort reflecting the author's continuing obsession with war was "The Sergeant," which was broadcast on April 29, 1952, on NBC's *Armstrong Circle Theater*. It centered around the agony of a soldier whose cowardly scream during combat costs the lives of most of his platoon. Does one moment of cowardice make a man a coward? It was a question that Serling would take up again, and more effectively, several years later in "The Rack."[22] Nevertheless, Serling steered clear of criticizing the war or the direction of American foreign policy itself.

When the apolitical Serling did take on the Cold War, as in "I Lift My Lamp," produced for *Hallmark Hall of Fame* in 1953, he appears to endorse it. The Bomb makes a dramatic appearance in another of his early works, "Mr. Finchley vs. the Bomb," originally written while Serling was at WLW. However, the squib, about an old man who refuses to vacate an atomic bomb testing site, only uses the weapon as a comic device to advance the story.

In *fine*, Serling made little history with *The Storm*. Nevertheless, it was good practice, and the initial productions that were produced from his scripts, and the local approbation he received for them— combined with his agent's encouragement—gave the young writer the confidence to think that he could do better if he wrote for television on a full-time basis.

Meanwhile, Serling grew even more unhappy with his WLW job.

Finally, one day in December 1951, Serling decided he had had it. As he later recounted it in the foreword to his collected plays, he finally decided to take the leap after he was assigned to concoct an audition show for a patent medicine show that was then the rage in Cincinnati. According to his later testimony, he read as far as the second paragraph of the advertising agency's work text—"This will be a program for the people. We'd like to see a real grass-roots approach that is popular and close to the soil"—and decided that was it. "The pattern of whatever future I had was very much in evidence. I was either going to write dramatic shows for television . . . even at the risk of economics and common sense, or I was going to succumb to the double-faced sanctimony of commercial radio, rotating words as if they were props, and utilizing one of the approaches characteristic of radio—writing and thinking downward at the lowest possible common denominator. That afternoon I quit the station."[23]

When Serling explained his decision to go to full-time freelance to his anti-TV wife that evening at a local Howard Johnson's, according to his admittedly sentimental account, she was fully supportive. "She knew it was a frustrating, insecure, bleeding business at best, and the guy she was married to could get his pride, his composure, and his confidence eaten away with the acid of disappointment. All this she knew sitting at a table at Howard Johnson's in 1951, and as it turned out, this was a scene with no dialogue at all. All she did was take my hand. Then she winked at me and picked up the menu and studied it. And at that given moment, the vision of medicine bottles, girl yodelers, and guitar-strumming emcees faded away into happy obscurity. For lush or lean, good or bad, Sardi's or malnutrition, I'd launched a career."[24]

The Serlings' joint optimism about television writing as a career, combined with their nationally broadcast wish to live in a house, led them to buy a ranch-style house in Wyoming Heights in April of 1952. At first, Serling, paralyzed by writer's block, wondered whether his typewriter was a monster.

Nineteen fifty-two, as it turned out, was a very good year for television. That spring, the FCC, in a newly expansive spirit, and, having satisfied itself that television's interference problems had been solved, lifted its four-year-old freeze on new television station licenses. The result was a modern-day version of the Oklahoma Land Rush. Hundreds of new licensees promptly rushed to stake out their piece of the ether, and the four networks—CBS, NBC, ABC, and DuMont (which would shortly be driven out of existence)—rushed to sign up new affiliates. When the dust cleared, CBS and NBC had signed up most of the two hundred new television stations, with ABC and DuMont a distant third and fourth. By the end of the year, the total number of stations had tripled, from 108 to 326.

Ownership of TV sets also exploded. In 1949, when Serling had written his first crude feature for WLW-T, only one out of twelve American families owned, or could afford, their own TV set. By the end of 1952, one out of every three American households were TV households; within three years, that ratio would expand once again to six out of ten. The TV antennae enveloping Cincinnati, which

Serling had breathlessly pointed out to his wife, were now prolif-
erating around the country. There was no such thing as "television
cities" anymore, since all cities worthy of the name now had at least
one station; media-rich Cincinnati, which already had two, gained
a third. There was only one television nation, linked by coaxial
cable. TV had moved out of the barroom into America's living room.

The question was, what was there to watch? Other than *I Love
Lucy*, or perhaps *Texaco Star Theater*, there was very little in the
way of new or original programming. Television's dominant program forms, including news and drama, were still all too imitative
and reminiscent of radio. "TV news" consisted of newsmen sitting
at their desks and reciting the news; occasionally they would get
up and walk around, but other than that, the "picture" wasn't much
different from what the radio-listening audience already received.
The most popular video genre in 1952 was the crime anthology
show, another transplant from radio; most of these shows, too,
retained their radio names. The extant dramatic anthology shows,
like *Kraft* and *Lux Video Theatre*, also tended to use material
grafted from other media, particularly the stage. The script editors
of these programs cried for more original writing, but it still wasn't
there. "It is only through good writing that television will grow,"
said NBC script editor Edward Barry Roberts in 1952, "and fulfill
its potential destiny as the most fascinating and the most important
means ever known of communicating information, entertainment,
and education. We are all waiting hopefully and impatiently for the
television artist-playwrights to appear."[25] Roberts and his colleagues would have to wait just a little longer for those "artist-
playwrights," most of whom, like Serling, were still learning the
demands, limitations, and potentials of the medium. When it came
down to it, there didn't seem to be much new or different about
television—yet.

Nineteen fifty-two was also a presidential election year, which
was fortunate for television. Carol Serling's distant cousin Robert
Taft was the odds-on favorite to win the Republican nomination
going into the convention that summer. However, the unsmiling
senator from Ohio and his obstreperous supporters foolishly ignored the television cameras that were carrying gavel-to-gavel
coverage of the quadrennial hullabaloo for the first time. This re-

dounded to the advantage of the far more telegenic former general and Supreme Allied Commander, Dwight D. Eisenhower, who won the nod.

Richard Nixon, the gimlet-eyed senator from California, was Eisenhower's uncontroversial choice for vice-presidential running mate, until word of an alleged Nixon slush fund suddenly darkened Nixon's candidacy. Significantly, Nixon turned to television to redeem himself, giving his now-famous "Checkers" speech ("Pat doesn't have a mink coat, but I always tell her that she'll look good in anything . . ."). Later, television would not be so kind to Richard Nixon, but for now it saved him.

That November Eisenhower and Nixon handily won the election, thanks in considerable part to a superior television campaign, and to Democrat Adlai Stevenson's inability to keep his speeches to the time allotted for them. The Eisenhower Era had begun. And so had the Age of Television.

6

THE TENSION AND THE GLORY (1953 – 54)

All things considered, I suspect the golden age for the dramatist is at hand. There is so much air to be illustrated, so many eyes watching, so much money to be spent, so many fine technicians and interpreters at one's command that the playwright cannot but thrive.
—Gore Vidal[1]

The most golden thing about television in that golden age was the power. We were allowed quantities of risk-taking which is the center of all art and theater. We had no medium and we had no rules, so we in effect created the medium ourselves . . . and when you're that young, you're immortal, you can't make a mistake. We had technical freedom, creative freedom, financial freedom. It was an ideal ground to create a mark on. Nobody could come and take it away from us because nobody knew how to do it but us.
—Fielder Cook[2]

It was over on Thursday or Sunday or whatever, and if the show was a hit, we would have a party and everybody celebrated, and if the show was a flop, we had a party and everybody celebrated, and the next day you got up and you started the next show.
—Ethel Wynant, CBS casting director during live television years[3]

Television truly came into its own in 1953.

The television year began with the widely publicized and widely anticipated birth on *I Love Lucy*, on January 19, of Little Ricky to Lucy and Ricky Ricardo—played by TV's reigning queen of comedy, Lucille Ball, and her TV-and-real-life husband, Desi Arnaz. Little Ricky's joyful debut, which coincided with the birth of the couple's real-life child, Desiderio Alberto Arnaz IV, found a

79

record-breaking 68.8 percent of TV set owners glued to their sets, making it the highest-rated show in television history. The inauguration of President Eisenhower the following morning drew markedly less attention.

In June, an estimated 70 million American viewers, plus millions more in Great Britain, gazed in puzzled awe at the telecast of a bona fide TV-cum-royal event—the coronation of Elizabeth II at Westminster Abbey in London. The blaring, glittering televised ceremonies seemed to symbolize both the beginning of the Second Elizabethan Era and of the Video Era. In contrast to the ushering in of George VI's, seventeen years before, which had been a media event of that day, his daughter Elizabeth's audience could now watch as well as listen to the ornate goings on, enhancing its sense of participation and further legitimizing the younger medium.

Meanwhile, in his cramped wire-entangled atelier atop New York's Grand Central Station, Edward R. Murrow was showing what TV news could do—when it had the guts—with his documentary show *See It Now* (a televisual version of his concurrent radio series *Hear It Now*) dramatically exposing such pressing problems as juvenile delinquency and rural poverty in hard-hitting, tautly focused programs. In November, Murrow and *See It Now* coproducer Fred Friendly began to tackle the country's greatest political ill, the guilt-by-association syndrome that was part and parcel of McCarthyism, with their powerful, carefully constructed newscast about the case of Milo Radulovich, an air force psychologist who had been wrongfully branded a security risk by McCarthyite government investigators because of his parents' political associations; the widely watched newscast spurred the Air Force into reinstating the wrongly maligned Radulovich. As Murrow and company proved, television, in the right hands, could be an active force for good.

Back in conservative Cincinnati, freelance television scripter and occasional CBS contributor Rod Serling, a fan of Murrow's since the latter's foreign correspondent period, followed the newsman's increasingly bold moves with great interest, mixed with some guilt over his own political passivity. "I was a strange, haunted middle-of-the-roader trying to find his way," Serling later said.[4]

Meanwhile, television drama (if not necessarily Serling's own work) was also coming of age. By 1953, six years after the first shaky dramatic anthology, *Kraft Television Theatre*, had appeared on the air, all the elements for a brief but fiery golden age of the genre had fallen into place: interest from network executives and sponsors, money for hiring actors and commissioning original scripts, the technology, the audience, and, above all, the creative talent.

The signal that a new era in television theater was at hand came in May 1953, with the production of Paddy Chayefsky's "Marty" on *Philco Television Playhouse*. Chayefsky's endearing drama focused on a lonely Bronx butcher, played by Rod Steiger, struggling to break free of his mother's clutches as well as those of his equally possessive bachelor friends while he conducts an off-and-on-again romance with Clara, an equally miserable schoolteacher, played by Nancy Marchand, who he meets one night at the Waverly Ballroom. Chayefsky's touching play displayed the singularity of the television medium, especially its capacity for intimacy, to powerful effect. In contrast to the outsized heroes and heroines Hollywood had been wont to offer, the people of "Marty" were life-sized characters whom TV viewers could welcome into their living rooms and identify with. The natural-sounding dialogue the author gave his characters enhanced the show's verisimilitude. "I tried to write the dialogue as if it had been wire-tapped," said Chayefsky.[5] "You want to go you should go," Marty says to his friend Angie, convincingly portrayed by Joe Mantell. "Well, what do you feel like doing tonight?" Angie asks Marty as they sit in a celebrated exchange at their favorite all-night beanery. "I don't know, Angie. What do *you* feel like doing?" is Marty's expressionless retort. "What do *you* feel like doing?" The famous love scene between Marty and the homely Clara gave viewers the same almost eerie feeling of *being there*. Serling, among others, would forever envy Chayefsky's uncanny knack for catching the rhythms of urban "backdoor dialogue," as Serling called it—as well as his fellow television playwright's ability to write affecting love scenes. Like most of his peers, Serling, too, envied the universal fame that suddenly accrued to Chayefsky as a result of the ground-breaking production.[6]

Clearly, "Marty" touched a nerve. Rod Steiger was staggered by the reaction to his performance. "People from all over the country and all different ways of life, from different races and religions and creeds, sent me letters," the actor remarked. "The immense power of that medium!"[7]

The enthusiastic response to "Marty" helped set off a gusher of drama anthology shows. By the following fall, there were no fewer than twenty-five anthology shows on the air, stuck into whatever production space—generally hastily converted radio studios—could be found in Manhattan's cramped canyons, transmitting original half-hour and hour-long plays into the ether. Many were good, many were bad, and a surprising number were very good—directed, performed, and staged *live*—in a continuum of teletheatrical activity that took place amid a frantic self-intoxicated world within a world whose hundreds of denizens sincerely felt they were making television drama into a new art form.

Thirty-five years later, the veterans of New York television, many of whom would go on to create even greater names for themselves in film or in other media, reverently recall that unique and unreal time—"when the creative people were in charge"—only accessible now on fuzzy kinescopes in the archives of broadcasting museums.

Producer Jerome Hellman, then working in the New York offices of the Ashley-Steiner Agency—the agency that Serling would later sign with—vividly recalled what it was like to be at the center of that swirling creative nova. "It [television] was a vital young industry about which no one knew a great deal, and it wasn't dominated yet by the money boys," said Hellman.

> It was really dominated by creative people, to whom New York City represented a kind of creative Mecca. So whether we had an interest in theater, in writing, in producing, in directing, in acting, whatever it was, we came to New York. That's where the energy and the vitality and the opportunity existed. So there was an explosive infusion of viable, creative talent at a time when there was a new industry being created, where the need for people was so voracious, that virtually anybody with talent, ability, and determination could force his way in the door and be seen. In my judgment it was a moment in time never repeated.[8]

"What we had was this wonderful confluence of superb acting talent, superb writing talent, and really emerging directorial talent,"[9] noted Hellman's colleague Arthur Penn. Like many of the directors who helped create the first great wave of television drama, Penn came from the theater, joining NBC's *Colgate Comedy Hour* as a floor manager in 1951 after attending Actors Studio, before getting his first chance to direct. Penn elaborated on how this unique "confluence" came about:

Since we were working out of New York on Sunday nights, that meant that all the Broadway shows were closed that night. And also, actors in plays signed on for a year at least. So what you had then was the cream of the theater actors often imprisoned—and I use that word advisedly—in a Broadway hit, eight performances a week. What we were able to do in the case of Philco was get the best of the actors who were on Broadway—Kim Stanley, Henry Fonda, Geraldine Page, Julie Harris. Names that are legendary in the theater who were desperate to do something else so they wouldn't go absolutely stale and crazy. They would work for $300 a week in live TV.

To be in a play was to be in a vertical community, and you couldn't try your craft or your skill with other people except on television. They were just wild to work together.

And then often, writers would write for specific actors. They were having things written for them although the money was absolutely minimal. But the pleasure of working together, and the opportunity to work with each other was very rich.

What was also happening was Actors Studio was forming. Here was exactly the same phenomenon: actors trapped in Broadway hits who had no chance to do any other kind of work, so they were desperate. So the Actors Studio was formed. And what was then emerging was a distinct New York acting style. And they were going to be stars within a very short period of time—Paul Newman, Marlon Brando, Jimmy Dean, et cetera. That's why live TV was able to function, because these were theater actors, not actors who needed four takes or five takes. They were able to just get up and go from eight o'clock to nine o'clock without stopping, performing a full play. They had the flexibility, the training, the sense that once they began performing the play, there was no stopping it, and that is what was consistent with live TV. There was no going back. We'd go on at nine and off at ten, and it was a complete living experience.[10]

Setting the "tone" for that remarkable assemblage of talent was a small group of dynamic, highly intelligent producers, most of whom had also come out of the theater. People like Fred Coe of

NBC's *Philco/Goodyear Playhouse*, Worthington Miner and Felix Jackson at CBS's *Studio One*, and, later, Martin Manulis and Herbert Brodkin at *Playhouse 90*. "It was the tone," said Penn, "that came from Herb Brodkin, and Fred Coe, and Tony Miner. The tone [*sic*] said, 'Get the good writers, and the good writers will bring the good actors, and the good actors will bring the good directors.' And there we were, that's how we became a circle. Each one of us would stimulate the other."[11]

Loring Mandel, who wrote for *Studio One, Philco/Goodyear*, and other shows, explained: "The people who were the producers at the networks, people like Felix Jackson and Tony Miner and Robert Montgomery and a number of others, these people had come from the theater, and they were 'show people,' in terms of their instincts, they understood drama, they were not numbers people, they didn't bother much with demographics, they were interested in pursuing ideas and drama on television. They were not bureaucrats in any sense of the word." The bureaucrats and the committees would come soon enough.[12]

Delbert Mann, the director of "Marty," who would also go on to direct the movie version of the TV play and other feature films, was another emerging director who came from the stage. Like Penn, Mann, if given his druthers, would have preferred to stay in "live." He described why:

> The studio in which we worked was very small. Sets had to be improvised and tucked into each other, together with the commercials, which were done live in the same studio. So the space was always a concern. Every little inch of space had to be used, cameras connected by cables to a specific outlet.
>
> You had to be very careful and plan how to get a camera under a cable to get over here to get another shot that you had to have, how to release this camera so you could get it over to the next scene, and a variety of physical problems of that nature that simply had to be thought out. And that's a world that really doesn't exist today. . . . The fact that you had to do a show from the beginning, all the way through, live, whatever happened, accidents or mistimings, or whatever, and get the show on and off the air as close to time as you possibly could, all that was unique to live television.[13]

"Doing an hour show every three weeks, casting it and adapting it and making it all come out at the right time was a terribly exciting adventure," said George Roy Hill, whose best-known TV work was a sprawling 1956 production of "A Night to Remember," a dramatic re-enactment of the sinking of the *Titanic*, which used over one hundred actors. "And you did so many you never worried about what you'd just fucked up, if you had. You were ready to go on to the next one—it was a manic experience."[14]

The audience played a key part in the live television experience, noted actor Richard Kiley, who would become a star in the 1955 *Kraft Television Theatre* production of Serling's "Patterns." "Instead of having eight hundred or a thousand people sitting on the edge of their chairs, you had millions upon millions upon millions of people watching you. It was scary—but thrilling," said Kiley.[15]

"It had that highly personal feeling about it," writer Tad Mosel agreed. "Because it was *live*, when you sat in your living room and looked at a live play, you really honestly had the feeling that Paul Newman was performing *for you*. Just for me, sitting here . . . and you saw he was nervous and you said, 'Oh, I hope he's going to get through it all right.' . . . It was like watching your children in a school play."[16]

Part of the thrill for both the audience and the crew was never knowing exactly *what* would happen. Kiley describes a typical live TV contretemps:

> We were doing a scene from *Anne of the Thousand Days* with Rex Harrison and Lilli Palmer. And I was playing Smeaton, who was supposedly the lover of Anne Boleyn . . . so there's one moment where Lilli Palmer is interrogating me. And she's staring me straight in the face, standing across this dock from me. And asking me if what I accused her of was true. And I look into those eyes of hers, and I'm supposed to absolutely crumble inside and with a great cry leap out of the dock and throw myself at the feet of Henry [VIII]. Well, I leaped out of the dock, and my pants caught on a gargoyle sculpture. So I had one leg hanging in the air, reaching for poor Rex Harrison, and I couldn't get to him. And do you know something? Those cameramen, those guys at CBS were so great. They saw instantly what had happened. They cut off

me, went to Rex, who didn't know what to do, and so he stood up and looked terribly stern.[17]

"What you had going then was a kind of ongoing emotional thing," said Kiley, "where you built and built and built and knew what you were doing. Which is, of course, the way the stage works. And then you have the additional luxury of the subtlety of being able to play things very subtly in front of the camera. You didn't have to project to the last row in the balcony. So you had the best of both worlds in a sense, that was why live TV was such a wonderful training ground for young actors and actresses. You were practicing your stage craft and learning film craft."[18]

Gore Vidal, who wrote seventy television plays and who wrote for both Fred Coe and Felix Jackson, also found the maniacal pressure of getting out a live television play exhilarating. "I'd go to the first reading," said Vidal, whose best-known video work was a 1955 *Goodyear* production of his parable, "Visit to a Small Planet." "And I'd listen to how everybody sounded, listen to the actors' complaints and talk to the director."

Then I'd go off and rewrite, because I didn't really know what the play was until I heard the actors' voices. The actors' voices were like the instruments of the orchestra. You've got a Kim Stanley, you've got a cello, and what you wrote is for a violin, so you alter it subtly for the cello. We were all very young and we all worked very quickly, so I'd come down with the changes. We'd go back to rehearsals and they were up upon their feet. And Nick [Dominick] Dunne, in the meanwhile, had put down the tapes on the floor which would show where the sets would be, the rooms and the doors and the walls, that was all we had for guidance. And I keep making changes, but not many from then on. Then you get into the studio, which is concentrated hell, and run through, which is generally the time of distinct disaster.

And then you have the nerve-racking time of before you go into the control room and the thing goes on live, which was a terrifying and exhilarating experience, then you go down to Hurley's and everybody got drunk. That's why there were so many alcoholics who came out of television. It was all the tension of doing it. There's no tension like that in the theater.

. . . You had eight days for the actors to get on their feet and for you to change it.[19]

"*The play was the thing*, always, to the end of live drama, the play was the thing, the most important element of the production," stressed Tad Mosel, another member of Coe's legendary stable. "If there were reporters, they interviewed the playwright. . . . The actors weren't asked to do that, because the play was the thing."[20]

To Mosel, the experience of being on the set when his "little play" went over the airwaves was glory enough. Mosel described his favorite moment of his weekly scriptwriting labors—watching the countdown:

> I would sit in the control room the night of the show. I'd sit way back against the wall, behind the director and the assistants . . . and beyond that a plate glass looking out at the studio. All the sets were in place, beautifully lighted, cameras were in position, the actors standing in opening position. And a hush would fall over everything. When the second hand of the clock would start around for that last minute, and it'd go all the way around and reach the top, then you'd begin. And this *rush* of music, and you'd hear this voice say, '*LIVE, FROM NEW YORK*,' and you knew that your little play was going out to forty million people. And there is no thrill anywhere in my life, anywhere, any time, of any kind, that will equal it. And I wouldn't miss that for anything. And that's why it was the golden age. . . . The *air* was golden, what was happening was golden.[21]

"Don't get the wrong idea," said Buzz Kulik, another veteran of that era who would go on to direct several episodes of *The Twilight Zone*. "There was a lot of crap around, and there was a lot of stuff being badly done. But the one thing there was was a kind of electricity and energy, a great kind of vitality in that period. I think it even existed in the framework of the audience. The audience was so excited about this new thing, that they brought a kind of energy and vitality to it also."[22]

Actor Roddy McDowall took a fond if more objective view of that time. "It was a wonderful playroom, like the early days of film. It was before it was so important and such a gigantic commercial asset to a lot of people, on such a gigantic level—there was room to do a lot of things and to fail. And out of those failures came an enormous amount of growth for a lot of people, especially young people. All of us were just a bunch of young kids throwing our hats into the air with nothing to lose. So we were able to commit without fear."[23]

"Sunday nights, we had the country," said Gore Vidal. "Monday morning you would be walking down First Avenue and every other group of people would be discussing *your play*."[24]

Serling, too, experienced and relished the delicious feeling of sitting in the control booth while his play was beamed out to 20 or 30 million TV theatergoers, and of overhearing New Yorkers discuss it the next day.

He, too, loved the theatrical experience involved in putting on a live television play. "There was something of the magic of theater in producing the live television play," Serling recalled with sentiment in a 1966 TV special about the "bygone age" of television drama, already a distant memory. "The bone-crushing schedules, the frantic adherences to deadlines, the missed camera shots, the shadow of the mike boom, the misplaced actor who missed his mark—they all comprised a flavor of opening nights. The mistakes, the boo-boos, the forgotten lines, but with it all that incredible and marvelous commotion that attends a Broadway first night."[25] Indeed, these things ultimately contributed to Serling's decision to move to the New York area himself.

Nevertheless, Serling opted to remain in Cincinnati and watch most of the action from the sanctuary of his own living room, where no one but Carol could see how nervous he was. Desperate though Serling was to break into New York television, he preferred to do so from afar, and let his work speak for itself, despite the increasing protestations of Blanche Gaines, who insisted that her charge move to the New York area as soon as possible to take full advantage of the city's video drama boom. Quite simply Serling was afraid. Or, as he put it:

> Between late 1951 and 1954, I lived in Ohio [commuting back and forth to New York]. This was expensive and time-consuming, but was a concession to my own peculiar hesitancy

about all things big, massive, and imposing. New York television and its people were *such an entity*. [Author's emphasis][26]

Serling's initial forays to Gotham were trips that tended to be brief and accident-filled. Once, the over-eager writer arrived at the offices of the J. Walter Thompson Agency for a story conference about one of his plays that was to be produced by *Lux Video Theatre*, and he became so flustered that he walked straight into a wall. Then the writer's luggage flew open, spilling his socks and underwear onto the floor and causing him to get even more redfaced. "Don't worry, little friend," Richard McDonagh, the *Lux* story editor, assured Serling, "these people are much more interested in the contents of that," pointing to Serling's head, "than your suitcase." Nevertheless, the experience did little to bolster Serling's confidence.[27]

Serling also made a fuss when he happened on the set of *Studio One*, where "Buffalo Bill Is Dead," his first contribution to that prestigious program, was being produced. Franklin Schaffner, the director, was unnerved by the annoying squeaky sound produced by Serling's tight shoes and asked that he be ejected, according to producer Felix Jackson, until Jackson pointed out to Schaffner that "that idiot *was* the writer."[28]

Perhaps such incidents weren't as unintentional as they seemed. Gore Vidal, another member of Jackson's *Studio One* stable—and another ham—vividly recalled Serling's vanity and exhibitionism. "Don't forget, he saw himself as a leading man, but he was much too short," said Vidal. "He had a lot of charm, was nice looking, had a lovely voice, and he was really sort of the star of his own inner drama," Vidal added.

Felix Jackson agreed. Jackson later recalled having tremendous respect for Serling as a writer. "But," he continued, "the thing about Rod was that he had this tremendous urge to be on the screen."[29]

In addition to trying to make meetings and causing pandemonium on the set, Serling, ever observant, also did pick up some good material during these trips to New York. His *Lux* play "Mr. Finchley vs. the Bomb," for example, was inspired by an eviction he observed in Chinatown. Serling also visited with his agent and surrogate mother, Blanche Gaines, in her offices on West Fifty-seventh Street. There Gaines would review the market with her up-and-coming client, as well as try to persuade him to move to New

York, to no avail. Then the writer would dash back to Ohio and the anonymity and relative security of Wyoming Heights.

Certainly Serling enjoyed the perquisites of being Cincinnati's most successful television scriptwriter, a position to which he acceded fairly rapidly. The sale of "Mr. Finchley" to *Lux* in April 1952, five months after his decision to go freelance officially, marked the end of his "hungry" period. All told, he sold thirteen scripts to *Lux* during 1952 and 1953. He also began making regular sales to the more established anthology dramas such as *Kraft, Studio One,* and *Hallmark Hall of Fame.* He wasn't rich, but at least he was making a living.

In August 1952, the first major article about Serling appeared in the *Cincinnati Post,* in conjunction with the *Hallmark Summer Theater* production of Serling's political drama "The Carlson Legend." If Serling was the star of his own inner drama, as Gore Vidal said, he kept his agonizing to himself—at least while he was in Cincinnati. Serling dutifully explained to his fellow Cincinnatians, perhaps not used to having many freelance writers in their midst, that he was just a working Joe, and compared television writing to working in the greeting card business, in that "Christmas sentiments have to be prepared in July and Easter and the burgeonings of spring have to be imagined in the dead of winter"—which goes a long way toward explaining the modest quality of much of his earliest video oeuvre. The *Post* noted the pay scale Serling rated as an up-and-coming television playwright: $600 for half-hour shows, and from $750 to $1,000 for an hour drama. "Checks for these amounts and for other freelance work . . . keep Mr. Serling from working in the usual eight-to-five manner."[30]

There was also a brief glimpse of the writer's chaotic household. Serling graciously accorded the credit for his initial success to his wife. "She's a psychology major [Carol was actually an education major], and knows how to treat a writer. She sees that I'm not interrupted when I sit down to write and doesn't mind if I get out of bed at night and prowl because an idea has struck me." He couldn't say the same, the writer joked, for his tiny daughter or cocker spaniel, "neither of whom has any respect for creative activity and scatter his thoughts with wails and barks whenever they feel like it."[31] Such was Serling's basic philosophy of parenting. He loved his daughter, Jody, as well as his second daughter, Nan, when she arrived in 1955; but he preferred to let Carol take care of their children.

For her part, Carol was happy to play the role of mother to the girls, perhaps as a result of her own parentless upbringing. Writing was Rod's job. Carol's was making sure that her husband could write—which meant keeping the girls (and the succession of Serling dogs) out of the way while he was pecking away. It was a family situation that was bound to create difficulties, and did, but during the Cincinnati days, it basically worked.

All in all, Serling's first year as a full-time freelancer was a striking success, yielding him nearly thirty individual script sales and close to twenty thousand dollars in income—four times his income for the previous year, not to mention four times Pearl Bentel's prediction of what he would earn if and when he became successful. Moreover, he was fast becoming a local celebrity. After the *Post* profiled him, Serling received invitations to speak before various Cincinnati civic-literary groups, including the Drama Circle of Cincinnati and the Book Review Club. He also was asked to devise a course on his brand-new craft for the Cincinnati College of Music. And he began receiving letters from long-lost friends and paraguys: was the Rod Serling whose name had appeared in the credits for *Lux Video Theatre* the same buck private who used to have a talent for telling off-color jokes? (A talent that Serling never lost.) There were also several requests for loans.

The following year was also a banner one for Serling. In January 1953, Rod won the thousand-dollar first prize in a scriptwriting contest sponsored by WTVN, the CBS affiliate in Columbus, Carol's hometown. The script, "Ward 8," had been previously tried out on local viewers (in a slightly altered version entitled "The Sergeant") to good effect on *The Storm*, which Serling cannily continued to use as his principal dramatic incubator.

That spring, the prolific scriptwriter broadened his audience—and his market—when he broke into *Kraft Television Theatre*—the granddaddy of dramatic anthology shows, with two dramas, "Next of Kin," a story about three soldiers killed in action and the wrenching effects on their families, inspired by a newspaper story Serling read; and "The Twilight Rounds," a gritty boxing drama. Serling's work also debuted on *Hallmark Hall of Fame*, another prestigious show that would become a regular outlet. Serling may not have been nationally famous yet, but by the end of the year he could boast of enough sales and regional celebrity to merit the title of the "Midwest's Top TV Scripter" from *Writer's Digest*, the Cincinnati-based writer's magazine.[32]

As a writer, Serling was still trying to find his voice, while learning the peculiar characteristics of the new medium he had adopted. Serling's characterizations were, still, often flat; his situations and resolutions contrived. He had yet to learn how to fully convert his essentially radiogenic imagination to video. His greatest strength was his ability to write vivid, crackling, if occasionally wordy, dialogue. He was also a very fast writer, a definite attribute in a medium that was devouring scripts. "It was easier for Rod to write a script than not to write a script," averred Gore Vidal.[33] By his own admission, he was still "one of the little guys" in the TV scriptwriting trade.[34] Paddy Chayefsky was the reigning heavyweight in the scriptwriting division.

That summer was a sweet one as the Serlings vacationed as a family for the first time at Carol's grandfather's cottage on Lake Cayuga near Interlaken, New York, starting a tradition that would continue for twenty-two years, until the summer of Serling's death in 1975. Serling also bought a thirteen-foot boat with an inboard motor which he spent much of the time puttering around in; it was the only time Serling ever relaxed, according to his wife. Later, when he became more successful, the thirteen-footer was replaced with a twenty-two-footer. It was "the only place I can recall [where] he didn't have a typewriter or a Dictaphone, when he was on the boat. And then he was thoroughly relaxed because he knew the telephone was far away and there was nothing he could do about it."[35]

That summer *Kraft* aired "Old MacDonald Had a Curve," one of the better-written Serling plays to date; it was the only pre-"Patterns" play that Serling thought well enough of to include in his 1957 published collection of plays. Half comedy, half fantasy with a soupçon of pathos, "Old MacDonald" was about an aging ex-ballplayer who is given a second chance at fame thanks to the freakish, *Twilight Zone*-ish gift of a seeing-eye curve ball. In addition to evincing his concern for the forgotten elderly, the play again displayed Serling's talent for writing convincing dialogue.

Several other radio and television works of Serling's from 1952 and 1953 also presage *The Twilight Zone* in other ways; but none more than "The Time Element," a fantasy he wrote for WLW about a man who finds himself back in time and tries to reverse the debacle at Pearl Harbor. Serling would later resurrect that play as the pilot for *The Twilight Zone*.

However, Serling generally steered clear of both fantasy and controversy during his Cincinnati period. Serling knew the limitations of the television medium and he accepted them, as he wrote in *Writer's Digest*:

Because TV is a mass medium you have to be governed by mass media taboos. Easy on sex. Easy on violence. Nix on religion. Gently does it on controversial themes. Sound strapped? I suppose it does at the outset. But experience brings acceptance and understanding.[36]

"How to write a TV script?" Serling asked. He answered himself:

First, pick up a textbook on the subject to learn the form. In thirty minutes, you learn the form and you're in business. From that point on you're a playwright. You write a legitimate story about interesting people with valid conflict and a valid resolve. You give your story mood, purpose, understanding, and honesty. That's what it takes. . . .[37]

Timid words for timid times. Serling, yet a conformist, at least on the surface, was not interested in breaking any ground or stirring up controversy.

Serling did take *some* chances. "Next of Kin" dealt in part with marital infidelity, a generally taboo subject on television. Another early teleplay, "Blues for Joey Menotti," had a prostitute as the female lead. And Serling's work did have its harrowing, even shocking moments—like the hair-raising scene in "24 Men to a Plane," when the haunted ex-jumpmaster is tortured by the recounting of his mis-jump; or the shattering climax of "A Long Time Till Dawn," Serling's melodramatic treatment of the juvenile delinquency problem for *Hallmark* in which the doomed, paranoid protagonist is unfairly machine-gunned to death on his girlfriend's balcony. Making the latter moment particularly memorable was the brilliant performance of a possessed young actor and Actors Studio graduate by the name of James Dean.

Serling, the haunted middle-grounder, began to find his way—and his voice—both as a citizen and as a television writer in 1954. He also finally conquered his fear of New York.

"In the spring, I plan to sell my house and move wife and kid to New York," he proudly stated in December 1953. "I've got the confidence now, I've made the contacts. I've got a bank account and a paid-for typewriter. And I need the security of being on the scene. I don't feel secure in Cincinnati."[38] To be sure, some of his New York colleagues didn't even *know* Serling lived in Cincinnati. Producer Martin Manulis, who worked with Serling on *Suspense* and several other New York-based shows in the early 1950s, before moving to the West Coast to produce *Playhouse 90* in 1956, couldn't understand why Serling couldn't come to his offices for a script conference for at least twenty-four hours, until he learned that the writer first had to fly in from Ohio. Manulis, who would later achieve fame for his collaboration with Serling on "Requiem for a Heavyweight," assumed that Serling lived in the New York area, like everyone else in New York television, and that Serling had been too embarrassed to tell Manulis otherwise (apparently, Manulis didn't read *Writer's Digest*).

Meanwhile, Serling had also grown gradually more uncomfortable with the Queen City's right-wing, conformist atmosphere, including the outspoken support for Joseph McCarthy and his witch-hunting ways. In March 1954, Serling was sufficiently stirred by that issue to publicly defend his hero, Edward R. Murrow, who had taken McCarthy apart on his now historic broadcast of *See It Now*. Murrow was pilloried in the Cincinnati press. Emboldened by Murrow's courage—as so many other haunted middle-of-the-roaders had been—Serling cut loose with an epistolary volley of his own in a vitriolic letter to the *Cincinnati Enquirer* on March 21, nine days after the Murrow broadcast.

"The *Enquirer*, Mr. Ratcliffe, Mr. Davis [two pro-McCarthy *Enquirer* columnists] and the rest of the 'Give-Em-Hell' Platoon share the one given reaction of their fair-haired senator," an enraged Serling wrote:

> . . . that of lumping all their critics [together as] "bleeding heart, pro-Communist, egg-head intellectual liberals. . . ." For

the benefit of all of these patriotic gentlemen, let it be submitted that not all of us who flinch at McCarthy's methods are Communists, pro-Communists, or even Communist excusers. . . .

We challenge McCarthy and his vocal cheering section on our morning paper to produce the name or names of any important Communists, not already pegged by other government agencies, who have been brought to justice through his committee's efforts. Our basic tenet of American justice that recognizes a man's innocence until guilt is proven will be with us long after the fog-horn echoes of the *Enquirer*'s and Joe McCarthy's campaign to delineate people in the Either-Or classification.[39]

McCarthy's own nationally televised reply to Murrow two weeks later was singularly unpersuasive, to the relief of Serling and many other emerging liberals. Nothing the obviously ill-at-ease demagogue could say in his defense—fallacious proof of Murrow's putative ties with the Soviet Union—or that he could dredge up could help; if anything, he hurt himself. The Murrow program proved to be the beginning of the end of Joseph McCarthy (although not of McCarthyism). And it had happened on TV.

In the spring, McCarthy's self-destruction continued before an amazed viewing audience during the sensational Army-McCarthy hearings, with a little help from a lawyer from Boston by the name of Joseph Welch. "At long last, have you no sense of decency, sir?!" the long-suffering army counsel had finally cried out at the hearing's climax, after the sneering solon had gratuitously smeared Welch's aide. The sputtering legislator couldn't reply.

In May, the U.S. Supreme Court sounded the death knell for southern nativism when it declared segregation in public unconstitutional. Perhaps there was some courage left in the land.

Meanwhile, in 1954, TV drama was also growing bolder, as well as more frankly politically liberal in tone. That spring, writer Reginald Rose caused a sensation on *Studio One* with "Twelve Angry Men," a tempestuous and mildly subversive teleplay about a jury of ordinary Americans and how they battle their way to a verdict of innocent for a "socially deprived" defendant, after originally thinking him guilty. The startling production, starring Franchot Tone and Jack Klugman, was as close to *agitprop* as TV had ever seen, and instantly made Rose TV's next writer-star, after Chayefsky. Like many of the better teleplays produced on anthology shows of the mid-50s, "Twelve Angry Men" was bought by a Hollywood studio—in this case United Artists—as the movie industry increasingly sought to co-opt television.

Serling was likewise concerned with intolerance and prejudice as themes and would deal with these at length in his later live work, as well as in *The Twilight Zone.*

But in 1954, he was more concerned with making a definitive dramatic statement on television about war—meaning World War II as well as the recently ended Korean War—this time *without* pulling his punches, and he finally did so in "The Strike," a searing antiwar play he wrote that spring for Felix Jackson.

"The Strike," which was broadcast on *Studio One* in June 1954, was Serling's most mature teleplay to date, as well as his bravest, effectively transposing his World War II experience, in particular his experience and observations atop Mahonag in 1944, to a more recent situation and making the lessons to be learned thereby apply to *all* wars.

The conflict in "The Strike" is an internal one. Major Gaylord (played by James Daly) is in command of a decimated regiment somewhere in the cold Korean jungle, valiantly attempting to hold his men together, even though many are critically injured and food and medicine are in short supply. He has sent out a platoon of twenty men who have lost radio contact with Gaylord's besieged command post, and their lives continue to plague his conscience.

Eventually, the order comes to retreat. The regiment and its nearly five hundred remaining personnel can pull out as soon as Major Gaylord gives the command for a massive air strike: the Air Force is to drop bombs where the lost platoon is believed to be. All through the night, the frantic Gaylord weighs his conscience—can he give the order that will kill twenty of his own men? Are the lives of those twenty men worth the others, including his own, that might be saved? And, ultimately, what sort of war is it that forces a man into making such decisions?

"The Strike" is filled with tense moments as Gaylord and his men repeatedly wrestle with the unanswerable questions that combat has forced them to confront: "Cowardice, conscience, morality, stupidity." Gaylord is unsure of what it is that seems to prevent him from executing his duties as commanding officer. As one of Gaylord's men says, "War stinks on any level. Only when you give commands—it stinks worse."[40] The responsibility of rank, whether in military or civilian life, would be an issue that Serling would return to many times in his work.

With "The Strike," Serling had finally put it all together: a gripping, well-turned plot, taut dialogue, believable characters—especially the beleaguered and besieged Major Gaylord, who is forced to make the toughest decision of his life—as well as a definite point of view, which had previously been missing from Serling's work. Particularly noteworthy, too, was the way Serling carried over his training as a radio writer, using aural details—in this case, the repetitive sound of the regimental radio man trying to make contact with the lost platoon ("Razor Red, this is Razor Blue, come in Razor Red . . .")—as an effective bridge between scenes.

Felix Jackson was so impressed with "The Strike" that he asked Serling to come up with a similar play, if he could, about the business world.

Serling eagerly accepted the challenge and went to work on the play that unbeknownst to him would finally make *him* TV's next writer-star.

He called it "Patterns."

7

PATTERNS
(1955 – 56)

There's no damn reason in the world to be nervous, he thought, later in the morning, as he walked toward the United Broadcasting building. After all I've been through, why should I be nervous now? He wondered what Hopkins was like. What did a man have to be like to make so damn much money? It's never just luck that lets them make it, he thought, and it isn't just who they know—I won't let myself fall into the trap of thinking that. Hopkins has got something, something special, or he wouldn't be making two hundred thousand a year. What is it?

—from *The Man in the Gray Flannel Suit*, by Sloan Wilson[1]

Nineteen fifty-five, as they say, was a very good year for television—indeed, it was a fascinating year for TV. Nineteen fifty-five, to cite a few memorable video moments, was the year that the brilliant, troubled nuclear scientist J. Robert Oppenheimer was interviewed on *See It Now*; the year that saw Mary Martin whisked into the nation's collective living room as Peter Pan—in color (if your family had a color TV set); the year in which the *Johnny Carson Show* debuted, as well as *The Millionaire*, and many other absorbing and entertaining new shows.

Of course, everything about TV itself, only in its seventh year as a commercial medium, was still fascinating in 1955, including the commercials. "Everyone was interested in TV—the educated and the featherbrains alike," John Crosby, the influential radio and television critic of the *New York Herald-Tribune*, later recalled of that time. "It was new and we were very innocent."[2]

That innocence would not last much longer. Indeed, one of the programs that debuted that year, an intellectually oriented quiz show known as *The $64,000 Question*, ignited a programming trend that would ultimately lead to TV's greatest scandal.

Nor were things very good for those on the broadcast industry's blacklist. McCarthy was gone, effectively removed from the national scene after the Senate had at last found the courage to vote his censure in December. But the specter of McCarthyism continued to haunt Network Row, thanks to the appearance of an organization called Attack, Inc., which was happy to keep the blacklist up to date.

Nineteen fifty-five was an especially strong year for serious television drama. It was the year of Paddy Chayefsky's "A Catered Affair"; the year that Humphrey Bogart appeared on television for the first time, playing the role of Duke Mantee—the role that he had made famous on Broadway—in a powerful adaptation of *The Petrified Forest*; the year that saw a gripping adaptation of Herman Wouk's novel and play *The Caine Mutiny*; and other teledramatic riches. TV had become the Broadway of the air.

However, the most notable dramatic television event of the season was undeniably Rod Serling's *Kraft Television Theatre* production of "Patterns."

Or, as Jack Gould, the television critic of the *New York Times*, put it at the time in his rave review of Serling's classic teleplay on January 16, 1955:

> Nothing in months has excited the television industry as much as "Patterns," an original play by Rod Serling. The enthusiasm is justified. In writing, acting, and direction, "Patterns" will stand as one of the high points in the TV medium's evolution . . . for sheer power of narrative, forcefulness of characterization and brilliant climax. Mr. Serling's work is a creative triumph that can stand on its own.[3]

If Rod Serling and his wife, Carol, had anticipated the critical and popular sensation that "Patterns" would stir that memorable night in January, perhaps they would have stayed home in Westport. But Serling, while reasonably proud of his latest effort, the seventy-first TV script of his that had been produced on network TV, and his fourth contribution to the long-running *Kraft* anthology, had no notion of how big "Patterns" would be.

Exhausted from moving family and possessions from Cincinnati to Westport, Connecticut, the aftermath of their first holiday season in New York, *and* Serling's thirtieth birthday, the Serlings had chosen to spend a few quiet days relaxing and visiting with friends and relatives in upstate New York during the third week of January. The night of the telecast found Serling in Ithaca, New York, at the home of a cousin, Frank Hammer, when the simple black-and-white credits for *Kraft* unrolled and Ed Herlihy, the mellifluous voice of *Kraft Television Theatre*, announced, " 'PATTERNS' . . . BY ROD SERLING," and dissolved to the play's first shot.

Though generally pleased with the production, neither he nor Carol was conscious of the impact of his words that night; nor did they have any notion of the pandemonium that was just then going on back at home in Westport, as Jody's teenage babysitter scrambled to answer all the calls coming into the Serling household that fateful Wednesday evening.

As Serling would later recount of that epochal moment in 1957, "It [the phone] hasn't stopped ringing since."[4]

In "Patterns," Serling had taken Felix Jackson's desire for a "Strike" about the business world to heart, effectively grafting his own doubts about success, and his essential decency, onto the figure of a rising young organization man, newly arrived in New York—like Serling. Then Serling has his protagonist discover his ethical breaking point in the Darwinian wilds of the corporate world.

"Patterns" and "The Strike" are essentially the same play, each dealing with the moral and ethical responsibility of rank—and of one human being to another.

"Patterns" is the story of Fred Staples, a young, ambitious, and sensitive vice-president who eagerly arrives for work in the high-rise New York offices of Ramsey and Company, a large, Gotham-based paper concern, after being lured to company headquarters from Cincinnati by the megalomaniacal, efficiency-minded Ramsey, the president of the firm—and a composite of "M," Serling's former station manager at WLW, and Colonel Rock Haugen, Serling's former regimental commander. The somewhat naive Staples and his perky and ambitious wife, Fran (clearly inspired by Carol Serling), who accompanies him on his first day of work, think that Fred is starting a challenging new job; actually, Fred has walked into a white-collar boxing ring.

Although he doesn't come out and say so, Ramsey has in fact hired Staples to replace another vice-president and his second in command, Andy Sloane, another industrial relations expert and the conscience of the company, "a battered, dying, yet strangely resilient man in his late sixties." Staples begins to get the drift of the situation as he watches Ramsey flog Sloane for criticizing a plant-closing order. Meanwhile, Staples and Sloane, who share the same offices and secretary, become friends.

Staples adjusts well enough to his new environment, but he is bothered by Sloane's predicament and can't understand why Sloane doesn't stand up to Ramsey. Nevertheless, he doesn't protest too loudly when Ramsey informs him of the real reason why he has brought him to New York. He doesn't quit because, as he admits to his wife, he *wants* Sloane's job; she is a quietly pushy woman who wants him to have it, too. Still, Staples's conscience continues to bother him—particularly after Ramsey unfairly takes Sloane's name off a financial report on which both of them worked. Standing up for Sloane—and working on Staples's sense of guilt—is Sloane's adoring and long-suffering secretary, who has been assigned to the younger executive against her will.

Ramsey fiendishly decides to use the issue of the report as a way of making things even more uncomfortable for Sloane, and at the next rancorous board meeting he berates Sloane, after the latter's feeble attempt to protest Ramsey's actions. Ramsey's philippic causes Sloane to have a heart attack; he slumps to the floor before the shocked executives, fatally stricken.

In the play's climactic scene, an embittered Staples, having seen all he wants to see of the big business world, and having already made up his mind to quit Ramsey and Company, returns for one final vengeful confrontation with Ramsey, to take his stand with the Andy Sloanes of the world and to put the baleful chief executive in his place:

FRED: Andy Sloane and I. The same pattern. We shared the same insecurities, Mr. Ramsey. The same sense of searching, worrying, apprehensions . . . so understand that before you put me in his place. It wasn't Andy's weakness that bothered you, it was his strength. It was his ethics . . . so you used Andy as your whipping boy to try to make him quiet. You played through his strengths to get to his weakness. You made him backtrack and knuckle down and you beat him to death. Because he had to compromise to stay alive—and for him to compromise kept him from living. You wanted him out, but you wouldn't fire him.

RAMSEY (nods): I'm not a human being, what else?

FRED: You're a washout! You're a genius, a production, organizational marvel with no compassion for human weakness. . . .[5]

Nevertheless, in "an anti-cliché ending to end all anti-cliché endings," as critic Andrew Sarris later put it,[6] the company head refuses to apologize for his ruthless ways. He also manages to persuade Staples to stay on anyway for the sake of the business. Staples, seizing upon the opportunity to justify Sloane, and to succeed him as the company conscience, grimly accepts Ramsey's challenge, realizing that it is what he really wants. His wife seconds the notion, while cheerfully reminding him that "there's always Cincinnati." Yes, the battered man agrees, "There's always Cincinnati."

There were many reasons for Serling's breakthrough to national celebrity with "Patterns." One of them was Serling's uncanny timing. His subject hit an especially sensitive nerve: when some were beginning to have doubts about the character and ethics of the faceless, all-powerful "organizational marvels" (in Serling's phrase) who now made America tick, Serling's play asked the crucial questions on everyone's mind. What made *them* tick? And what were the men who worked for *them* like? Both *Executive Suite*, one of the most successful films of 1954, and *The Man in the Gray Flannel Suit*, one of that year's most acclaimed novels (which would also soon be made into a popular film), addressed these concerns. America was preoccupied with big business, warts, deformities and all. In 1955, *Time* made Harlow Curtice, the driven president of General Motors, its "Man of the Year." The Organization Man, as the species was called, was also a subject of intense interest in academe, where David Reisman's sociological tract by that name had become an influential book, as had its companion, C. Wright Mills's *White Collar*.

Thus, a hard-hitting play about big business was bound to stir up interest. Moreover, "Patterns" *was* daring for its time, and for television. The upper-echelon skirmishes of *Executive Suite* and *Gray Flannel Suit*, nasty as they got, were gentle in comparison to the literally life-and-death struggle that Serling had set behind the closed doors of the fictional Ramsey and Company.

Although Ramsey and Company actually had been inspired by the political power struggles of WLW, it could just as easily have stood for the paternalistic major networks, the ruthless Ramsey himself for either RCA chairman David Sarnoff or CBS's master manipulator William Paley.

Indeed, "Patterns," which Serling had written on order for Felix Jackson and *Studio One*, had been turned down by Paley's network—to both Serling's and Jackson's dismay. "Rod Serling cut to the core of it. . . . It was quality, the reality of business, and that didn't sit well with CBS at that time, and they turned it down. . . . And it went to *Kraft*," said Jackson.[7]

Yet future Serling critiques of television would be even less oblique. Nor would they end on such an affirmative ending as Staples's final, dogged decision to "fight me [Ramsey], take over if you can. And watch the business grow from your efforts . . . beyond your wildest dreams." Actually, that ending had been tacked on by Serling at the suggestion of *Kraft* story editor Arthur Singer—along with numerous other suggestions from both Singer and director Fielder Cook that Serling incorporated. (Cook would later claim to have written 40 percent of "Patterns.")

Originally, Serling had Staples quitting Ramsey's organizational crucible and New York and returning to Cincinnati. Serling doubtless liked the new ending better, not only because it was less predictable, but also because it in fact reflected his own personal optimism, in the winter of 1955, about the future of television and the prospect of putting his own creative stamp on it. Staples, as he would say, "*is* me."[8] Future Serling critiques of both the American economic system and American television would actually be far more "Marxist"—a label the *Wall Street Journal* tacked on to him the day after the telecast.

"Patterns," as Felix Jackson said, was a quality play. More important, it was a quality *television* play, making full use of the medium's unique limitations and potentials, particularly its potential for intimacy. Serling's frequent, written-in close-ups, which would soon become one of his televisual signatures—along with his crackling dialogue—brought the millions of *Kraft* living room viewers face to face with his sweaty, agonistic characters in a way that Hollywood could not. And, of course, "Patterns," unlike *Executive Suite, was* done live. Ed Begley's "live" on-screen heart attack was *quite* convincing.

To be sure, the superbly wrought production values of "Patterns" also contributed greatly to the program's impact. Serling had been very fortunate in the cast and crew that *Kraft* and J. Walter Thompson put together—and the fine ensemble work they delivered. Bringing Serling's script to vivid reality were the intelligent, convincing performances of young Richard Kiley, an actor who had already appeared in another Serling play, "Summer Memory," as Staples; veteran actor Everett Sloane, best known for his work with Orson Welles in *Citizen Kane* and *The Lady from Shanghai*; and Begley, whom many television viewers had already seen on Broadway in such plays as *All My Sons* and *Inherit the Wind*, in the demanding roles of Ramsey and Andy Sloane, respectively. Director Fielder Cook, in addition to assisting with the script, deftly kept the action moving at a pounding pace. Audiences liked the rapid scene transitions and montages of hectic business executives. "It was the first time in television that we were able to visually cut through to the drive and energy of the finer movies," Cook later said. Cook was so pleased with the result that when the play was over he turned on an intercom and shouted in a "hysterical voice" (according to Richard Kiley), "This is the greatest show I have ever seen in my life!!!"

Other professionals watching that night were also impressed. "It was like watching a very, very good movie," Jerome Hellman remembered. "It was so good in terms of content, and so good technically. You know how sometimes everything clicks? Well, my memory of it is that everything clicked on that show. And you sat there and said, 'Wow,' and were totally riveted. And that's a rare experience."[9]

It added up to a watershed event, both for television and particularly for Serling, who, as author of the play, after the manner of the theater, received the lion's share of the glory. Jack Gould's raise-the-rafters review in the *New York Times* four days afterward (Gould had not seen the play himself and had to watch it on kinescope) certified Serling's ascension to TV stardom. Gould topped himself by urging the show's producers to restage and retelevise

"Patterns" at the earliest possible opportunity: "A repeat performance at an early date should be mandatory," he wrote. NBC, eager to associate itself with what had become such a prestigious production, was all too happy to comply with the critic's unprecedented request. And one month later, on February 9, 1955, the entire original cast reassembled and proudly went through the paces again, the first time in TV history that any play or any author had been so honored.

And this time the chain-smoking, coffee-slurping author was indeed on the set, nervously watching "his little play"—which in the meantime had become quite a *big* play—go out to another 20 million viewers.

Suddenly—literally overnight—Serling had made it in Big Television, and made it big. Indeed, by the time the writer boarded the train from Westport for New York to attend the historic rebroadcast of his teleplay, he had already been inundated, by his own delirious estimate, with twenty-three offers of TV assignments, three movie offers, and fourteen requests for press interviews—and more invitations to lunch at 21 and drinks at Sardi's than he could count.

And "like a kid in a candy store," Serling eagerly—and in retrospect somewhat stupidly—grabbed them all.[10]

Serling's enthusiasm was understandable. After all, this was what he and Carol had left Cincinnati for: to make it big. Now—in one fell swoop—he had.

He accepted all offers, and immediately became overworked, overpressured, and overexposed.

Indeed, 1955, the year of "Patterns," would turn out to be one of considerable turmoil for Serling. Partly this was because of his own childish nature and downright inability to say no—a weakness that would continue to haunt him for the rest of his career; partly it was the result of his justifiable fear that he would burn out, and that he had better produce as much as he could while he was still able; partly it came from the inevitable pressure on him to repeat his success with "Patterns"; and partly it was the result of trends within the television and movie industries that were threatening New York television and its ability to generate hits like "Patterns"—as well as playwrights like Serling, Chayefsky, and Reginald Rose.

Actually, by January 1955, the days of New York television were already numbered. Pressure and interference in program content from both network headquarters and equally timorous commercial sponsors and their agency representatives were increasing. Three years before, the sponsors of dramatic anthology shows didn't much care about the story line; they were more interested in seeing that their commercials were broadcast without a glitch. "The sponsors never used to be much involved," said Jerome Hellman, "nor the advertising agencies: they were busy producing live commercials. I remember a time [in the early 50s] when you'd be doing a show in one studio, and they'd be producing their commercials in the next studio. And they were too busy watching the foam on the beer disintegrate or the grease in the pan evaporate to even bother to look in on what you were doing."[11] Now, with more money and viewers on the line, sponsors and ad agencies had suddenly become very involved in programming, and they didn't like what they were seeing on the anthology shows. The agonistic characters and down-beat themes of the "ashcan" school of TV writing, as Chayefsky, Rose, and Serling were derisively called—or television's "Angry Young Men" (a phrase imported from the British)—diluted, and indeed subverted, the commercial message the sponsors were send-ing to viewers. And the sponsors and ad agencies were more and more willing to come out and say so.

As television historian Erik Barnouw later noted:

> Most advertisers were selling magic. Their commercials posed the same problems that Chayefsky drama dealt with: people who feared failure in love and business. But in the commercials there was always a solution as clear-cut as the snap of a finger: the problem could be solved by a new pill, deodorant, tooth-paste, shampoo, shaving lotion, hair tonic, car, girdle, coffee, muffin recipe, or floor wax. The solution always had finality.
>
> Chayefsky and the other anthology writers took these same problems and made them complicated. They were forever sug-gesting that a problem might stem from childhood and be involved with feelings toward a mother or father. All this was often convincing—that was the trouble. It made the commer-cials seem fraudulent.[12]

Sometimes the changes the sponsors wanted were astonishingly frivolous: one cigarette company wanted Serling to excise the word "lucky" from his script, fearing it might aid a competing cigarette.

Another sponsor, in an incident which Serling would frequently cite as proof positive of Madison Avenue philistinism, would ask Serling not to have the Russian soldiers in "Dark Side of the Earth," his 1956 teleplay about the Hungarian Revolution, smoke *too* many cigarettes lest it give their product an evil connotation. Sponsor objections were often more substantive, dealing with theme and approach. Thus, as Barnouw wrote, "During 1954–55, anthology writers and directors feared sponsors and their agencies increasingly intent on interfering with script matters, dictating changes, writing plot details."[13] Then, in late 1954, Reginald Rose found himself engaged in a bitter behind-the-scenes battle over his teleplay about racial prejudice, "Thunder on Sycamore Street." The play, inspired by an actual incident that had recently taken place in Cicero, Illinois, was about a group of suburban neighbors who were so perturbed when a black family bought a home on their block that they banded together to stop the move, and eventually resorted to outright vigilantism to accomplish their end. In the final, blue-penciled version that went out over the air, the black intruders had been changed into a white ex-convict and *his* family.

"You cannot write about adultery, abortion, the social values of our times," Paddy Chayefsky complained in December 1954. "Or almost anything that relates to adult reality—that downbeat type of drama is almost as taboo as politically controversial stories." At least partly because of the Comstockian climate, Chayefsky decided that year to get out of television writing altogether. His "A Catered Affair," broadcast in February 1955 on *Philco/Goodyear*, was his last teleplay.

Writing for television had become too much of a grind, the dramatist declared in the foreword to his collected plays: "A successful hour dramatist may do four, five, or six shows a year with a thin hope—a very thin hope—of reselling one of his scripts to the movies. He has no guarantee that his next year will be as fruitful; in fact, most writers live in a restrained terror of being unable to think up their next idea. . . . Very few television writers can seriously hope to keep up a high-level output for more than five years."[14]

Chayefsky decided that he had had enough and returned to his true love—the theater. Twenty years later, he would wreak his revenge on the medium he helped spawn in *Network*, his vitriolic 1975 film satire of Network Row. "Prior to Paddy Chayefsky, most of us were considered to be two-headed hacks who wrote around the clock and used boy-girl situations in any one of five thousand different routine matters, but Paddy gave us stature," Serling said on *Mike Wallace Interviews* in 1959. "I respect his decision to leave."[15] And thus the man who had helped create New York television left in a huff. He was followed closely by Gore Vidal and several other writers.

Besides, Chayefsky and numerous of his writing peers had no interest in moving out west—which is where, it increasingly appeared, both the medium and the genre were headed. By early 1955, the movie industry, having decided it couldn't beat television, had decided to co-opt it. It had the space television needed in Hollywood, it had the stars, and it had the technical expertise to do what it thought was better—or at least cheaper—than could be done in New York. Live TV was too wasteful, movie industry executives pointed out to network executives. How can you show a rerun of a live television play? And increasingly, network executives began to listen; CBS had already tacitly made the commitment to moving drama out to the Coast by building Television City, a massive, in-house production facility just outside of Hollywood off of La Brea Avenue. Also, in a landmark move in 1954, ABC and Walt Disney Studios had formed a partnership to make one-hour filmed shows on the West Coast that would serve to promote Disney films and Disneyland (which would open in July 1955).

All this was very distressing to the proponents of New York television, especially the major New York–based television critics, who considered live television as almost a cultural resource.

And then Serling stepped into the ring with "Patterns," confounding Chayefsky's morose predictions, and became not only television's writer of the moment, but its reigning Angry Man.

It was a role Serling reveled in, as well as one that suited his self-dramatizing tendencies. But it was an onerous one during the first year of his "reign" as a video heavyweight, as he struggled to meet the New York critical establishment's expectations of him, as well as his own engorged expectations of himself.

Serling *was* capable of other quality hard-hitting plays, as he proved soon enough with "The Rack," his play about courage and prisoners-of-war, which was aired on *The United States Steel Hour* on April 12, 1955. The writer had been interested in treating this sensitive and controversial subject ever since the shocking news of

Top: Sam Serling, circa 1935. *Bottom left:* Ann Goodman, left, and Esther Serling in Binghamton, 1939. *Bottom right:* Rodman Serling, about five, atop his motor scooter, one of many gifts from his doting parents. *(Courtesy of Ann Goodman)*

A meeting of the Binghamton Central High School Debate Team at adviser Lloyd Hartman's house. *(Courtesy of Lloyd Hartman)*

Top left: Rod's brother, Robert, at Antioch College—which Rod would also attend— in the early 1940s. *(Collection of Antioch College) Right:* Sam and Esther Serling in Florida during World War II. Sam would die of a heart attack while driving to Syracuse on the last day of the war.

Top: The gung-ho para-trooper, at 5′4½″ the short-est member of the 511th Parachute Infantry Regi-ment, before shipping out to the Pacific. *Bottom:* Private Serling, fellow trooper Richard Loughrin, and another trooper in Leyte after the successful relief of the island, 1944. Serling suffered the first of two in-juries on the hellish island. The war would always be his main inspiration—and trauma. *(Courtesy of Richard Loughrin)*

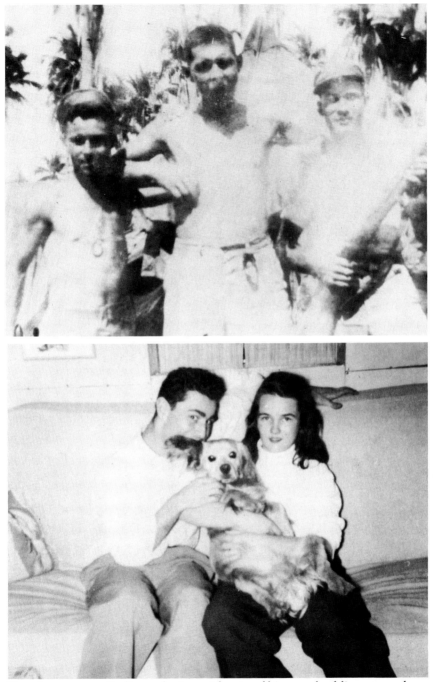

Top: A war-weary Serling, relaxing with two of his para-buddies, somewhere in the Pacific. *(Courtesy of Jerry Shea) Bottom:* Trailer life. Rod, Carol and spaniel in their cozy but primitive kerosene-heated trailer at Antioch College, circa 1949. *(Photo by by Barbara Agranoff)*

The life of the party. Serling, twenty-nine, at a party for a scriptwriting class he taught in Cincinnati, June 1953. The gorilla imitation was a Serling perennial. *(Courtesy of Bill Myers)*

The video playwright conferring with Robert Huber, director of *The Storm*, an original dramatic series broadcast over WKRC-TV, Cincinnati, December 1951. Serling used *The Storm* as an incubator for the scripts he would send to the networks in New York. *(Courtesy of* The Cincinnati Enquirer*)*

Rod Serling and Van Heflin, the star of the United Artists version of Serling's hit teleplay "Patterns", on the set in New York. *Bottom:* the *Daily News* liked the movie, but not too many others did. *(Photograph by Bill Myers)*

Serling after winning his third Emmy for "The Comedian," with CBS casting director Ethel Wynant (who would later help him cast *The Twilight Zone*) and the equally proud members of the secretarial pool at Television City, February 1958. *(Courtesy of Meredith B. Brucker) Bottom:* The writer-cum-host of *The Twilight Zone* hamming it up.

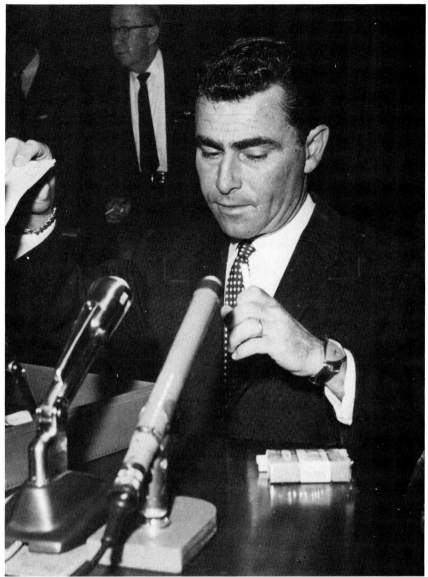

Serling preparing to testify before the Federal Communications Commission, January 1960, during the commission's hearings on radio and television programming. *(U.P.I.)*

Opposite page: Claude Akins and Jack Weston look skyward in the classic *Zone* episode, "Monsters Are Due on Maple Street," from the series' first season. *(U.P.I.)*

Joseph Schildkraut and Alma Platt in the third-season episode "The Trade-Ins." *The Twilight Zone* may have been the greatest actors' showcase in TV history. *(CBS)*

Serling and Mickey Rooney take a break on location for *Requiem for a Heavyweight,* New York, 1962. Although well received, the film was neither the critical nor the commercial knockout that Serling, who was beginning to tire of TV, had hoped for. *(CBS)*

The writer on the set of *Night Gallery* at Universal Studios. Initially excited about the series, Serling became disillusioned after he realized that he had no creative control over the show. *(Courtesy of* The Cincinnati Enquirer*)*

Rod Serling took on a lot of strange assignments in his sprawling career, but none was odder than the role he played in a 1971 episode of *Ironside* as Thyros, owner of a magic store. *(Courtesy of* The Cincinnati Enquirer*)*

Top: Serling's greatest joy during his twilight years was teaching. Here he is with some of his students at Ithaca College. *Bottom:* A deceptively healthy-looking Serling at his home in Interlaken, summer of 1974. One year later he would suffer the first in a series of heart attacks, leading to his death while tending his garden. *(Photograph by* Ithaca Journal/*Michael Parkhurst)*

American prisoners-of-war "breaking" while in the custody of the brutal North Korean regime had soiled the country. How did their captors get them to "confess" and "turn"? And were these men truly traitors? The subject was a natural for Serling. And now, at the urging of the New York–based Theatre Guild, which produced *Steel Hour*, he took it on. The Pentagon, uncomfortable with the subject matter, refused to give technical cooperation to the writer.

The result was a strong play, but not quite as strong as "Patterns." Perhaps trying too hard to be Freudian, Serling had decided that his protagonist's problem stemmed from childhood, to paraphrase Barnouw—in this case the imprisoned army captain and ex-POW's relationship with his militaristic father, a career army man.

"The Rack" centers around the court-martial of Captain Ed Hall, Jr., a dedicated and much-honored officer who is accused of treason: during his four years in a Korean prisoner-of-war camp, Hall could not help but collapse and cooperate with the enemy in order to survive. The feelings of his dominating but loving father are mixed—he is genuinely relieved to see his son, but loathes him for turning Communist. For his part, Hall is not optimistic about his chances for freedom: he *did* collaborate with the enemy and knows that next to nothing can justify such behavior.

The one person who believes in Hall is his counsel, Lieutenant Wasnik, who is convinced that Hall was justified in committing treason in order to save his life. The outcome of the court-martial remains unclear until the end, as both sides bring up their heaviest moral artillery. In spite of a passionate plea by Wasnik on his behalf, Hall is convicted—as an example to future prisoners of war. Leaving the courtroom, he confronts his father, who is finally able to set aside his political prejudice and to forgive his son.

From an artistic standpoint, "The Rack" continued along the same stylistic lines that Serling had developed in "The Strike" and "Patterns." At the forefront was the combative dialogue and inspired use of the court-martial setting: Serling's natural penchant for speeches seemed particularly suited to this arena. His ability to present two equally convincing yet opposing arguments in the play's final moments almost perfectly rendered the difficult moral ambiguity of the issues involved.

Also typical of Serling was his emerging compassion for all people, particularly those entrapped by "the system." As in the best of his writing, the true forces of evil were completely unseen (a device he would use to startling effect several times in *The Twilight Zone*). Rather than confronting a physical enemy, what these characters must battle is the regimentation and structure of the faceless organization that determines the course of their lives. This was where Serling was his most "angry"—in his frustrated attempt to understand how militarism and militaristic power structures—like big business, the sporting world, and network TV—are intolerant of change, weakness, and any notion of exceptions to the rule.

"The Rack" did have its flaws, which probably seemed much greater when held up next to "Patterns." The subplot with the father is initially presented as the most important issue for Hall—and presumably the basis for his "weakness"—but is ignored until the end, where its resolution seems contrived. Neither was the play explicitly political (no one questions that the Communist North Koreans are "the bad guys"), instead dealing with the moral and ethical questions of courage and cowardice.

Finally, even though Serling's talent for dialogue was evident, the philosophy behind the words still seemed a bit simplistic and uninformed. Moral arguments are often reduced to simple, clichéd metaphors that basically go unexplored (somewhat lessening any aesthetic impact they might have had). This may also account for the slightly padded feel of the work: certain scenes and characters seem redundant or unnecessary, and the trial itself occupies only the final third of the play.

In spite of these flaws, overall the teleplay is one of Serling's more original and sensitive scripts. Ultimately, Serling's script offered compassion for the victims of this "system" and of the war, even if it could not offer justification and understanding. This humanist stroke is the most effective and potent theme of the play.

"The Rack" sufficiently impressed Metro-Goldwyn-Mayer to persuade it to buy the story for a screenplay. But it failed to appease Serling's New York press; and the reviews were generally poor. It did, however, provide a major boost to the acting career of Paul Newman, who played the role of Captain Hall in the filmic version, and would remain a lifelong friend.

As a result of "The Rack's" failure, the pressure on Serling to repeat his first dramatic video knockout simply increased.

"Overnight successes are almost always something special," Serling later wrote, in explaining his post-"Patterns" agony. "They hit some kind of basic nerve of reaction . . . some fantastic universality.

. . . In my case, the first reviews of the shows after 'Patterns' were charitable. It was as if the critics were wary of throwing bricks at a successful author for fear their analysis might be incorrect. (After all, this is the guy who wrote 'Patterns.')"[16]

Matters weren't helped any by the writer's extreme sensitivity to negative or lukewarm reviews. "He was extremely sensitive to criticism," his brother, Robert, who would also become a writer, remembered, "unlike those writers who can laugh at critics all the way to the bank. I've seen him open his mail after one of his scripts was aired, sift through twenty-five rave reviews, and center dourly on one bad review which put him in a blue funk for several days."[17]

Or, as his thin-skinned brother recalled, "After a time, when the comparisons [with "Patterns"] were obviously negative, the needle was unsheathed. It got longer, it probed deeper, and I began to bleed."[18]

The "bleeding" began in March, when the critics took apart "Garrity's Son," a play he wrote for *Ford Theater*, and "The Champion," a boxing story aired on *Climax*. Then came the critical failure of "The Rack" in April.

By June, J. P. Shanley had taken to derogating Serling as "rapidly becoming the most prolific dramatist on television." "This time," Shanley said in his review of Serling's teleplay "To Wake at Midnight," "Mr. Serling was dealing with the subject of neo-Nazism and some of its consequences. His script, entitled 'To Wake at Midnight,' had brief moments of power and credibility. For the most part it was custom-tailored writing. The pieces of the plot were put together neatly, but the assembled product had no real style. . . ."[19]

One of the reasons why "To Wake at Midnight" may have seemed "assembled" is because Serling, in an effort to keep up with the increasing demand for his work, had ditched his typewriter (which he had always hated) for a tape recorder. With a recorder, he could, in effect, "write" as quickly as he thought, which was very quickly indeed. Dictating helped Serling capture the dialogue for his plays, which he enjoyed "acting out." Unfortunately, it often led him to overwrite, and his work lost much of its smoothness and continuity, at least at first.

Next came the positively nightmarish experience of the making of the movie version of "Patterns," when, in outspoken director

Fielder Cook's colorful phraseology, veteran producer Jed Harris "raped" the novice screenwriter.

"You couldn't destroy Rod," said the director. "Rod was made out of strengthened steel and tungsten. You couldn't destroy Rod."

But, like anyone, you could bully him, and you could wear him down. Now [co-producer Michael] Myerberg and Jed Harris bought this property and took it to United Artists and said "We will give you a cheap movie—$500,000—and will do it with the originals, Fielder and the whole thing, it'll be the new generation this that and the other," so they get $500,000.

I was very busy working, and I wanted to talk to Rod about the script because I had a lot of things I wanted to do with Ramsey—I wanted to open up, for Rod, the other side of Ramsey that Rod wouldn't have time to write in forty-eight minutes. The old mother that Ramsey went home to every night, things that I just couldn't wait for Rod to write. But Harris told Rod not to talk to me until the first revisions were done.

He [Harris] passionately felt the writer belonged to him. He would be the mediator between us. Rod was sent to Atlantic City—Jed loved taking writers to Atlantic City—and disappeared in a hotel suite for about two or three weeks. At any rate, out of it came a screenplay, which was delivered to me.

I opened up the screenplay, and it said in big black letters on the title page, "The Bitch Goddess, Success, by Jed Harris and Rod Serling." I read about 25 pages, and I put it down, and I wrote on the front of it, "I resign from the picture, this is cannibalism," sent it back to Michael Myerberg, and I went back to work.

Rod said he was overbooked with work. But no one, after going through what Jed Harris had put him through, would ever go near the script again, and I don't blame him. It's called writer rape.

I sat down with Jed Harris and Michael Myerberg, and I said "I haven't got a writer. Nobody can write this except Serling. Mr. Harris cannot write it because he is not a writer, and this is Rod Serling's screenplay."

The producers agreed to Cook's terms and flew Serling in for the rewrites. But Serling apparently still felt queasy about dealing with Harris again. Cook continued:

I think Rod was there for two or three days, but he couldn't stay. So I sat down with Jed Harris, and took the original "Patterns" script, and put this scene back and threw this other one out, and made Harris initial each page until I got to the end of the scenario. I cut out everything that Jed put in, I cut his dialogue, leaving a "Patterns" which wasn't a great deal different than the one on television. But on all of the other levels that Rod could have been so brilliant in he never achieved because Harris suffocated him.[20]

The reviews for the film were good. The *Daily News* gave it five stars. But United Artists did little to promote it and it quickly sank from sight. Serling had a somewhat happier experience with the film industry in the fall when he went to Hollywood on assignment from MGM. He "liked" Hollywood, he told a reporter from the *Cincinnati Times-Star*. "We had a swimming pool and a tennis court. Did a little work, too . . ."[21] He found Hollywood amusing. "I think he was amused by the idea of a writer of proletarian origins and left-of-center thinking dictating his dialogue to his secretary while they were both sitting in his swimming pool," said Serling's friend Don Freeman, TV critic of the *San Diego Tribune*. Serling enjoyed playing the part of the chic, terribly intense New York television writer.[22]

By late 1955, Serling, too, could see that the television industry was moving west, and he and Carol realized that if he wanted to stay in the industry, they would ultimately have to move once more.

In the meantime, Serling, who had been wooed by the larger talent agencies since "Patterns" had aired, also decided to change agents.

Serling made his feelings clear to a stunned Blanche Gaines in an unemotional personal letter: he simply needed a bigger agency that would know better how to handle the career of a major talent, which he had become. He needed someone with a little more *weight*. Serling felt that he could obtain those services from the elite Ashley-Steiner agency. "We never encouraged Rod to leave Blanche," said Jerome Hellman. "There was certainly no meeting with Rod where anybody 'gang-banged' him or individually 'banged' him or anything else. He was a guy who was very ambitious and determined to go all the way to the top, and felt at that point in time that he couldn't get what he needed from this person who had been so nurturing and supportive in the early years. Rod had reached a point where he was almost an industry. She [Gaines] didn't have the capacity to deal on that level. She wasn't into packaging, she wasn't a powerful negotiator, she didn't bring these other skills to the table. [But] I know Rod had to have tremendous feelings of guilt about that."[23]

Three years later, those feelings of guilt would show up in "The Velvet Alley," Serling's scathing autobiographical study of the rise and corruption of a television writer, in which Jack Klugman, playing a Blanche Gaines–type of agent, has a fatal heart attack shortly after his services are terminated by his suddenly successful, gone-to-Hollywood client.

And still, the critics had continued their tattoo: When would Serling write another "Patterns"?

By year's end, *Newsweek*'s television critic was still in Serling's camp, but only barely. "Although none of the new scripts was quite up to the high standard set by Serling's study of big business in 'Patterns,' " he noted in his tepid year-end review, referring to the dozens of scripts Serling had dashed out, "they showed that after six years at his trade, the man is not only willing to tackle any dramatic subject or mood but is likely to handle it skillfully."[24]

At that point, the beleaguered writer had few remaining literary pretensions. "I don't have the imagination most writers have," Serling said to the *Newsweek* reviewer. "At his best," the article continued, "he feels he has given something approaching universality to his subject, as in 'Patterns' with its scrutiny of 'old age afraid of competition from youth.' "[25]

"My future is unquestionably in TV," Serling concluded. "I like movies as a change of pace, but TV is much more intimate. You're looking at people close up, physically and psychologically, and there aren't as many taboos."[26]

Of course, there *were* quite a number of taboos in television, and the number was growing larger, as Serling would discover.

Outwardly, Serling seemed like a happy man to his neighbors in Westport, particularly the neighborhood children. "I would say he was happy, and I was surprised when he moved," said George Githers, one of the neighborhood children. "He seemed open and happy and no signs of any kind of unrest."[27]

"The Serlings [seemed to have] a good relationship, and they seemed very happy. He struck me as a gentle man.

"He was always very nice to me. We used to play on the mountain outside his house, and I got to be friendly with him. He didn't strike me as 'angry' at all. . . . He had a natural affection for all of the kids in the neighborhood, and maybe because I was the only Jewish kid in the neighborhood, particularly me."[28]

If Serling had reason to be angry, Githers believes, it may have been because of Serling's Jewishness. Apparently, Jews were still something of a novelty in the upper-class, mostly Gentile community. "Westport didn't have many Jews at that time, and there was some hostility from some of the older Westport people. There was so much pressure to conform, and there was a lot of tension for everyone to look the same. I think that had an effect on him in terms of his writing."[29] To be sure, many of the settings of Serling's more memorable *Twilight Zone* tracts on prejudice are played out in upper-middle-class suburban towns that are reminiscent of Westport. Additionally, after nearly ten years of marriage, domestic strains had begun to show. Nevertheless, the Serlings were still a cohesive family unit.

Serling was of course thrilled in early 1956, when it was announced that he had been nominated for the Emmy Award for Best Television Writing for his script of "Patterns." However, he was angered by the treatment he received three months later, when he and Carol traveled to New York to attend the ceremonies: when Serling's name was read as the winner and the exalted author stepped up to the stage to receive his statuette, he discovered that there was no one there to greet him.

"After the applause had died down," Serling told reporter Gene Shalit years later, "I remained there on the stage with a hollow feeling in the pit of my stomach, realizing, as did everyone else, that there was no one on stage to give me the award. Somewhere along the line, plans had gotten fouled up, and Ed Sullivan, who was to hand me the Emmy, had been called off the stage by a photographer. So there I stood, lonelier than I ever shall be the rest of my life, wondering what the hell I should do next. There was a ripple of laughter from the audience—embarrassed laughter. And finally, a gentleman from the firm of Price-Waterhouse, which handled the vote tabulation, in a perfect spasm of compassion, grabbed an Emmy off the shelf and shoved it into my stomach, like a quarterback handing off a football."[30] Another less sensitive writer might have shrugged off such an incident, but Serling felt deeply slighted.

Serling had two bruising encounters with the censors early the following year that made him realize just how small the window for creating compelling and socially relevant television drama was becoming, when two of his teleplays, "The Arena," a drama about senatorial infighting, and "Noon on Doomsday," an attack on racial intolerance, were mangled by various intermediaries before they reached the air.

" 'The Arena' took place in 1956, and no juggling of events can alter this fact," Serling recalled sarcastically a couple of years later.

> So, on the floor of the United States Senate (at least on Studio One), I was not permitted to have my Senators discuss any current or pressing problem. To talk of tariff was to align oneself with the Republicans; to talk of labor was to suggest control by the Democrats. To say a single thing germane to the current political scene was absolutely prohibited. Several million viewers got a definitive picture of television's concept of politics and the way government is run. They were treated to an incredible display on the floor of the United States Senate of groups of Senators shouting, gesticulating, talking in hieroglyphics about make-believe issues, using invented terminology, in a kind of prolonged, unbelievable double-talk. There were long and impassioned defenses of the principles involved in Bill H.R. 107803906, but the salient features of the bill were conveniently shoved into a corner of a side-of-the-mouth sotto voce, so that at no time could an audience have any idea what they were about.[31]

Previously, Serling, in keeping with the conformist sentiments he had expressed in *Writers' Digest*, might have been disposed to accommodate such censorious demands as the price of working in a mass medium. Now, as TV's leading angry man, he felt more inclined, or even *obliged*, to publicly fight such officiousness.

Serling was even more shocked and angered by what happened that year to "Noon on Doomsday," which was inspired by a murder case then in the news—the Emmett Till case, in which a young black boy had allegedly been kidnapped and killed by two white men who went to trial and were exonerated on all counts.

Later he described to interviewer Mike Wallace what happened to his script: "In 'Noon on Doomsday,' which was based on the Till case, I wrote the script using black- and white-skinned characters initially, then the black was changed to suggest 'an unnamed foreigner,' the locale was moved from the South to New England —I'm convinced they would have gone to Alaska or the North Pole and used Eskimos except that the costume problem was of sufficient severity not to attempt it. But it became a lukewarm, emasculated, vitiated kind of a show. I went down fighting [the sponsor, U.S. Steel], thinking in a strange, oblique, philosophical way 'Better say something than nothing.' "[32]

Nor was Serling pleased by the critical reaction to "Noon on Doomsday," which failed to satisfy even the critics back in Cincinnati. " 'Noon on Doomsday' is high caliber," Henry Furst, the critic of the *Cincinnati Times-Star* opined, "but probably will not win the lavish praise heaped on 'Patterns.' "[33]

No matter what he did, it seemed, he still was in the shadow of "Patterns."

8
THE BIG GREEN
(1957)

Rod's plays are often drawn from the day's headlines. He was disturbed when he read the sad reports of Joe Louis wrestling. He's writing a play about it, "Requiem for a Welterweight." . . .
—Earl Wilson, *New York Daily News*, April 6, 1956[1]

A significant night in the inner—and increasingly public— drama of Rod Serling's life and career had arrived. It was 6:59 P.M., Pacific standard time, on the evening of October 11, 1956, and in Studio 6B of CBS Television City in Los Angeles, the large Bulova clock was winding down.

Russell Stoneham, assistant to *Playhouse 90* producer Martin Manulis, began the countdown as the second hand approached twelve.

"Ten, nine, eight . . ."

Three thousand miles away at the home of friends in Connecticut, Rod Serling, the author of that evening's *Playhouse 90* presentation, "Requiem for a Heavyweight," was pacing and chain-smoking.

Serling was usually this way when one of his plays was about to go out over the air, but tonight he was especially nervous.

This was it, he figured. Either he knocked them out—"them" meaning the television critics who had been on his back for a year and a half to deliver another "Patterns," as well as the millions of *Playhouse 90* viewers who were hoping to see the Serling punch that night—or *he* would be knocked out of the video ring.

Adding to Serling's nervousness—as well as the cast and crew's —were his doubts about the acting ability of Ed Wynn, the aging

118

comedian and vaudeville star, who was slated to play the crucial role of the trainer, Army, who fights to keep as much as possible of his beaten charge's pride in Serling's ring melodrama. He had done poorly in rehearsals—poorly enough for Serling to threaten to withdraw his name from the credits if Wynn stayed. But Wynn had stayed, at the insistence of producer Martin Manulis, whose idea it was to cast Wynn in his first dramatic role.

Back in the studio, a hush had fallen on the complicated expressionist set that had been built for the production of Serling's pugilist drama.

In the wings, Jack Palance, playing Serling's tragic hero, the washed-up boxer Mountain McClintock, was waiting to make his agonized entrance. The rest of the cast—Wynn's son Keenan, playing Maish, Mountain's unscrupulous manager, and Kim Hunter, the social worker who attempts to rescue the battered boxer from his sordid world—studied their lines. They, too, were nervous. So were Manulis and director Ralph Nelson. "Requiem" was the second show of the season for Manulis's newfangled ninety-minute program (Serling's adaptation of Pat Frank's "Forbidden Area" had been the first, broadcast a week earlier). CBS president Frank Stanton, who had originally conceived the idea for the show, was also fidgeting back at network headquarters.

Back in Westport at the home of his friends, the Bergs, Serling could almost hear Stoneham continue the countdown in his merciless voice.

"Seven, six, five . . ."

Serling drank a lot of coffee over the next ninety minutes. He also went through approximately two packs of Salem cigarettes.

As with most of Serling's plays, the idea for doing "Requiem" had come from the news, particularly from the sad reports that ex-heavyweight boxer Joe Louis had started wrestling for a living. Of course, aging boxers had engaged Serling's sympathies ever since he hung out with Joe Matesi in the army; a washed-up fighter had been among his favorite characters since Antioch, when Serling had made such a fighter the centerpiece of his first published short story. That is why the news about Louis had struck a special chord with him.

But Serling didn't want to write just another play about a washed-up boxer—he had already done that. He wanted to write a play using the Louis character shaded with some of the characteristics of other heavyweights he had known or seen, like Ezzard Charles and Matesi, and translate them and the sport of boxing into something larger and more metaphorical.

"Four, three . . ."

Critics later debated whether Serling wanted to create an indictment of the sport of boxing or an indictment of the American system. Probably he wanted to do both.

Most of all, he wanted to get the critics off his back. He wanted to prove to himself and to the world that he was indeed a heavyweight. "Requiem for a Welterweight" wouldn't have made it—it didn't sound right. So his next literary knockout punch became "Requiem for a Heavyweight."

"Two, one . . . Cue Music. Cue Announcer!"

"LIVE, from Television City in Los Angeles, Playhouse Ninety presents . . .

"REQUIEM FOR A HEAVYWEIGHT.

"BY ROD SERLING . . ."

To reprise the plot: Mountain McClintock (Palance), after fourteen frustrating years in the boxing ring, is told by the boxing commission that he must give up fighting—another serious blow could leave him blind. He puts his faith in his longtime manager, Maish (Keenan Wynn), who, unbeknownst to either Mountain or trainer Army (Ed Wynn), has lost money by betting against Mountain. Eager to pay off his debts, Maish makes plans to have Mountain begin a career in professional wrestling.

In the meantime, Mountain turns to an unemployment agency, where his unique situation—the only work he has ever known is fighting—moves a sympathetic social worker, Grace Carrie (Hunter). Grace tries to convince Mountain that perhaps he would be better suited to teaching boxing at children's camps. Enamored of the first female he has had any sort of relationship with, he tentatively agrees.

Maish has arranged an audition with a wrestling promoter, however, and Mountain is torn between his loyalty to his manager and his own convictions about the phoniness of wrestling. He is proud of the fact that he has never taken a dive and doesn't want to lose that small claim to dignity. Desperate, Maish blames Mountain for his financial woes and says that the fighter owes him. Seeing Maish's true colors, Mountain abandons his wrestling engagement and, upon Grace's advice, returns to his hometown in Tennessee, knowing that at the very least, he has not sold out either his principles or his talent.

Serling had given "Requiem" everything he had and almost everything one could want from a television play: a simple but intricately built plot, with two effective lines of conflict (the conflict within McClintock as he agonizes over his future and his principles, and the conflict between Maish and his seedy creditors). In short, it was a great story. It had compelling, three-dimensional characters. It had crackling dialogue. It had a lot of dramatic close-ups.

The reigning TV critics also thought it worked. Jack Gould of the *New York Times* wrote: "It was an artistic triumph. . . . Mr. Serling wrote a searing, inspired indictment of the worst side of the prizefight game. . . . It had immense power and poetry, and is certain to win many a prize."[2]

Ben Gross of the *New York Daily News* was also impressed: "A bitter, mordant, and yet moving play, relentless in its exposure of the utter heartlessness of the commercialized fight game. . . . Pulling no punches, this drama of hard-boiled realism stripped prizefighting of its championship glamour."[3]

Finally, there was John Crosby of the *New York Herald-Tribune*, who enthused: "['Requiem'] had the distinction of packing an awful wallop and setting a pace for casting, direction, settings, and production that I can only hope will be a regular thing." Crosby especially singled out Palance's performance as Mountain: ". . . underneath the faltering speech lies an essential decency and humanity that commands your respect and affection. Both author and actor collaborated here to create a genuinely moving and real person."[4]

To Serling "It was the accolade of a lifetime." "Requiem" gave Serling the validation and revalidation he needed. Serling's friend Del Reisman, later script supervisor on *The Twilight Zone*, recalled Serling's excitement and pride. "I remember I had a conversation with Rod after 'Requiem,' and he said he was so pleased because he had taken some shots after 'Patterns,' and no one could take shots with 'Requiem' because he had done it all, he was at every rehearsal, and it was his baby. He was really pleased, and he really made a point of saying 'I wrote this.' "[5]

"Requiem" was the talk of the town that night, John Crosby later recalled. "I remember walking into '21,' a fairly sophisticated beanery, one day in the 1950s and finding the whole restaurant buzzing with talk about 'Requiem for a Heavyweight.' . . . It set the whole town talking much in the same way Al Jolson used to when he'd walk out on stage of the Winter Garden and knock 'em dead in the 1920s."[6] Serling had knocked 'em dead. And for a brief moment, his demons were stilled.

Four months after that memorable evening, at the beginning of 1957, Rod Serling was comfortably ensconced in a rented nine-bedroom house complete with swimming pool in Beverly Hills, still basking in the acclaim for "Requiem" and the California sunshine, and awash with offers to write for both television and movies. He was indeed a happy man—or as happy as anyone as intrinsically insecure as Serling could be. And who wouldn't be? He was rich, he was famous, and he was Hollywood's hottest writer.

Although the movies paid more, and to many writers, had more status—and although he made noises about writing a stage play, and in fact had made several abortive efforts to do so—Rod Serling's heart continued to belong to television. Specifically, it belonged to *Playhouse 90*, where he had become one of the chief writers-in-residence along with such other imported New York writers as Tad Mosel and Reginald Rose.

Television City, the last outpost of live television, was an exciting place in the late 1950s, with three different plays simultaneously in production and disparate casts and crews dashing about the $12 million facility. As Martin Manulis, who was the show's producer for its first two years, recalled: "One show was having a reading and starting its rehearsals from its first reading, one was already rehearsing on the floor, and one was in front of the cameras for three-day rehearsal prior to air."[7]

"Well, it was a very glamorous place," remembered Dominick Dunne, who had moved from New York to California with Manulis to help him put on the ninety-minute spectacular. "There was still a feeling in Hollywood that TV was the downside to the movie industry. But those of us who were nurtured in live TV and then went out there didn't have that feeling at all."[8]

As for the show itself, Dunne recalled, "We had some stinkers. But when it was good, it was great. And more often than not, they were good rather than bad. People weren't into formula, like they are now. Guys were writing the best play that they could write for the hour and a half they were writing for."[9]

Like many of Serling's colleagues, Dunne was annoyed by the writer's attention-getting mannerisms around the *Playhouse 90* set. "He used to slurp his coffee," according to Dunne. "He would be watching a run-through of a live TV show, and he would be a foot away from the actors, and he would be drinking coffee out of a cup, and he would make a loud slurping sound—it used to be very unnerving. It used to drive me crazy. I used to think, 'What must the actors think when he sucks in the coffee like that?' I always thought it was a slight affectation. It was as if he was calling attention to himself and his importance.

"At the same time, he was a talented man. No one ever denied that!"

And Serling? "He was a star himself," said Dunne. "The secretaries were *all* mad about him."[10]

One of those young secretaries, Virginia Cox, agreed. "He was a really nice guy, not at all superior," said Cox, who later became professor of English at the University of Wisconsin. "Always very nice to the people in the office. Like secretaries, we really gossiped and tore everybody apart. But everybody was fond of Rod."[11] Serling returned this affection by often making the secretaries in his works his most sympathetic female figures.

That fondness grew after *Playhouse 90*'s broadcast of "The Comedian," directed by John Frankenheimer, on February 14, 1957. The elaborate production proved once again that Serling still had the magic touch when it came to adaptation, too, this play being based on a 1952 story by Ernest Lehman (who had written *Executive Suite*).

Sammy Hogarth (Mickey Rooney) is the egomaniacal comedian, about to put on his first ninety-minute television special. Hogarth masks his fear and insecurity by yelling at his head writer, Al Preston (Edmond O'Brien), and his Milquetoast brother, Lester (Mel Tormé), who is the butt of Sammy's on- and off-camera jokes. Lester wants Sammy to drop his trademark Lester-bashing monologue, and he begs Al for help. At first, Al refuses, reminding Lester that Sammy employs both of them and feeds them well: "When you've been living on caviar, you build up an immunity to Mulligan's stew."

Meanwhile, Lester's wife, Julie (Kim Hunter), exasperated with her husband's weakness, walks out on him, after telling him that Sammy has repeatedly propositioned her—even at their own wedding.

Lester eventually resorts to blackmailing Al (who has "stolen" some material from a late partner for Sammy's special). Al tells Sammy that he needs to drop the offending monologue, but Sammy brazenly refuses to abandon his act. Al then finds Julie at Sammy's house, drunk, waiting to see if she can "convince" her brother-in-law, through sex, to drop the monologue.

The day of the show arrives, and Al finally admits to Sammy that he stole the material. Sammy fires Al and arranges for the dead writer to get credit. Al explodes, telling Sammy that the comedian will always be hungry for attention, "addicted to laughs, adulation, and the love of forty million people"—but that he will never be truly loved by anyone. Sammy is wounded, but won't admit it.

During the telecast, Lester, desperate for revenge and anxious to prove himself to his wife, walks out on stage during the monologue, but Sammy's brilliant improvisation saves the show. Afterward, Al gladly leaves the world of Sammy, and Lester is reunited with Julie. But their joy is short-lived: the cold-blooded comedian, seeing the two embrace, begins ordering Lester around again. To Julie's chagrin, Lester acquiesces to his still-powerful—and more successful—older brother.

At the heart of the bravura production was Rooney's standout performance—his first on television. Getting that performance required all of John Frankenheimer's considerable directing skills, as Kim Hunter recalled. "Rooney was used to film and used to more or less doing what he bloody well wanted to [on camera]. Rooney's attitude was 'Who is this young whippersnapper director?' Johnny finally won Mickey over, and got Mickey to trust him. He had to make Mickey understand that in live, you can only do it once. Johnny finally got to him and got him to understand that he had to make choices, because the camera has to know where you're gonna be, what you're gonna know. 'I have to know,' Johnny said. Johnny could get that trust from Mickey. It was marvelous to watch. He was an actor's director, and there aren't too many in television and films."[12]

In adapting "The Comedian" for television, Serling retained the basic plot and characters of Lehman's story—only a few minor traits are changed. In the story, Sammy is physically imposing, a feat that would have been impossible to convey with Mickey Rooney (in spite of his stature, however, Rooney is no less frightening as Sammy Hogarth).

The story is told solely from the point of view of Al Preston, and the characters of Lester and Julie are not as fleshed out as they are in Serling's script. Utilizing the visual medium's ability to use multiple points of view, Serling's characters, through monologue and dialogue, seem much more psychologically "real" to the viewer than they do to the reader, who must filter each of these characters through Al's eyes. Obviously, Serling's gift with realistic dialogue was an advantage in adaptations: where the written word can rely on interior monologues or narration, video and film must use both the spoken word and the picture to convey crucial story or character information.

For the most part, these changes are the standard ones that must be made when adapting from a written to a visual medium, and by the time of "The Comedian," Serling had obviously learned the basic rules of adaptation. However, there is one major break with Lehman's story: in the final scene of Serling's teleplay, Lester walks on stage with Sammy, who clowns for a minute then quickly cuts to a commercial, sensing danger. In the story, on the other hand, Lester begins to feebly slap Sammy in the face. At first, Sammy can clown, but as the puny Lester gets more and more physical, Sammy loses control and ends up beating his brother senseless in front of the entire country, ruining his career. Lehman allows Sammy's own maniacal personality to betray and ultimately destroy himself. Serling's Sammy, however, continues to be the bad guy to his brother and those unable to escape his wrath, and never realizes the terrorizing effect he has on people (aside from a chastising monologue from Al, which seems to be Serling's replacement for Lehman's final scene).

In the end, Serling's ending is more realistic—there is no happy ending in the form of Sammy's comeuppance. Serling's ending also seems more in keeping with Serling's continuing preoccupation with moral ambiguities. The triumph in Serling's work is that one man —Al—is finally able to stand up to Sammy and escape his dominance; the agony is that Sammy, the consummate professional (and another representative of the increasingly greedy world of network television), will retain his power over those who know him for what he is and continue to be loved by those who believe him to be merely a comic.

Three weeks later, abeaming, Serling bounded up to the podium of the 1957 Emmy Awards to accept the Best Television Writing award for "Requiem." All told, the production won five awards that night, including Program of the Year and personal awards for Manulis, Palance, and director Ralph Nelson.

And this time, the Board of Governors of the Academy of Television Arts and Sciences ensured that there was someone there to give the writer his trophy.

Next, Serling plowed into a lucrative assignment from MGM to write a Western, *Saddle the Wind*, for Robert Taylor and John Cassavetes. The film, an adaptation of a story by Thomas Thompson, cast Taylor and Cassavetes as two brothers with different temperaments and different ideas about how to protect their land and their honor; with Taylor as the wiser older brother who would rather talk things out and Cassavetes as the hotheaded (and apparently demented) youngster who would rather shoot first.

Casting Cassavetes, the young Method actor, against the taciturn Taylor was Serling's unorthodox idea. According to the director, Robert Parrish, "I remember once he said, 'Jesus, we got this square star'—Taylor was square as a post, see?—'Let's get this guy I know called Cassavetes. To have him and Robert Taylor in the same picture will either be a total disaster, or it will have something interesting in it.' "[13]

The result could be described as an interesting disaster.

"Taylor wasn't difficult," Parrish remembered. "He was just boring. And the more wooden he got, the more 'Actors Studio' Cassavetes would get, just to annoy him. Cassavetes was always respectful, but you knew he was putting on Taylor all the time."[14]

Rounding out this odd movie crew was the rich and totally inexperienced producer Armand Deutsch. Serling's sense of humor was especially welcome in preproduction conferences with the naive and slightly pompous department store heir. "Deutsch was probably the wealthiest guy in Hollywood at the time," Parrish recalled. "He wanted to be another Dore Schary, but he lacked any experience in movie making. Deutsch felt that if he got on his feet, and walked from one end of the room to the other, that this would energize both us and the picture. Anyway, one day, Deutsch was walking from one end of the room to the other, talking all the time, and Rod just kind of walked behind him—right behind him. He made about three trips across the room before Deutsch even realized it. Deutsch was so confused, he said, 'Where's Rod?' And Rod, surprising him, said, 'I'm here, Ardie, I just wanted to hear every word you say.' " Later, Parrish would be one of Serling's first choices for directing the pilot episode of *The Twilight Zone*, and he ended up directing two episodes in the show's first season.[15]

"I gave better dialogue to the horses than the actors," the novice screenwriter later said of *Saddle the Wind*, which he also called "Stop the Fart."[16]

Nevertheless, MGM thought highly enough of his work on the film to sign Serling to a $250,000, four-picture contract.

The Serling phenomenon had spread to the publishing industry as well. That spring, Simon and Schuster also brought out Serling's first book, *Patterns*, an anthology of television plays. Richard Grossman, who was Serling's editor on the book, vividly recalled Serling's pugnacity. "He had the air of people I had known in boxing. There's this special kind of alertness that boxers have, because of a need to anticipate where people are coming from, that carried over into his social life. His eyes moved like a boxer's, for one thing. He bore right into you, which is why I think he became such an effective TV personality. When he stared into that camera, he was really looking at you. And, of course, there's something about little boxers. . . . They're associated with fast-moving, feisty little things, and he certainly was that. He was a feisty little guy."[17]

He was profiled in glossy magazines, like *Vogue*. "Rod Serling, a revved-up, good-looking playwright of thirty-two, straddles both coasts of the country, whiffing out tight scripts for both TV and the movies," enthused the April 1957 issue:

> His now-famous TV drama for *Playhouse 90*, "Requiem for a Heavyweight," won the Sylvania Award and may be a Broadway play. Ever since "Patterns" and "The Rack," Serling has been happily in the chips which amount now to $130,000 a year. In Westport, Connecticut, where he lives most of the year with his wife and two small children, he builds model airplanes, goes water skiing in the [Long Island] Sound, and talks his terse plays into a Dictaphone. Paraphrasing slightly the words of Ben Hecht in his book *A Child of the Century*, "Every writer is a frustrated actor who rehearses his lines in the auditorium of his skull."[18]

The "revved-up, good-looking" author was illustrated by a photograph of himself aswirl in cigarette smoke, *à la* Edward R. Murrow.

Unfortunately, Serling's vanity was beginning to get the better of him, according to his neighbors from Victoria Avenue in Cincinnati, the Marmers, when they came to visit the Serlings during one of Rod's increasingly rare hiatuses between movie and television writing assignments.

"They came into New York and picked us up to see *The Diary of Anne Frank* on Broadway," Phyllis Marmer recalled. "Of course, Rod had gotten third-row center seats. Anyway, we were walking along the street to go to a restaurant before we caught the train home to Westport, and Rod said he would like to be recognized. That everybody knew him by 'Rod Serling,' but they didn't know what he looked like."[19]

"He wanted adulation," continued her husband, Saul. "He wanted people to say 'Hey, there's Rod Serling' like 'Hey, there's Clark Gable.' "[20]

"He wanted the recognition. Carol hated it, but Lord, he wanted it."[21]

For most writers, the disassociation between name and face is one of the boons of their profession, without which they cannot observe real life. Not for Rod Serling. Eventually, as narrator and host of *The Twilight Zone*, he would get his wish and more: he would become an American icon.

In 1957, however, he was already sufficiently famous to cause a stir at Chasen's, as the Marmers discovered the next time they visited the Serlings, in California, later that year.

> We wanted to go to an intimate place for dinner, just to be with them. But what he did that evening was put on a performance the whole time we were there. We walked into Chasen's, and instead of getting an intimate table in a corner, he made sure he was seated in a place that was recognizable. He talked to the *maître d'* and said "Can we sit in this particular area?"
>
> As we walked in, we had to go past a lot of people, and they all said "Hello," or "Hi, Rod," "Nice to see you Rod." He was just two feet off the ground.

So we finally sat down, finally ordered. And then we would start to talk, and he'd say "Oh, just a minute" and he'd go over and talk to somebody. Then he'd come back and sit down and we'd start to talk again. . . . It was always "Who's recognizing me?" Claire Trevor came over to the table. The fact that we were eating didn't matter a bit. "Rod, darling, could you get my son into this next play you're writing?" she asked. Now if that had happened here, in Cincinnati, he would have laughed at it, I mean he would have realized how phony it was.[22]

Could Serling have both respect and recognition from his peers *and* the approbation of the movie industry? Perhaps he could—in Hollywood. By the summer of 1957, Serling had made up his mind. He was going west. He and Carol began shopping around Los Angeles for a house, albeit not without reservations.

Eventually, they decided on the Virginia Bruce mansion, located in the hills of Pacific Palisades only minutes from the sands of Malibu Beach. The house had everything a once-hungry writer could possibly want: nine bedrooms, a tennis court, Japanese gardens, and, of course, a swimming pool. The Serlings moved there with their two daughters and support staff in December of 1957.

Serling felt guilty about leaving New York for Los Angeles—the land of mink swimming pools, as he used to kiddingly call it around that time. But that was where the business was. The golden age of television was essentially over. Video had left New York—and most of the other "angry" young writers who had participated in the brief, exhilarating video moment had left for less restrictive, if not necessarily more lucrative, pastures. Hollywood had won the battle for television's body, just as it once had radio's, if not its soul. And New York had lost something very special.

"It wasn't until the middle fifties when Hollywood suddenly realized not only was television not going to go away," said Tad Mosel, "but that it was going to get bigger and keep growing, and already it had changed the living habits of the entire world. So then they [Hollywood] kind of moved in with the money, and when they moved in with money, all television changed."[23]

Said Paul Bogart: "What happened was the movie business said, 'We've got to get this back.' And it did."[24]

And alone among his peers, Rod Serling decided to follow his star, along with the industry, to its new capital.

"Television's last angry man," *New York World Telegram* critic Harriet Van Horne dubbed him.[25] That certainly sounded impressive (even if it wasn't exactly true: there were other writers with consciences, like Ernest Kinoy and Reginald Rose, who continued to write for the medium, but did not require of themselves to play the role of public controversialist to the extent that Serling did). Serling would be the one to show what the medium was capable of doing, no matter how painful it was. As usual, television's Last Angry Man saved his greatest wrath for network censors and sponsors. By 1957, he had acquired a reputation as one of the strongest critics of sponsor interference.

The TV industry responded in kind. In a 1957 *Television Age* article, "Billion Dollar Whipping Boy," "Rod Serling," the magazine opined, "considered by some as the top scripting talent uncovered and nurtured by television, lamented that commercial TV programs won't buy a script which has 'the faintest aura of controversy' about it, and insisted that the writer is constantly 'hamstrung' by 'taboos and imposed dogmas' that emanate from the sponsor." After noting Serling's complaints about the treatment of "Noon on Doomsday," the magazine declared: "Trade observers, balancing Mr. Serling's complaint against the proposed reason for sponsor 'pressure' in this instance, cannot help wondering whether he would have felt the same about such 'unreasonable' pressure if, in addition to the script's author, he was also one of U.S. Steel's stockholders."[26]

It wasn't just vanity or self-interest that motivated Serling to stick with the medium when many of his cohorts were abandoning ship. Rod Serling genuinely *believed* in television. "I think that of all the media, TV lends itself most beautifully to presenting a controversy," he told J. P. Shanley of the *New York Times* in 1956. "You can just take a part of the problem, and, using a small number of people, get your point across."[27]

As critic Andrew Sarris later wrote, "Television was the biggest sociological game in town, and Serling wasn't giving up on it without a fight."[28]

Serling may have moved to the land of mink swimming pools, but he wanted the American public and his video expatriate friends to know that, although he was going *to* Hollywood, morally and aesthetically, he was not *going* Hollywood—that he was still a *New York* writer—at heart. Thus, shortly before moving to Los Angeles, Serling wrote an article for the *New York Times Magazine* comparing New York live television drama to the made-in-Hollywood filmed type that was increasingly dominating the nation's airwaves. "It is unquestionable," Serling wrote, "that New York cared more about quality. Too, New York respected its writers more [this from the writer who was not allowed on the set of "Patterns"]. The writer of the filmed television play was never and is not now an identifiable name. This is in sharp contrast to the New York live TV writer who has been granted an identity, an importance, and a respect second only to the legitimate playwright."[29]

If Serling had any regrets about leaving the video Great White Way, they weren't evident to Jerome Hellman, who had also moved to "the Big Green" in late 1957. "I was having lunch with Rod at the Beverly Hills Hotel when the attendant brought up this big, white Lincoln Continental," said Hellman. "He looked at me and he said, 'Yeah, yeah, I know what you're thinking, I've gone Hollywood. But I like all of this.' It was funny because he felt it was necessary to justify it. He must have had funny feelings about it, but he was real clear about the fact that he liked it. That's what he felt, that's why he said he was here, because he wanted to be and he liked it. He liked the sunshine, he liked the fact that he was tan. He liked it all. He liked the convertible, and why not?"[30]

9

THE VELVET ALLEY (1958)

Hollywood is a place of ritual, a place where the secrets of power are of magical significance, a place where superstition, sex, and money mingle, where human values are distorted and sometimes lost. It is, in short, a part of that modern cultural continent we all inhabit, a place where in exaggerated form we can see our own communities.
—Hortense Powdermaker[1]

Rod Serling was on the coast-to-coast NBC tubes on Sunday, and his interview with Martin Agronsky was refreshing and revealing.

The former Binghamtonian, whose Hollywood contract is for a quarter of a million dollars, got his start in the WINR studios knocking out scripts for the "Dr. Christian" radio series.

Sitting in lush Hollywood surroundings, beside his swimming pool, Mr. Serling appeared young, handsome, nervous, and rich.

"This," he said, pointing to the luxury around him, "is just the gravy of what I'm doing."
—"Serling Proves Money Is Great," *Binghamton Press*, March 18, 1958

A week before the 1958 Emmy Awards presentation, Rod Serling told a reporter, "A guy who wins one Emmy has defied the law of averages. When he wins a second one, he has beaten the law of averages. Winning a third one means that he has proven that the law of averages doesn't exist."[2] The following week, Serling indeed proved that the law of averages *didn't* exist, by collecting his third consecutive Emmy for Outstanding Dramatic Writing, this time for "The Comedian." But he wasn't smiling—in fact, he had to limp to the stage this time as a result of having a car door close on his leg.

*   *   *

To be sure, the Rod Serling who received his third Emmy in March 1958 was not the same man whom the National Academy of Television Arts and Sciences audience had seen the year before, still aglow with "Requiem" accolades.

Serling's mother, Esther, had died only two weeks before. She had been suffering from high blood pressure for months. When the end came, on March 5, Rod was as much relieved as grieved. She was buried on a cold, miserable day in Syracuse.

His mother's death seemed to trigger new self-doubts, which winning a record third Emmy couldn't quell. In his own estimation, he remained an incomplete writer. Among Serling's many insecurities regarding his chosen profession, he was particularly bothered by his inability to write for women. "I remember that Rod had a great tendency to underwrite his women's roles," said Kim Hunter. "I called him on it and he admitted it. I thoroughly enjoyed doing all his work, really, but I did say to him, 'It's all very well you having great women's parts, but it'd be better if you could write them as well, too!' He said to me, 'That's why I love you in my shows, because you fill in all of the things I can't write.' "[3]

"I don't think he understood women," said his former secretary, Virginia Cox. "I think he was locked into a male vision. I just don't think women interested him that much. I think he loved them, I think he liked them, I think he got along well with them. I just don't think the female experience interested him. That wasn't the genesis of his creativity. He could not write a love scene. It was part of his limitation, he resented it, he was frustrated by it, he wanted to transcend it, and he could not.[4]

"What he was best at," said Cox, "were combat scenes. I think the real source of his writing was somewhat limited to his war experience, that was the thing he felt most deeply about, and the thing he wrote best about. When he got away from that, he was less sure. He wanted to be a Paddy Chayefsky, he wanted to deal with complex moral issues, and he did not feel capable of that.

"He would say things to me like, 'Ginny, why can't I write a love scene?' " Cox remembered. "And he couldn't, it was true."[5]

Ethel Wynant, the former casting director for CBS, who cast many of Serling's shows (including, later, *The Twilight Zone*), agreed: "He didn't write very well for women. He wasn't much interested in women. I think he had some interesting women's parts, but they were only facilitators to move the story along."[6]

Wynant also noted the importance of the war experience in Serling's work. "If Rod had written 'Marty,' " she speculated, "that's what it would have been about. He would have had a scene with Joe Mantell [the actor who played Marty's companion] where he would have said, 'Goddam it, give me a break. I don't want to sit around here each Saturday night, I wanna get laid. And the only way I'm gonna get laid is if I take Nancy Marchand out, cause nobody wants to lay her. And that's better than not getting laid.' Paddy didn't write that way. And it might have still been a very good play if Rod had written it. It would have been a lot more intense. There wouldn't have been a lot of 'What do you wanna do tonight, Marty?' "[7]

Director John Frankenheimer, once a close friend of Serling's, also recalled Serling's self-doubts. "Yes, I remember him saying, 'John, why can't I write a love scene?' He never believed in himself as a writer. He always had doubts, and he could never solve that demon in himself. He could never accept that he was a very talented man."[8]

Serling once again used his combat experience as the basis for his next *Playhouse 90* telepic, "Bomber's Moon." Directed by Frankenheimer, starring Robert Cummings, Martin Balsam, and Rip Torn, the play purported to tell "of the minute tragedies of a few who stand in the backwash of battle."

"Bomber's Moon" is the name of a pub in World War II England where American servicemen hang out between bombing raids on Germany. Colonel Culver (Cummings) is a hardened veteran who calls bereavement "wasteful" and finds cowardice appalling. Young Lieutenant Harrison (Torn) is grounded by Culver for his past cowardice, even though the fun-loving Captain Rierden (Balsam) believes that his friend Culver is being too harsh.

On the next mission, Rierden is killed taking Harrison's place, and an infuriated Culver tells the guilt-stricken Harrison that he should kill himself in shame. Later, he gets a better idea: Harrison should be the one to attempt a dangerous, one-man mission to prove his mettle. The lieutenant reluctantly agrees and succeeds in his mission—but is killed. Culver breaks down: "I killed Harrison . . . I thought if I could kill Harrison, I could kill that dirty part of myself." Before he is sent home, his superior explains that guilt and grief are a necessary facet of combat and leadership, "an ache we carry in our gut that no medic can cure."

The reviews of "Bomber's Moon" (which took its title from a phrase in one of Edward R. Murrow's wartime broadcasts—"It's a bomber's moon tonight") were sufficiently positive to allay some of Serling's insecurities. "There's nothing wrong with TV theater that quality writing can't cure," wrote UPI television critic William Ewald on May 23, 1958. "The astonishing thing about 'Bomber's Moon' was that it managed to sock its way home despite the familiarity of its material.

"I'd heard the story before . . . but Serling's writing pinched it all alive. He is the kind of writer who is not afraid to linger over a moment that will twitch life into a character—a wise-guy pilot admiring himself at length in a mirror; a lieutenant holding a salute ten seconds, fifteen seconds, until his C.O. [Commanding Officer] sees fit to return it; a silly joke about Anthony Eden injected during a serious moment in a bomb shelter."[9]

One week later, CBS offered its star playwright another one-year exclusive contract, which called for him to write a minimum of three television plays for *Playhouse 90* at a rate of ten thousand dollars per script. The network also offered him 40 percent ownership in a science fiction series that it was considering doing with Serling called *The Twilight Zone*.

Then Serling ran into another censorship storm on his next *Playhouse 90* script, "A Town Has Turned to Dust," in which he once again tried to meet the subject of racial prejudice head on. "By the time the censors had gotten to it, my *script* had turned to dust," Serling lamented afterward.[10]

The reviews for "A Town Has Turned to Dust" were generally good. Nevertheless, its censoring left Serling angrier than ever at his network and agency handlers. "We're developing a new citizenry," the writer told the *Cincinnati Post*, "one that will be very selective about cereals and automobiles, but won't be able to think."[11]

"They [the network and agencies] wanted to sell products," observed Don Freeman, "and Rod wanted to sell ideas."[12]

There was an increasingly cynical tone to Serling's pronouncements about television after "A Town Has Turned to Dust." Serling was wearying of the "Angry Man of television" role. He was also wearying of television, which seemed to be given over entirely to Westerns and quiz shows.

"A final note to any aspiring television writers," Serling declared in another article. "Do westerns and make your horses gray and if you have any burning desire to write of anything that has two sides to it, do a magazine piece on window cleaning."

"Writing is a frustrating, nerve-racking, lonely business," Serling told *Cosmopolitan*. "I figure the creative active life of a writer can't be measured in terms of whole generations. Perhaps in six or seven years I'll be burned out."[13]

Serling's prediction would prove uncannily accurate.

To be sure, within the CBS hierarchy were some who still loved him. Serling was briefly cheered by a laudatory article about television by CBS Vice-President for Programs Hubbell Robinson, one of the few remaining champions of "serious television" at network headquarters in New York, that appeared in the July 1958 issue of *Esquire*. In his piece, Robinson included Serling in a short list of "those who have given television its greatest moments." He also put "Requiem for a Heavyweight" at the top of his list of the medium's twenty-five masterworks.

Robinson himself was doomed, soon to be replaced by incoming CBS president James Aubrey (also known as "The Smiling Cobra"), whose programming credo was, "The more interesting the programming content of a television show is, the more it interferes with the commercial message."

"Success is a terrible attack on your sense of values," the jaded playwright told *Time*. "You get teed off because the heater of your swimming pool doesn't work."[14]

Serling decided to put some of his mordant thoughts about Hollywood and television into a teleplay that summer. He called it "The Velvet Alley." Beware the "velvet alley" of video success—like all Hollywood success it could also corrode a writer's original values.

"The Velvet Alley" was telecast on *Playhouse 90* on February 2, 1959, and told the story of Ernie Pandish (played by Art Carney), who, at forty-two, is trying to eke out a living as a television dramatist. His supportive agent, Max (Jack Klugman), finally hits paydirt and sells one of Ernie's scripts to a prestigious show that originates from Hollywood. Ernie is enamored of the glamour and attention he receives in California. After his show makes him instantly "hot," he decides to stay, in spite of Max's warnings that he should return home.

Months pass, and successful plays continue. Ernie becomes rich and famous, but finds himself more and more irritable, and more and more caught up in the business, unable to give any attention to his wife, Pat. Desperate for guidance, he is sweet-talked into dropping Max and signing with a large, flashy agency. Crushed, Max returns to New York. Equally disillusioned with her husband, Pat follows him.

Later, on the day Ernie wins an Emmy, Max dies of a heart attack. Shocked, Ernie returns to New York and begs his father to come back to California with him—he is the only family he has left. Steve Pandish refuses and berates his son for throwing away the things that were really valuable to him. The end of the play finds Ernie Pandish as "successful" as he could ever have dreamed of—but weeping, shattered, and totally alone.

"It's all so true," said Saul Marmer, although Serling would publicly insist otherwise. "Just what he would write about in 'The Velvet Alley' is what he became. Carol saw it coming. She kept him even in Cincinnati, she kept him on an even keel in Connecticut, but she couldn't in California. She did threaten to leave him."[15]

"I remember him telling me he took a lot of those argument scenes from his own domestic life," said Don Freeman. "There's a line in there, 'It's all Disneyland out here.' And Rod said, 'You know, Carol actually said that to me.'"[16]

Nevertheless, Serling insisted that any resemblance between him and Pandish was coincidental. "One of the basic problems in this industry is that it never trains people for success," he said in a statement issued by CBS. "Suddenly everything's all whipped cream and marshmallows and mink coats and swimming pools. You can't throw this down a gut and expect ready digestion. But to Ernie Pandish, identity became equated with money, and I don't think I'm that way. He traded off certain values: I haven't."[17]

The play made Serling distinctly unpopular with many of his television colleagues. Californians, Serling found, had very thin skins indeed.

"I won't argue the show's relative merits as a piece of drama and the antiquity of its theme makes it indefensible in the area of originality," the embattled writer wrote in his defense in the monthly bulletin of the Writers Guild of America.

But as to the honesty of its theme and the legitimacy of its people—this I will defend. The chorus of disapproval elicited in these climes after the show made me observe what is a rather odd phenomenon in Los Angeles and particularly in the movie industry.

It suggests a kind of clinical defensiveness and hypersensitivity not known in the East. You can knock New York in front of New Yorkers and they'll yawn at you. You can bitch volubly to the residents of Chicago—and they'll grin at you. But have the temerity to suggest that Hollywood, California, and its environs and industries have special problems—and this conjures up a chorus of professional knockers whose critical judgment seems to be based more on geographical pride than any analytical and established criteria of good theater.

All television writers don't lose agents and divorce wives and wind up over-fed kooks full of neuroses. But to criticize a piece because a certain protagonist does wind up this way—is like criticizing *Death of a Salesman* because all salesmen don't commit suicide.[18]

Serling also won praise—and criticism, especially for his subject—in 1959 for his acidic portrait of union racketeerism in "The Rank and File." Years later, *World-Telegram* TV critic Harriet Van Horne would remember the play as one of Serling's most powerful. "I remember a Serling play called 'Rank and File' on that greatly missed series, CBS *Playhouse 90*," Van Horne wrote in 1975. Van Heflin played the lead.

The story detailed the grubby rise of one Kilcoyne, a Depression-scarred factory worker.

We watched him change from a hungry, beaten man to absolute czar of an international brotherhood, a Hoffa–style union. Along the way, Kilcoyne has paused at many a moral crossroads. Ultimately, gross ambition devours the gentle idealist. We see it all in searing flashbacks.

The first scene . . . is still vivid in memory. Here was a shabby, shuffling picket line on a cold, rainy day in the 30s. Now and then the men put down their signs to warm ungloved hands over a fire in a refuse can.

Suddenly the guards order Kilcoyne to take his hands off the factory fence. He refuses. Before your eyes, his fingers are brutally smashed. He still refuses to remove his hands. 'In that moment, I tell you he was a giant,' we hear the union lawyer remark in the next scene. Then, slowly, the giant disintegrates before our eyes.[19]

But Serling's time for speaking truth to power—at least via TV —was running out. There wasn't much market in television for plays like "Patterns" and "Rank and File" as the fifties came to an end. The live television anthologies that Serling had once thrived on had all but disappeared; eight of the top-ten-rated shows of the '58–'59 season were Westerns, one was a detective show, and one was a comedy-variety show.

In the meantime, the television quiz show scandal had struck, and everyone from President Eisenhower to the National PTA was wringing his hands over the subject of network programming. Who controlled it? How could it be improved?

In 1960, the Federal Communications Commission, prodded into action after a decade of leaving the television industry to its own devices, decided to hold hearings on the subject, and as TV's most prominent writer—and critic—Serling was invited to testify.

Serling furnished numerous examples of "ludicrous and timo- rous" interference with his work for the commissioners, like the time when an insurance company objected to a suicide in one of his scripts, and the notorious instance, during the rehearsals for "Requiem," when one of the sponsors, the Ronson Lighter Com- pany, asked Serling to change the line "Got a match?" to "Got a light?" And, Serling added, "The food people don't want anything which might reduce the appetite."

For his part, Peter Allport, vice-president of the Association of National Advertisers, criticized "The TV writer for advocating the 'magazine concept' of divorcing advertisers from any control over program content and restricting their activity" and stated that ad- vertisers had not only provided the financial support possible, but had also contributed significantly to much of the program direc- tion.[20]

"If the sponsor chooses the play as a kind of piggy back on which he wants to use his commercial, then he has to respect the form he has chosen," Serling replied.[21]

Allport fired back in The New York Times: "Serling has produced some wonderful shows, [but] the situations he describes are not as serious as [he] claim[s]. The advertiser is a pretty good judge of what he wants his name attached to."

In truth, Serling *was* assailing the wrong enemy. By 1959, the program control pendulum had swung back to the networks, partly because of the advent of multiple sponsorship, and partly because the networks had become more jealous of the product they were putting out. But sponsors still made a better target. *Television Age* identified Serling as the chief industry critic and called for an industry counteroffensive against the complaints of television critics and writers.[22]

Serling was encouraged in his attack on the increasing commercialism by his angry counterpart in CBS News, Edward R. Murrow. In 1958, shortly after his program *See It Now* was canceled, Murrow delivered a blistering speech to a group of his broadcasting peers. "There is no suggestion here," Murrow cried, "that networks or individual stations should operate as philanthropies. But I can find nothing in the Bill of Rights or the Communications Act which says that they must increase their net profits each year, lest the Republic collapse. . . . I am frightened by the imbalance, the constant striving to reach the largest possible audience for everything; by the absence of a sustained study of the nation. . . . I would like television to produce some itching pills rather than this endless outpouring of tranquilizers. . . . Let us have a little competition. Not only in selling soap, cigarettes, and automobiles, but in informing a troubled, apprehensive, but receptive public."[23]

The days when CBS—or the television industry—would tolerate an Edward R. Murrow *or* a Rod Serling were obviously numbered. Serling may have wanted to be the Norman Corwin of television, said Loring Mandel, but, Mandel pointed out:

> Rod had something that Corwin didn't have, which was the layer of bureaucracy that grew continually, that separated him from people like Paley. In the time that I wrote, I never got as high as Paley or Stanton. You just didn't get up that far, and they didn't get down that far. The people that you were dealing with were functioning, and you could have a certain amount of contempt for them. . . . We were able to play one another's bureaucrat off against another. Corwin never could, cause there weren't any bureaucrats then.
>
> I'll give you one example of bureaucracy.
>
> In 1956, CBS initiated a writer's development program that lasted one year. I believe that Rod was in it, I believe that

Reggie [Rose] was in it, and I was the junior of something like eleven writers. We were given guaranteed annual salaries, and in exchange we were to produce nine outlines for one-hour shows. And CBS could ask us to write four or five of those scripts should they be picked up by any of the shows on the air. We never saw a creative person. The only person we dealt with at CBS was a man named Gilbert Ralston, and he was in business affairs.

We would give this material to Gilbert Ralston, and he would put it in the CBS mail distribution system, so when it got to the shows, it came in like something unsolicited from the mail, and almost none of that material was ever done. It was almost a total waste of time as far as CBS was concerned, because they never made the connection between the program and the creative people they needed. It was all done through business affairs.[24]

Fortunately for Serling, a creative escape presently appeared in the form of *The Twilight Zone*.

10
ENTERING THE ZONE
(1959)

ROD SERLING, one of television's most famous playwrights, brings you an extraordinary dramatic series, THE TWILIGHT ZONE, defined by the author as "The land that lies between science and superstition, between the pit of man's fears and the summit of his knowledge. You will find the bizarre, but the believable; the different, the shocking that is yet understandable. Its tales must be shown; they cannot be told. And each carries with it its own special surprise." In tonight's drama—a small-town main street lies deserted at midday . . . and a frightened man asks, "WHERE IS EVERYBODY?"

> —CBS newspaper ad for the premiere of *The Twilight Zone*, October 2, 1959[1]

The years 1959 to 1961 were a period of creative turmoil for American politics and culture, as the country went from the Fabulous (and rather complacent) Fifties to the Scientific Sixties, from Eisenhower to Kennedy, from black-and-white to color.

Television was an American institution by 1959, with sets located in nine out of ten American homes. The television industry itself, though, was in a state of upheaval, the result of the public uproar over the unfolding quiz show scandals. Americans were deeply shocked on November 2, 1958, when Charles Van Doren, a Columbia University history instructor, scion of one of America's great literary dynasties, and star contestant on *Twenty-One*, admitted to Congress that he had been given the answers to the questions asked on the quiz show by the program's producers. Even President Eisenhower was disturbed, and he called for further investigations. For the first time in its short history, the television industry was on the defensive. To brighten their tarnished public image, network executives hurriedly provided money and time for news and public affairs programming. Indeed, 1959 to 1961 were great days for the network news divisions.

The same could not be said for network drama, where the same leveling trends that had set in continued. By the end of 1959, television and television drama emanated almost entirely out of Hollywood. Only one live television drama remained on the air. Viewers apparently felt willing to confront reality on *The Huntley-Brinkley Report*, but preferred not to be reminded of the fast-changing world the rest of the evening. Hence the continued popularity of shows like *Gunsmoke*, which continued to be the top-rated program.

The years 1959 to 1961 were full of creative turmoil too—and high achievement—for Rod Serling. Television's prophet-outcast adopted the mantle of master fantasist—or video Aesop—using the television set as a prism through which to view America's tormented soul. It was these years that saw the birth and fruition of his masterwork and icon: *The Twilight Zone*.

Serling was cautiously optimistic about his new venture into television auteurism as he made the publicity rounds for *The Twilight Zone* during the summer and fall of 1959. One stop was Mike Wallace's interview show.

Like many New York intellectuals who had admired Serling as the conscience of the industry and as one of the last ties to the golden age of television drama, Wallace viewed Serling's decision to become involved with a filmed fantasy series as a sellout. "So you've given up writing anything important for TV?" Wallace derisively asked.[2]

"If by important, you mean to try to delve into current issues, you're quite right," Serling answered, sounding defensive. "But I'm convinced that this will help my career. In eleven or twelve years of writing, I can lay claim to this: I have never written beneath myself. I have never written anything I didn't want my name attached to."[3]

I stay in TV because I think it performs the function of providing adult, meaningful, exciting, challenging drama without dealing in controversy. I think it's criminal that we are not permitted to make dramatic note of social evils that exist, of controversial themes as they are inherent in our society. I think

143

it's ridiculous that drama, which by its very nature should make a comment on those things which affect our daily lives, is in a position, at least in terms of television, of not being able to take that stand. But these are the facts of life, and they can't look to me or Chayefsky or Rose or Gore Vidal or JP Miller or any of those guys as the precipitators of some big change.[4]

"Is television good?" Wallace asked Serling.[5]

"Some television is wonderful. Some television is promising, exciting, and has potential," Wallace's chain-smoking guest answered. *The Twilight Zone*, he was sure, would turn out to be that kind of TV.[6]

Curiously, Serling told Wallace that his dream project involved writing a stage play about the McCarthy period. Serling would talk a lot about writing for the legitimate theater for the next two decades, but would do very little about it—mostly because in his self-conscious view, it *was* the more legitimate form. It sounded good to say that he was writing a play, even though he never got around to it.

But he knew that his singular talents were best fitted for television. As Buzz Kulik, a TV and movie director who frequently worked with Serling over the years, put it:

> [Rod's] kind of style, pithiness, and drive of his writing lent itself peculiarly to television. I believe there was a kind of writing that was purely wonderful for television, and there was a group of guys who wrote peculiarly for television. . . . And I think Rod recognized that, and I don't think he ever seriously sat down and said 'Okay, I'm really going to write a play.' He was a creature of the medium and he never felt more comfortable than when he was working in the medium."[7]

The process of getting *The Twilight Zone* on the air had actually begun—none too auspiciously—two years before, when CBS, which had a prior first-purchase-rights deal with Serling, had bought a script for a time travel fantasy from him entitled *The Twilight Zone*: "The Time Element," with a view toward possibly expanding it into a series. Serling's story, an expansion of the same script he had concocted for *The Storm*, was about a man who dreams that he goes back in time to Honolulu just before the Japanese attack on

Pearl Harbor. He tries, in vain, to warn the Army of the imminent debacle—and winds up getting killed in the attack. At the time— 1958—the story was considered too "far out" by the West Coast CBS brass and was put on hold. Although science fiction and fantasy programs like the video version of *Lights Out* and *Captain Video* had enjoyed a limited success with viewers before then, Serling's proposed show was considered déclassé for the man who many considered television drama's counterpart of Edward R. Murrow. To Serling's keen disappointment, it was shelved.

That might have been the last anyone heard of *The Twilight Zone* or "The Time Element" if not for Bert Granet, the new producer of *Westinghouse Desilu Playhouse*, a filmed anthology show produced in Hollywood. Granet felt that his show needed more prestige. An admirer of Serling, he arranged a meeting with him via their mutual friend, director Robert Parrish. Did Serling, perchance, have an unproduced script in his back files that he still wanted to do? Serling mentioned the shelved "Time Element" script. Granet was "ecstatic," he recalled. And he was even happier after CBS quickly agreed to sell him the *verboten* Serling teleplay.[8]

Then came the difficult job of persuading Westinghouse and its conservative ad agency, McCann-Erickson, that "The Time Element" ought to be aired. Many of the original objections to *The Twilight Zone* were then resurrected. "The network people and the agency people didn't like unfinished stories, like 'The Time Element,' which left the audience hanging," Granet remembered. "I can't tell you how much they didn't want to do it." They liked their stories neat and wrapped with a bow." Nevertheless, Granet's persistence, along with his belief in the theatrical potential of the oddball Serling script, overcame all obstacles.[9]

On November 24, 1958, *Desilu Playhouse* presented an hour-long production of "The Time Element." William Bendix starred as the deluded man who goes back in time to Pearl Harbor, and Martin Balsam was the unbelieving psychiatrist who tries to persuade the protagonist that he is the victim of delusions. Allan Reisner (who was also later to direct an episode of the *Zone* series) was the director.

"I'm not making any supernatural claims in this story," Serling said before the telecast. "What my central character experiences is just an extension of something that's happened to all of us. For example, who hasn't had that chilling moment of recall in which a new occurrence seems to be something that's happened before?"[10]

Apparently, a lot of television viewers had. The show caused a minor sensation. Within days *Desilu Playhouse* was deluged by over six thousand letters of praise. The critics were also approbative. "Rod Serling is one of the pioneer television writers who still stays in the medium, even though he is as articulate as video's expatriates about TV's limitations," Jack Gould noted approvingly in the *New York Times*.

> The humor and sincerity of Mr. Serling's dialogue made "The Time Element" consistently arresting. And Mr. Serling wisely left the individual viewer to work out for himself whether the play's meaning was that even with fresh knowledge of the past no one will heed its lesson, that to be out of step with the crowd is to only invite ridicule.[11]

"Mr. Serling had his troubles in Hollywood over script censorship," the critic concluded. "But where other dramatists either capitulate or retire, he manages to achieve a great deal through the subtlety of his approach. What he might do with no shackles could be most exciting."[12]

The powers-that-be at CBS apparently agreed. Impressed by the audience and critical reaction to Serling's show, CBS decided that it might have been too hasty in dismissing Serling's venture into fantasy and suggested that he write another pilot for his shelved *Twilight Zone* anthology series.

Serling already had one ready to go: a downbeat play called "The Happy Place," about a future society that puts its aged citizens to death. Written the week following his mother's death, the script was one of Serling's most morbid, and was rejected by the network. "When I met with him [to discuss "The Happy Place"]," William Self, then CBS's head of West Coast programming, recalled, "I told him I didn't like it. It dealt with euthanasia, and I told Rod that for a pilot, the advertisers and sponsors would think it was just too serious. We actually had kind of an initial falling out about that. Rod went away for a few days. Then he came back and gave me another script, and it turned out to be 'Where Is Everybody?' "[13]

Inspired by a walk he had taken across a deserted movie set, Serling came up with the second idea for a series pilot. "Where Is Everybody?" features Earl Holliman as an apparent amnesiac (actually an astronaut in training who has begun to hallucinate after spending four hundred hours in an isolation chamber), wandering around an eerie, just-deserted town, seeking desperately to establish his identity from the few clues available. Only at the end of the show, as his Air Force handlers rescue the now-berserk space cadet from the isolation chamber, do *we* learn his actual identity.

"When he first said he wanted me for a science fiction show," remembered Holliman, "I thought I would be one of twenty guys on a spaceship."[14]

General Foods liked "Where Is Everybody?" and in February 1959 signed on as principal sponsor. Kimberly-Clark, the Kleenex manufacturer, later joined on as alternate sponsor after Serling pitched in with a sales campaign of his own that emphasized the story-telling qualities of the show. People watch television to be entertained, Serling said, and *The Twilight Zone* entertains them.

Serling only wanted to do *The Twilight Zone* if he could have total creative control of the show, and thanks to some hard bargaining by his agents at Ashley-Steiner, that is exactly what he got. The contract he signed bound him to write 90 percent of the scripts for the show's first three seasons. It was a task that would have daunted most Hollywood writers, but not Rod Serling. Ultimately, he would write over 90 of the 156 episodes over the show's five seasons. Jonathan Spota, manager of Jonathan Winters, remembered running into a joyous Serling the day after the *Zone* deal was inked. "You wouldn't believe how happy he was."[15]

Serling celebrated by spending a weekend in Las Vegas. While Carol was having good luck nearby, he became enslaved by a merciless one-armed bandit, an incident he would turn into one of his first *Twilight Zone* episodes, "The Fever," about a penny-pincher who becomes obsessed by a diabolical slot machine. The machine consumes all of the man's money, invades his dreams, and eventually, as his screaming wife helplessly watches, "chases" him out of his hotel window—". . . in the Twilight Zone." Ideas for other episodes for the show's first cycle came to Serling in a similar random fashion. Another walk through a movie back lot gave Serling the notion for "Walking Distance." A conversation about astronauts with the wife of a friend at a cocktail party resulted in "I Shot an Arrow into the Air." Serling even worked on the series while he slept. He kept waking up to write down ideas he had in his dreams in a notepad by his bed.

Meanwhile, he had put together a first-rate production team, headed by veteran producer Buck Houghton, who would produce the first three seasons of *The Twilight Zone*; unit production manager Ralph W. Nelson (not the director of "Requiem"), who would remain for the duration of the show's run; veteran cinematographer George T. Clemens, who was coerced out of semiretirement to try to film Serling's bizarre scripts (which frequently called for bizarre special effects on a very limited budget). Later in the show's run, many others, including Serling's old friend Ethel Wynant, would join the *Zone* production team for a time.

And thus it went. The Serling household was on a virtual war footing during the months leading up to the show's debut, when the first cycle of episodes was being produced. Every morning, Serling would awaken at five or six o'clock and begin dictating scripts, often acting out *all* the parts, while pacing around his new home office, a glass-enclosed lanai down by the pool.

Visitors who encountered Serling in midcreation would often leave open-mouthed in awe at Serling's sheer prodigiousness. One of those visitors was Chester Erion, Serling's East Coast Dictaphone repairman.

"It was something to behold," said Erion. "When he was writing and talking into the machine, he was not only giving the story line right out of his head without any notes or anything, but at the same time he was saying 'Camera One will move in from this side' and adding in all of the directions for the cameras and everything, including the movements of the actors. I'd be working on one machine while he was recording on another."[16]

"He was an extraordinarily energetic person, just exploding with ideas," said Del Reisman. "Buck and I would joke about Rod's prolific talents a lot. We would kid each other and say, 'I just talked to Rod and he's working on something and we'll probably have a script this afternoon.' I'm exaggerating, but only a little. He would come up with a script in a matter of days, and this is an original, in three or four days, starting with nothing. He worked awfully fast. Once he got the idea, and he had it in his mind where he wanted it to go, he just went."[17]

"I rather imagine there were times when he dictated *Twilight Zone* scripts in an hour or two," Serling's friend and associate (and former Westport neighbor) Dick Berg remembered. "I know for a fact that he could work at that rate. Once he had the fix on what his story was, he was able to improvise at almost the rate of speed it would take the director to stage the scene. The people would absolutely materialize on the spot, the dialogue would flow out. . . . It was fascinating. He was the most natural storyteller I ever met."[18]

Unfortunately, not all of the ingredients in Serling's mania for work were natural. "My image of Rod is with a cigarette and a Coke bottle in his hand—the original Coke with all of that caffeine," Del Reisman said. "He must have stimulated the Coke rather than the other way around. Obviously, he wanted that constant stimulation that he got from it."[19] By that time, Serling was smoking four packs of cigarettes a day.

After five or six hours of writing, he would hop into his Continental and race down to the MGM back lot in Culver City to preside over the day's shoot, usually not returning until late at night.

One of the first episodes filmed was an occult Western called "Mr. Denton on Doomsday," about an aging gunslinger who briefly regains his sharpshooting powers via the gift of a magic potion from a mysterious vendor named Henry J. Fate. One of the supporting characters, a bully, was played by Martin Landau. Landau recalled the crew's—and Serling's—excitement as the executive producer/ writer sat down at a table on MGM's Western set and read through the script in sequence.

"I remember Rod sitting at the head of the table," Landau said. "And we read and we stopped and we discussed and he'd rewrite and we'd reread and refine it. Of course, for Rod to sit down for any length of time was hard—he was so wired.

"For a writer to be present on the set of a *television* show," Landau pointed out, "and the cast to all be there, reading their roles in sequence, was so unusual. It gave us a feeling that he cared. It gave us a sense of camaraderie. And it made for a show of real quality."[20]

Actress Janice Rule, a transplanted Actors Studio product (like Landau), played the lead in "Nightmare as a Child," another one of the early *Zone* episodes. She also recalled the Broadway "feel" of the show: "The air was charged with all of our creative energies in that one piece of work. Nobody was thinking about anything except the work itself. You were doing the thing at hand, that was the most important thing in the world going on. That whole quality carried over into *The Twilight Zone*."[21]

The play was still the thing on *The Twilight Zone*. As Serling later put it, "Scripts were written with an eye towards the literacy of the actor and the intelligence of the audience."[22]

Adding to Serling's excitement—and his nervousness—as the first thirteen episodes were being shot was the widespread perception on the part of critics and interviewers that by doing *The Twilight Zone* Serling was somehow debasing himself.

EX-ANGRY YOUNG MAN REBEL NO MORE, the Associated Press announced over a story about Serling's departure from the realm of straight drama for *The Twilight Zone*.

No, he wasn't entering *The Twilight Zone* for the money, he countered. Yes, he admitted to Mike Wallace that he stood to enrich himself if the series succeeded. But he also stood to lose a lot if it didn't. As proof, Serling cited the fact that he was trying to get out of one of his lucrative deals with MGM. *The Twilight Zone* would *not* be your ordinary thirty-minute series, Serling promised. These would be "high quality, extremely polished films." They just wouldn't be controversial. "There won't be anything controversial in the new series," he told Wallace, in words that seemed directed toward reassuring his worried sponsors more than anything else. He was tired of "acting the role of tired nonconformist. I don't want to fight anymore. I don't want to battle sponsors and agencies. I don't want to fight for something I want and have to settle for second best . . . which is in essence what the television writer does if he wants to take on controversial themes."[23]

The only person who continued to exercise any control over him, he happily admitted in press interviews, was his wife. "She uses a rapier to puncture my ego," he told the *New York Times*. "Although she has no part in this business and wants no part of it, she's an unerringly accurate critic. She also picks flaws in my grammar. When she says, 'You used a conjunction there and it's wrong,' she destroys you."[24]

"How do you criticize a man and make him love it?" asked a reporter from the *Binghamton Press* of Carol Serling during a meeting with both Serlings. "You don't! Or if you do, you have to be pretty careful," said Carol. "Sugar coat your comments with a praise. But frankly, I'm trying to learn to give over all criticism. It burns the heck out of him, especially when I'm right!"[25]

"I certainly respect her critical opinions," Serling continued affectionately. "You know she never criticized my work until after we were married."

"You didn't do any writing until after we were married, dear," she chided.[26] Her obedient husband didn't correct her.

Serling had difficulty surrendering the "angry man of television" role entirely, his publicist, Owen Comora, recalled. "I remember he went on a talk show in Pittsburgh, and he started complaining about how impossible it was to put on a meaningful drama when it was interrupted every twelve minutes by dancing rabbits with toilet paper. I could have killed him! After all, Kimberly-Clark, one of our sponsors, was the country's leading toilet paper manufacturer!"[27]

Nevertheless, the writer-producer managed to maintain an amiable relationship with his sponsors, he assured Wallace on CBS. "We have a good working relationship, wherein questions of taste, questions of the art form itself, questions of drama, I'm the judge. This is my medium and I understand it. I'm a dramatist for television. This is the area I know. I'm trained for it, I've worked for it for twelve years. The sponsor knows his products, but he doesn't know mine. When it comes to the commercials, I leave that up to him. When it comes to the story content, he leaves that up to me. In eighteen scripts so far, we've only had one minor line changed."[28]

October 2, 1959, was premiere night—the date of departure, Serling joked. That Friday night at ten, NBC's *Gillette Cavalcade of Sports* was back for its eleventh season. ABC, inspired by the popularity of NBC's *Peter Gunn*, introduced *The Detectives*, a hard-driving, New York–based action program starring Robert Taylor. CBS countered with *The Twilight Zone*.

The 18 million viewers who tuned in to the unorthodox new program heard a sinuous off-camera voice describing "a fifth dimension . . . as vast as space and timeless as infinity. It is the middle ground between light and shadow, between science and superstition . . ."

Serling need not have worried about the critics. With few exceptions, the press loved the show. Cecil Smith of the *Los Angeles Times* called the show "the finest weekly series on television."[29] "In the field of imaginative drama, Rod Serling has few peers," Jack Gould wrote in the *New York Times*.[30]

The general audience was another matter. Serling had hoped for at least a 21 or 22 Nielsen rating and a 33 share, but the numbers *The Twilight Zone* put on the board at first were much lower than that—low enough for the *Zone* team to worry about the show's survival.

Serling and the rest of *The Twilight Zone* team had a particularly rough night the Monday following the series' third episode, when the show was trounced by *77 Sunset Strip*, getting an abysmal 16.3 rating. Serling began to breathe easier when, one night in November, the *Zone* beat its competition on both of the other networks. The show was not a ratings hit, nor would it ever be. But, surprisingly, it did gradually build up a loyal following, particularly among teenagers. "The appeal to children was a complete surprise to us," said Buck Houghton. "We never thought of that. I don't think CBS did, either; it was on at ten o'clock. We got a lot of nasty notes from parents saying 'You're keeping the kids up!' "[31]

In the meantime, *The Twilight Zone*'s immediate prospects began to improve, in spite of the fact that Serling would occasionally still lambaste the increasingly ratings-and-revenue-based mentality of networks and sponsors—as he had during his testimony before the Federal Communications Commission. The sponsors were content to let Serling speak his mind, particularly because the ratings continued to improve modestly. In spite of their inability to understand some of the more arcane scripts, Kimberly-Clark and General Foods each announced in February that they would remain as sponsors, at least for a while longer, and the show was renewed. Three months later, however, Kimberly-Clark jumped ship, claiming the show wasn't doing the job it wanted. Colgate-Palmolive immediately signed on to fill the breach. Nevertheless, because of the show's offbeat content as well as its generally mediocre ratings, *The Twilight Zone*'s sponsorship would continue to gyrate wildly throughout its five-year run.

Meanwhile, the unusual show continued to create a buzz within Hollywood. Actors told their agents to get them a part on Serling's show. "The parts were so *interesting*," said Claude Akins, who appeared in two episodes. "With other series, you'd look at the script and think 'Oh, wow, I only did this part last week.' But not with *The Twilight Zone*."[32]

"You're never any better than the situation, and he created such a great situation for performance," remembered Jack Warden, who also appeared in two episodes. "That was one of the reasons so many actors wanted to work with Rod, because the parts were exciting and the situations were so different. When my agent said anything about a *Twilight Zone*, I said, 'Oh God, take it.' I didn't even have to read it, I knew it'd be something exciting to do."[33]

In some cases, episodes of *The Twilight Zone* were custom-made for certain actors. Buster Keaton had an episode written for him. So did Agnes Moorehead.

Directors also flocked to the show. "Those scripts were so well-honed by the time we got them, that it was just a pleasure to go in and shoot them," said Richard Donner, best known as the director of *Superman* and the *Lethal Weapon* films, who directed four *Twilight Zone* episodes (including "Nightmare at 20,000 Feet" and "The Jeopardy Room").[34]

Donner and the other directors also liked Serling's flexibility. "Rod encouraged you to do whatever you thought [would] be imaginative with his scripts," said Douglas Heyes, director of nine episodes (including "The Eye of the Beholder," "The Howling Man," and "The Invaders"). "I was able to try all kinds of things that I had always wanted to experiment with. . . ."[35]

"Most of my effects were done right there in the camera—on the set," Heyes continued. "*Twilight Zone* made it possible to do that. They encouraged you to give your best. Many of the things I tried would not have been possible in any other atmosphere, but on *The Twilight Zone* I had this freedom—thanks, mainly, to Buck Houghton and Rod. I sat in on every cutting session. They worked right with you on the cutting, and it came out the way you wanted it. I was spoiled early on because Rod encouraged me to do everything I could."[36]

Unlike his live television days, Serling also knew when to get out of the way of his directors. "There are very few writers or producers who can stay away, but Rod was amazing that way," said Buzz Kulik, who directed seven episodes. "Rod would never come onto the set because he felt that it would be intrusive. Every once in a while I would hear from him, if he had seen some dailies or something. It was an amazing organization. Working the way those people worked was just a sheer joy. They had Ralph W. Nelson as production manager, absolutely a brilliant old man, and Buck, and Rod. And they would get nine scripts and put them together, and get them in as good shape as they could, and then you'd shoot them.

153

Most shows you would be getting pages the day you start shooting, or they would still be writing when you were shooting. Never on *The Twilight Zone*. That work was done and it was ready to go. It was such a well-oiled, organized operation."[37]

Perhaps the most extraordinary thing about the first season of *The Twilight Zone* to viewers, and indeed about the show in general, was the degree to which Serling *was* able to use the show to make statements about the current human condition—without being explicitly "controversial." As Carol Serling put it, "Rod felt that drama should be an assertion of social conscience. He found that in *The Twilight Zone*, through parable and suggestion, he could make the same point that he wanted to make with straight drama."[38]

Case in point: Serling's haunting disquisition on fear and raw prejudice, "Monsters Are Due on Maple Street," with Claude Akins and Jack Weston, broadcast March 4, 1960.

One quiet summer day on Maple Street, a meteor speeds overhead causing a failure of all power equipment—cars, electricity, telephones. The residents gather and try to explain the outage, and a young boy who reads comic books says that humanlike monsters from outer space have invaded—indeed, already walk among humankind. At first, the adults laugh this off, but then they begin to point fingers at each other: Who is the monster? The accusations become stronger. "Look, you all *know* me," Goodman, one of the Maple Street residents, desperately reminds his neighbors. The other residents continue to accuse him: why does he keep such strange hours, walking around early in the morning looking up at the sky?

> GOODMAN (shouts): You fools. You scared, frightened rabbits, you. You're sick people, do you know that? You're sick people—all of you! And you don't even know what you're starting because let me tell you . . . let me tell you—this thing you're starting—*that* should frighten you. . . . You're letting something begin here that's a nightmare!![39]

Finally violence erupts, with one neighbor getting shot. Nearby, two aliens discuss how their experiment in fear has proved successful; one little power failure, and Maple Street—and every other street like it—will destroy itself.

"For the record, prejudices can kill and suspicion can destroy,"

Serling intoned in his closing narration, while the little neighborhood below—which could well have passed for Wyoming Heights or Westport—continued to self-destruct; "and a thoughtless, frightened search for a scapegoat has a fallout all its own—for the children, and the children yet unborn. And the pity of it is that these things cannot be confined to the Twilight Zone."[40]

The first season also contained more meditations on the threat of nuclear war by the author, who joined the antinuclear group Citizens for a Sane Nuclear Policy in 1955, and was one of the most active members of its Hollywood chapter. The first "place" the Bomb was dropped on American television was in a memorable episode called "Time Enough at Last," a morbidly ironic tale that aired November 11, 1959. This time, unlike "Mr. Finchley vs. the Bomb," Serling wasn't pulling his punches on the nuclear threat.

Meek Henry Bemis (Burgess Meredith) works as a bank teller, but is always getting into trouble because of his passion for reading. One day, while he is in the bank vault, the Bomb drops. He emerges as the only survivor, but is unsure if he *wants* to live at all. He is about to kill himself when his eyes alight on the ruins of a library. He is in heaven! After arranging his books for the years to come, he settles down to open the first one—and breaks his glasses.

Many of Serling's characters are named after other figures in his life. The central figure in "Nightmare as a Child," a story about a schoolteacher who confronts a stranger from her past, is named Helen Foley, after Serling's junior high school teacher and mentor. Denton, the ex-gunslinger hero of "Mr. Denton on Doomsday," is named after Serling's childhood friend Herbert Denton. Various other tableaux from Serling's life also pop up. The Ithaca, New York, bus station puts in an appearance in "Mirror Image," an episode about a woman who encounters her doppelgänger while waiting for a bus to nearby Cortland. And, of course, there are also many references to Binghamton, most notably in "Walking Distance" and "A Stop at Willoughby," the latter about a harried New York executive who dreams of a Binghamton-like town called Willoughby while taking the train home to Westport.

The first season was, all in all, another knockout performance. Serling and his crew had proven that television could be both commercially successful *and* worthwhile.

On June 21, 1960, the National Academy of Television Arts and

Sciences awarded Serling, who had written twenty-nine of the season's thirty-six episodes, his record fourth Emmy for Outstanding Dramatic Writing. Serling's gamble on launching his little oddball show had paid off. Later, he called it "the happiest moment of his professional career."[41] Once again, congratulatory telegrams poured in from all over the country.

Ominously, there was no telegram from Serling's own network.

No television season would be complete without a controversy involving Rod Serling, and Serling unwittingly provided one on May 20, 1960, with his last teleplay for *Playhouse 90*. In "In the Presence of Mine Enemies," an overly talkative but occasionally moving drama about the Warsaw Ghetto, starring Charles Laughton, Susan Kohner, George Macready, and Robert Redford, Serling committed, in the eyes of many, the gross indelicacy of including a sympathetic Nazi (Redford, in his television debut).

Leon Uris, author of the novel *Exodus*, led the charge against a surprised Serling with a telegram to CBS president Frank Stanton, demanding that the negatives of the production, which he called "the most disgusting dramatic presentation in the history of American television," be burned. Serling promptly jumped into the fray with his own broadside, a scathing but respectful letter to Uris in which he claimed he had been maligned and personally offended by Uris's suggestion that his work was anti-Semitic. Charles Beaumont, a writer for *The Twilight Zone* and a personal friend of Serling's, rallied to his defense, saying that Uris's accusations were "hysterical, vicious, and wholly irresponsible. As for his demand that CBS burn the film, the author of *Exodus* would do well to remember that that sort of thing was one of Herr Goebbels' specialties."[42]

Amidst the uproar, few noticed that "In the Presence of Mine Enemies" was the last production of *Playhouse 90*, which had been canceled thanks to an edict from CBS's new chief executive, James Aubrey. With the show's demise, the golden age of live television dramas officially came to an end.

Meanwhile, to the envy of his former colleagues, Serling seemed to be having his dramatic cake and eating it too, in that "middle ground between science and superstition . . ."

11
ACME
(1960)

"On this planet, or wherever there is human life, perhaps out among the stars, beauty is in the eye of the beholder. Lesson to be learned . . . in the Twilight Zone."
—from "The Eye of the Beholder," first aired November 11, 1960[1]

Serling reached the pinnacle of his power and creativity both as a writer and as a producer during *The Twilight Zone*'s second season, 1960–61, for which he was to win his fifth Emmy. Serling, feeling relaxed, left Los Angeles for his traditional summer break along Lake Cayuga with Carol, Jody, and Nan and the two dogs the family now owned, Beau, an Irish setter, and George, a dachshund.

The summer of 1960 was another pleasant one for the Serlings, at least on the surface. Serling's artistic and financial gamble on the show had been vindicated, and now, for a blissful few weeks, Rod once again had time to go boating around Lake Cayuga as the girls giggled at his habitual klutziness with the controls. Now there was time, for once, to play with his daughters, to assure them that they weren't being neglected in the glare of Serling's fame. Time to tend to the vegetable garden he had begun to grow behind the house, to meet friends down the lake for dinner in Ithaca. Time to take a spin down Route 17 to Binghamton, seventy miles away, to hang out with his buddies from the 511th, Vernon Hartung and Jerry Shea; or to drive over to the West Side and walk around the old family house at 67 Bennett Avenue.

But Serling's respite was brief, and he was never far from Carol's control. One friend recalled that whenever Serling visited Binghamton, he had to check in with her every few hours. Carol had devolved almost entirely into a mother figure for her husband. Even the letters he wrote to her when they were apart have a formal, filial quality. Serling had already begun to rebel against his wife by indulging in occasional liaisons with other women.

The morning after a visit to Binghamton (usually following a sleepless night), Serling would shut himself into the narrow trailer attached to the cottage and begin dictating scripts again.

Soon he was headed off to Tompkins County Airport to catch the first leg of the long transcontinental trip back to Los Angeles —to his second family, his *Twilight Zone* family, back at the offices of Cayuga Productions—sad to be leaving his upstate sanctuary, relieved to be returning to work and to be free from Carol's control.

Cayuga Productions, the company Serling had formed to produce *The Twilight Zone*, had a number of new elements for viewers for the second season of *The Twilight Zone* that debuted on the last day of September 1960.

One was the eerie new theme music especially composed for the program by Marius Constant. The new, improved, surrealistic credits pulled viewers through an exploding, Dali-esque space, reaching the exploding titles as Constant's metronomic and very catchy theme ticked on and Serling's clipped voice warned viewers:

You're traveling through another dimension. A dimension not only of sight and sound, but of mind. A journey into a wondrous land whose boundaries are that of imagination. That's the signpost up ahead! Next stop . . . THE TWILIGHT ZONE![2]

Another feature that also quickly caught on with *Twilight Zone* viewers was the new on-camera role for Rod as narrator-host. During the first season, he had only served as an off-screen narrator (aside from a brief cameo in the season's final episode). Bothered by the show's mediocre ratings, CBS came to the conclusion that the show needed a charismatic and enigmatic "host"—like Alfred Hitchcock, who had become an icon hosting *his* anthology show, *Alfred Hitchcock Presents*—as a means of tying its disparate episodes together.

Orson Welles was one of the first possibilities considered. Serling was a longtime fan of Welles, and was excited about the idea—except that Welles, then in exile from Hollywood and living in England, initially claimed he wasn't interested. Serling was too busy with his writing and producing duties that summer to go to London himself and attempt to convince Welles, so Ted Ashley of Ashley-Steiner went instead.

"I went to London to try to convince Orson Welles to do the show," remembered Ashley. "We ate in this restaurant in Soho, but he never wanted to get around to the business at hand. I think we started around twelve-thirty . . . and it was something like three o'clock and I had to cut the lunch short.[3]

"So finally we started talking about the narrating job. And I told him how Charles Barry [an associate of Welles] had said that last week, Orson said he would like to host the show.[4]

" 'Well,' Orson said, after letting out a burp, 'that was *last* week. This is now, and now I don't feel like doing it.' "[5]

With Welles out, Serling, the ham, decided that maybe *he* should give the host role a try. And so on September 30, after the intriguing prologue for that evening's episode, "King Nine Will Not Return"—a thriller about a former World War II bomber pilot (Robert Cummings) who thinks he sees the crewmen of his old bomber—the visibly nervous author stepped into the frame and into nearly 20 million *Zone* homes, and began punching his lines out: "This is Africa, nineteen forty-three," he declaimed. "War spits out its violence overhead and the sandy graveyard swallows it up. Her name is King Nine, B-25, medium bomber, Twelfth Air Force. On a hot, still morning she took off from Tunisia to bomb the southern tip of Italy . . ."[6]

Viewer response to Serling's new role as on-camera host was enormous. With his huge eyebrows, dark, Jewish good looks, intense demeanor—and that *voice*—Rod Serling indeed looked (and sounded) like the guy who created *The Twilight Zone*. Or, as Frank Stanton put it, "He was the only writer I had ever met who looked like his work."[7]

In his own way, Serling was every bit as weird—and fitting—for *The Twilight Zone* as Hitchcock had been for his show.

"I've heard from other directors that he was a basket case when he came down [to the set] to shoot his lead-ins," said Douglas Heyes. "But I never got that impression at all. He'd always have it perfectly memorized. I think he really had fun doing it. I think he had a lot of theatricality—and it's right up there on the screen."[8]

Sydney Pollack, then an actor who played a feature role in the second season episode "The Trouble with Templeton," agreed. "I think Rod was a performer at heart. He certainly had a sharp sense of theater. That was present in his conversation. He knew what would or could achieve an effect with an audience. He was sort of a master of understatement in those lead-ins. They were very stylish in their day. He had a good sense of humor—that's why he was great to talk to. I remember bumping into him at some particularly miserable party, and it was such a relief to bump into someone who was as miserable as I was and joke back and forth about it!"[9]

Serling's new hosting abilities began changing him in ways that were both predictable and not. America had never had a recognizable writer-star before, and the surprised and gratified host of *The Twilight Zone* found himself being stopped for autographs whenever he went out in public—a development that satisfied his cravings for recognition but particularly upset his wife and caused her to dread going out with him. Like it or not, Serling was no longer a mere writer; he was now a TV "personality."

To his former colleagues from New York, Serling's decision to go on camera was in some ways inevitable. Many felt that his new turn before the lights was just another symptom of Serling "going Hollywood." "He ended up as a performer. *Twilight Zone* was a platform for his performing," said Gore Vidal, in retrospect.[10]

The lead-ins also did Serling very little good with CBS's new president, James Aubrey. Serling's quirky dramatic anthology show represented the antithesis of the kind of lowest common denominator "broads, bosoms, and fun" programming that Aubrey and his fellow network executives were bringing to television. A product of the ABC telefilm action-adventure factory, Aubrey had actually been part of the programming team that had been responsible for *77 Sunset Strip*, Serling's chief Friday night competition, so it could be said that Aubrey had a personal prejudice against Serling's show.

And it was Aubrey who had decided to pull the plug on the network's most prestigious dramatic program, *Playhouse 90*. It was Aubrey, too, who had, with apparent relish, dismissed Hubbell Robinson, the CBS programmer most responsible for the inception of *90* and *The Twilight Zone*, via a closed-circuit farewell.

Del Reisman, who began his stint as associate producer of *The*

Twilight Zone at the beginning of the show's second season, remembered the telecast well. "Here was Hubbell on the monitor
saying, 'Today, I have decided to step down,' and so on, and 'The
Smiling Cobra' [as Aubrey was known at CBS] was sitting behind
him, smiling. I'll never forget that moment. It was like a Tom and
Jerry cartoon with the feathers flying all over the place."[11]

With Robinson's departure, an era had officially ended. "[Under
Aubrey] it was all cost accounting," recalled Emmy-winning television writer Loring Mandel. "Aubrey said, 'Why should we pay
twenty-five cents a head for fourteen million people to watch *Playhouse 90* when we can get fourteen million people to watch old
movies at ten cents a head?' *That's* why *Playhouse 90* went off the
air. That's why drama went off the air. The people like Hubbell,
and Felix Jackson, and John Houseman [who had also produced
for *90*], and any number of others, people who were skilled in drama
who were producers were all pushed out. When Aubrey came in,
virtually every producer who had any theatrical qualifications at all
was pushed out."[12]

Zone director Buzz Kulik agreed. "Aubrey, in my opinion,
changed the entire complexion of television, much for the worse.
He was the one who killed live television because it was not financially remunerative compared to situation comedies. He went to
film right away and made all those sitcoms, and there would be
syndication and all kinds of other ways of making a buck with it,
and you could do it more cheaply than doing the *Playhouse 90*s
and the *Twilight Zone*s and the *Climax*es we were doing. He also
had a very strong personality, had his own ideas and theories, and
put them through. He was a one-man government, his was the right
way, everybody else's was the wrong way."[13]

With Robinson—who had once called Serling one of the hopes
of the medium—gone, Rod Serling had lost his most influential
patron at CBS. What William Lewis, the CBS vice-president in the
1930s, had been to Norman Corwin—an internal, corporate
patron—Hubbell Robinson had been to Rod Serling in the mid-to-
late-1950s. Now Robinson was gone, and the in-house perception
of what had been Serling's home network had drastically changed.

Until then, Serling had been considered "one of the jewels in the
CBS crown," according to former CBS programming head Mike
Dann. "He gave CBS as much character as Lucille Ball and Edward
R. Murrow."[14]

"Aubrey wouldn't have given a guy like Rod creative run of the house in terms of development," said Del Reisman. "It just went against his grain. He really wanted to be in charge." Serling's new hosting duties put a face on his unwelcome strain of TV auteurism.[15]

During his overt Angry-Man years in the late 1950s, Serling's major grievance with commercial television had been censorship. Indeed, that was one of the major reasons Serling had entered *The Twilight Zone*. As he had hoped, this was no longer a major concern. Aside from the normal standards and practices, where potentially offensive words or phrases were excised by a network censor at an early stage of revisions, both the networks and sponsors left Serling and his crew alone as far as thematic or stylistic concerns went. As Carol Serling put it, "The TV censors left him alone, either because they didn't understand what he was doing or believed that he was truly in outer space."[16]

Serling did continue to exercise fairly complete creative control over his show. Instead of resorting to censorship, Aubrey, who was apparently determined to see Serling's one-man show canceled as soon as possible, began to make Serling's life miserable by pulling in the financial reins. Under a complex formula, the production costs of *The Twilight Zone*—an average of fifty thousand dollars per episode—were jointly underwritten by CBS and the show's two sponsors (whoever they happened to be at the time), with the network assuming the accountant's role.

Thus, as the second season progressed, Serling and Buck Houghton found themselves being visited more and more by inquisitive network representatives. Often, the only way the producers could bring the show in under the agreed-upon budget, once the sets and costumes had been pared down to a workable minimum, was by cutting out entire speaking parts.

"Jim Aubrey was a very, very difficult problem for the show," said Reisman. "He was particularly tough on *The Twilight Zone*, because for its time it was a particularly costly half-hour show. I spent a lot of time with Buck trying to reduce scripts, some by Rod, by one speaking part or two speaking parts because we were just about to start shooting the show and we were over budget. And Aubrey was real tough on this subject even if it was a small number of dollars."[17]

Ironically, by forcing Serling and Houghton to keep the show as sparse and unembroidered as possible, Aubrey and his auditors probably enhanced the show's storytelling power and its effectiveness. Nevertheless, Serling didn't like anyone looking over his shoulder; the collision course between him and the network had been set.

The new Serling lead-ins also increased the creative pressure on Serling to continue the high quality of writing he and his cowriters had achieved the previous year. Now his face was on the show: it had to be good.

Fortunately, the general process of producing *The Twilight Zone* was somewhat smoother the second time around (financial pressures notwithstanding), as a result of the increasingly smooth teamwork between Houghton, director of photography Clemens, Reisman, Nelson, and the rest of the *Twilight Zone* crew.

Doug Heyes credited Serling's producer with being the best line producer in the business. "Houghton was knowledgeable in all of the craft areas," said Doug Heyes, "[including the] below-the-line areas such as budgeting. Buck really brought something to the series that had a lot to do with the look. When you got into postproduction, Buck was a good, professional, workmanlike producer, and was a major factor in the look of the show."[18]

"As Rod found out that I knew what I was doing," Houghton recalled, "he produced less and less." According to Houghton, Serling was seldom at casting or postproduction meetings. "I'd show him the final copy of the pictures but sometimes he wouldn't look. He'd say, 'I'm sure it's fine.'"[19]

Serling also had total confidence in George Clemens, who, as director of photography, was probably more responsible than anyone else for the distinctive "metaphysical" look of the show. Clemens would win an Emmy for his work that year.

Heyes, who directed five episodes in the second season, including Serling's famed parable "The Eye of the Beholder," described how Houghton's "well-oiled machine" worked in practice:

> The actors got two days of rehearsal. First, with the director around the table, in the morning. The second half of that day we worked on a stage, not the stage we were shooting on, and started blocking action using functional furniture with tape marking off the sets.

The second day they actually had the sets built, and we were able to block it out on the stage we were going to film on. They might still be putzing around painting while we were working.

With George Clemens and the key grips and the electricians and so forth watching, we would rehearse. George would be telling the gaffer where to put the lights and so forth, in a soft voice, not interrupting our rehearsal at all. For example, in "The Eye of the Beholder," I wanted the effect of the bandages being unwrapped from the main character's point of view. I showed this problem to Clemens, and said, "We've got to get something around the camera that we can unwrap." So he got a fishbowl, and when we shot that sequence he was prepared for it. When things like that occur to you on the set while you're shooting, which is usually the case in television, you can't put them together in time. We were able for two days to anticipate problems that would come up during photography.[20]

With things under control on the set, Serling could concentrate on the scripts.

Searching for non-Serling scripts for the second season of *The Twilight Zone* was much less difficult, thanks to the contributions of the small stable of writers Serling had put together. During the first season, Serling had put out an open call for scripts to satisfy the non-Serling script quotient. This had proved disastrous as thousands of unsolicited scripts, mostly from nonprofessionals, streamed into Cayuga's offices. A wiser Serling then began showing screenings of the show to select groups of West Coast writers. From these screenings and meetings emerged three writers who became regular contributors to the series—George Clayton Johnson, Richard Matheson, and Charles Beaumont. The three writers' contributions were increasingly noticeable during the 1960–61 season.

George Clayton Johnson, an ex-logger-turned-beatnik, wrote "A Penny for Your Thoughts," a beguiling tale about a man (Dick York), who, with the freak flip of a coin, can hear people's thoughts. The brilliant, quirky TV writer Charles Beaumont contributed "The Howling Man," wherein a man (H. M. Wynant) discovers—and misguidedly frees—an imprisoned man (Robin Hughes) who turns out to be the devil; and "Shadow Play," about a man (Dennis

Weaver) condemned to die who is convinced that his impending peril is all just a bad dream. The fantasist Richard Matheson, already of *The Incredible Shrinking Man* fame and the most established in Serling's co-writers group, penned the classic episodes "The Invaders," an almost entirely silent episode starring Agnes Moorehead as a woman besieged by tiny creatures who turn out to be representatives of Earth (an homage to Moorehead's all-talking radio classic "Sorry, Wrong Number"); and "Nick of Time, a striking piece, starring William Shatner and Patricia Breslin, about a couple driving across country who are distracted by and temporarily obsessed with a luncheonette fortune-telling machine.

By now, *The Twilight Zone* format was fairly simple. As Richard Matheson described it, "The ideal *Twilight Zone* started with a really smashing idea that hit you right in the first few seconds, then you played that out, and you had a little flip at the end: that was the structure."[21]

The things that happened in *The Twilight Zone* had to be weird, but believable or *almost* believable. As George Clayton Johnson put it, "These were realistic fantasies about seemingly average people on average streets—a timid book clerk, a frightened old woman, an ambitious pool shark, a desperate old man in a rest home—each of whose lives would be tilted by some extraordinary magical factor."

When I started to write for *The Twilight Zone*, I adopted Rod's format. There was an attempt to match the amount of time with the amount of space taken up. If you wanted a lingering shot of a couple of trees, then you wrote half a page of florid description of those trees, and the shot would be there. If you just threw it away in a line, "There's a bunch of trees," that only lasted for an instant on the screen. So there's a matching, and the trick was learning how to apportion that and be poetic at the same time.

The thing with scripts in those days is that they were not written for a mass audience, but an audience of one—the producer. And if the producer said "Yes" to your script, then you could do rewrites on it until hell wouldn't have it, but at least you had a job and everything went well. Ultimately, these scripts became very real experiences because they were dramatized to the point where you learned about what the story was about on the last word. There was a format you could see: a certain amount of white space to the page; a certain amount of speeches to the page; a certain amount of length to the paragraphs of description; a certain amount of bated breath. The author was telling you a story and you could sense his presence, even though it was just stage directions, because of the use of metaphor.

Serling caught that quality very very well, a kind of dark and *mysterioso*, threatening and tense situation. He could put together a scene where the threat would grow: We're in an atomic bunker and is the Bomb really going to go off? Serling could build suspense through the kind of tone he worked with. He was the master so there wasn't any argument about how the scripts should look.[22]

As for the three Johnson stories that Serling adapted in the show's first season, Johnson said, "He felt free to invent or change, as an editor might, but he would start with my idea or my conclusion or some emotion that I had generated which he identified with."[23]

Indeed, Serling's adaptations usually diverged so much from the original that there was no question that they were still his scripts. In spite of this, Serling was still thorough about giving proper credit. "Some stories he bought and changed so much that he needn't have bought them in the first place," said Buck Houghton. "He was meticulous about proper credit. There's one show that was based on a conversation with a friend at a cocktail party ["I Shot an Arrow into the Air"], and Serling gave her on-screen credit for the idea."[24]

"There was a sense that we were making something absolutely dandy," said Johnson, "and we needed everybody working to do it right. I also believe that Rod had the ability to hire top-notch people."[25]

One famous writer who didn't think everything was so dandy was veteran fantasy writer Ray Bradbury, who contributed only one script to the show ("I Sing the Body Electric," which had been submitted in 1959 but was not produced until 1962). Bradbury was infuriated when Serling and Houghton rejected other scripts he had written for the show on the basis that they would be too difficult and expensive to produce. The aggrieved, and possibly jealous, older writer later loudly accused Serling of plagiarizing from his work.

"My impression of that situation was that Serling screwed Bradbury," Johnson recalled. "In some way, Bradbury was promised something, and something else happened, and poor Bradbury was the screwee and there was no way that Serling knew how to make it up."[26]

> I think Serling was intimidated and in awe of Bradbury, and I don't think that Serling was the star that Bradbury was in that field of writing. Serling didn't know how to deal with crowds the way Bradbury did [for instance]. I think that when he was around Bradbury, he felt Bradbury to be the greater celebrity. I think that a lot of Bradbury was used in *The Twilight Zone*. A lot of his most unique and most Bradburian ideas were common property. The field was so heavily marked by Bradbury there was no way Serling could walk across it without stepping in some of Bradbury's footprints. I stole from Bradbury. I'm sure Beaumont did, too. We all stole from him. Bradbury was the seminal influence.[27]

Serling's "gremlins," as he liked to call his co-writers, formed a kind of club within a club on *The Twilight Zone*, as actor William Shatner recalled. "There was a group of five or six of them called 'The Green Thumb,' " said Shatner. "I was allowed in because I had done some Richard Matheson and George Clayton Johnson stuff. But the best of them was Beaumont. He was their mentor, and they met at his house. And he'd say 'Let's do this!' and they'd all charge out into the night to do something or another.[28]

"These guys were on the fringes of success. If they had been more successful, they wouldn't have been what they were. They were a rat pack on the fringes of the successful writers. They were doing shows like *The Twilight Zone* while other people were doing movies or whatever. They also did a lot of motorcycling."[29]

Serling reveled in the role of paterfamilias of this unique, talented group. Of course, sometimes even a paterfamilias can get mad.

"He was very professional about accepting suggestions from us," said Del Reisman. "But there were times when he would be very upset and say, 'No, no, I like it the way it is.'[30]

"He had a temper and sometimes he would go through periods when he was relatively uncommunicative. He would want certain

167

things done and he'd get annoyed that they weren't done his way, he'd get upset. We were a family, and like we did with our families, you got angry, you got pissed off at your family because you were with them all the time. So when Rod would get pissed off, he'd show it. He didn't blow up or anything. He was human: he had his moments of irritation and temper and they were visible."[31]

However, in general, *The Twilight Zone* family, Serling included, was a happy one, and when the manic executive producer did visit the set, usually after filming a group of his host spots, he usually was in a chipper mood.

Serling was particularly admired by his actors. "What Rod did," said Reisman, "that I think the actors especially appreciated was that he made himself available—and the actors had confidence because if there was a problem, there he was."[32]

If Serling wasn't physically available, for example when he was back East, he was always a phone call away, ready to lend assurance, or, if necessary, to exert his executive authority, as actor Cliff Robertson discovered during a rare set dispute between director of photography George Clemens and himself that broke out while the *Twilight Zone* company was filming "A Hundred Yards Over the Rim" on location in the Mojave Desert in March 1961. The second season episode, one of the numerous Serling scripts using the accident of stepping backward—or forward—in time as its principal plot device, was supposed to be about a Jacksonian era pioneer (Robertson) whose search for medical help for his dying son takes him "a hundred yards over the rim" of the next hill and smack into present-day New Mexico.

A stickler for authenticity, Robertson had carefully researched the historical background for his role and had concluded that his character, Christian Horn, ought to wear a stovepipe hat (instead of the cowboylike outfit the wardrobe department had proposed) and brought one with him to the set. Clemens, looking through the lens, thought Robertson's headgear made him look ridiculous and said so. "I was scared we'd be laughed off the screen in the first scene," he recalled. Robertson, sticking by his guns, insisted on wearing it, and director Buzz Kulik agreed. Producer Houghton took Clemens's side. Production stopped. There was only one solution to the stalemate: call Serling.[33]

"Let Cliff wear the hat," Serling ruled after hearing both sides, much to Clemens's and Houghton's dismay and Robertson's delight.[34]

"Rod was very sensitive to the artist's needs," Robertson recalled, still savoring his triumph. "He was not one of those producer types who ran roughshod over actors. He really backed us up." Fortified by Serling's decision, Robertson went on to turn in a bravura performance—and Clemens and Robertson wound up patching things up.[35]

It was such positive experiences that made "repeaters" of actors like Robertson: actors and actresses who appeared in *The Twilight Zone* more than once. Noted performers who made more than one detour through *The Twilight Zone* during the show's five seasons would include Burgess Meredith and Jack Klugman (4 appearances); Martin Landau, Fritz Weaver, Lee Marvin, Anne Francis, Claude Akins, Jack Warden, William Shatner, Inger Stevens, George Grizzard, Joseph Schildkraut, Ed Wynn, Dick York, and Jack Weston (2 appearances each).

"That second year, I can't think of anyone who turned down a chance to do the show," said George Clemens. "Even if they had to cut their pay in half."[36]

Serling was more likely to hang out with actors, with whom he felt more sympathetic, than with his writers, who tended to make him feel insecure. One of the actors with whom Serling felt especially simpatico was his fellow ex-paratrooper Jack Warden. "He wanted things right," Warden remembered, "and yet he had a lovely way of telling you. He wasn't adamant about it. He'd listen to you. And a worker! God, he worked all the time." Like many of Serling's friends and colleagues, Warden was bothered by Serling's intense chain smoking. "I've never seen anyone smoke like Rod. I don't think I ever saw him without a cigarette in his hand, always taking those deep inhalations."[37]

As chief writer, Serling continued in his role as video Aesop, using the show as a personal bully pulpit to comment metaphorically on the aspects of human behavior and the human condition that made him angry. Thus, his morality play, "The Eye of the Beholder," directed by Doug Heyes, which first aired on November 11, 1960.

In a dark hospital room, a woman (played successively by Maxine Stuart and Donna Douglas) awaits the results of cosmetic surgery that will finally make her look "normal." As her bandages are removed, her surgeon and nurses recoil in horror—"No change. No change at all!"—though the woman appears quite beautiful.

Then the lights come on and we realize that the drama has taken place in another world, a world whose inhabitants are (to us) gargoyled. Only then do we understand the lesson of the episode:

"Beauty *is* in the eye of the beholder, in this year, or a hundred years hence," as Serling says in his closing narration. "On this planet, or wherever there is human life, perhaps out among the stars. Beauty is in the eye of the beholder. Lesson to be learned . . . in the Twilight Zone."[38]

Serling's roots as a radio writer were especially evident in "The Eye of the Beholder," director Heyes noted. "That was like a radio show because you only heard voices. I didn't even look at the actors when they came in for interviews. I sat with my back to them and listened to their voices because I knew I wouldn't be seeing their faces—I cast it as if I were casting a radio show. They all had to have very sympathetic, warm voices."[39]

The second season also featured Serling's stirring, frightening cautionary tale about the power of the state, "The Obsolete Man," broadcast June 2, 1961, which directly descended from Archibald MacLeish's "The Fall of the City."

In a futuristic society where books have been banned, the Chancellor of the state (Fritz Weaver) has declared a humble librarian, Wordsworth (Burgess Meredith), "obsolete," and sentences him to death. Wordsworth, as his final request, has the Chancellor join him shortly before his death. To his horror, the future *Führer* finds himself locked in a room with the librarian—reading from the Bible—and a ticking bomb. Seconds before the explosion, the Chancellor breaks down and yells, "In the name of God, let me out!" Wordsworth allows the Chancellor to escape and is himself killed. But the librarian has triumphed: moments later, a court pronounces the *ex*-Chancellor obsolete and a furious crowd tears him to pieces.[40]

All told, the second season, during which Serling adapted or wrote twenty scripts, was another outstanding personal, as well as team, achievement. The Academy of Television Arts and Sciences again recognized this, nominating Serling once again for Outstanding Writing Achievement in Drama, an award that he won on May 16, 1961.

For Serling, this unprecedented fifth Emmy, and the second for his *Twilight Zone* writing, was especially sweet. The year before he had the novelty factor going for him—as well as a sizable CBS advertising campaign. This time he felt, quite rightly, that he had won on his own merits.

Serling was characteristically magnanimous in accepting his fifth Emmy, taking pains to give credit to his principal co-writers.

"I want to thank three writing gremlins who did the bulk of the work: Charles Beaumont, Richard Matheson, and George Clayton Johnson," he said as the audience at the ceremony applauded.

"Come on over fellas," he exhorted his smiling gremlins, "and we'll carve it up like a turkey!"

"Rod was generous," George Clayton Johnson said, looking back. "He'd done the bulk of the work, and though Charles and Richard and I joked about making a visit to Rod with a hacksaw, we all knew whose Emmy it was."[41]

12
ICON
(1961)

"People stop me, question me, ask for autographs," he says. A note of bitterness crept in: "Next year, I'm going to do the commercials— 'In the Twilight Zone, nine out of ten doctors recommend you smoke . . .' " He laughed. "They'll say I've really sold out."
   —from an interview with Serling by Cecil Smith of the *Los Angeles Times*, April 23, 1961

By 1961, *The Twilight Zone* had become something of an institution. The phrase had passed into the mainstream of American language: "Man, I was in the Twilight Zone!" boxer Archie Moore exclaimed after being knocked out in a 1961 match.[1]

In March of that year, Secretary of Defense Robert McNamara warned the Communist bloc about starting "twilight zone" wars. "Man," a startled Serling proclaimed after hearing that. "Now we really have arrived!"[2]

Indeed, *The Twilight Zone* actually seemed to have won the Kennedy Administration's seal of approval, as expressed by maverick FCC chairman Newton Minow in the latter's celebrated "vast wasteland" speech of May 1961. That was how Minow described the current video landscape, especially in dramatic and children's programming. But he identified a few exceptions—one of them, *The Twilight Zone*.

Nevertheless, Serling had become disillusioned with the *Zone* and the *Zone* phenomenon; and the sheer exhaustion of having written so many of the first three seasons' scripts had begun to set in. He had also become increasingly disenchanted with the network that had spawned him, CBS.

"I have to have a special feeling about CBS," Serling had told Mike Wallace in 1959 when he was defending *The Twilight Zone* and his special association with CBS.[3] Earlier, he had also iterated these feelings before the FCC.

But the era at CBS that Serling had had such a feeling for was now over. Hubbell Robinson's forced departure confirmed that. So, for that matter, had the resignation of fellow TV critic and chain-smoker Murrow, who had quit the increasingly pressurized confines of CBS management in 1961 to accept a position with the Kennedy Administration as head of the United States Information Agency, after his show, *See It Now*, was canceled by William Paley and the powers that be.

Only one year before, in an apparent surge of gratitude, the creator of *The Twilight Zone* publicly thanked CBS in an article in *TV Guide* for giving the show "a legitimate chance to prove itself and allowing it to get into high gear."[4]

However, by the end of 1961 those proprietary feelings were fast disappearing, largely as a result of his increasing fights with Aubrey and his men over money.

Like any good producer, Serling generally managed to shield the rest of his crew from network-induced problems. "They didn't bring their fights with CBS to me," said Doug Heyes. "That was one of the great things about *The Twilight Zone*. I had total freedom. Sometimes I would think of an idea that would make the episode more *Twilight Zone*-y [but] that would require some expense. I remember one episode, 'The Chaser,' in which I devised a huge bookcase that must have doubled the budget, but they [Serling and Houghton] never blinked an eye. They just said, 'Okay, great!' I didn't have to argue with anybody over the money—*they'd* argue about the money and let me have it! I knew that they were having problems with Jim Aubrey, but they kept them away from me. My responsibility was to get the job done."[5]

Serling was so determined not to let budgetary problems get in the way of putting out the best *Twilight Zone* possible, according to George Clemens, that he occasionally made up for the cost overrun on expensive sets out of his own funds. "Rod would say, 'Don't worry about the budget,' " said Clemens. " 'I'll take care of it.' And he did. I'd ask him, 'Do you want me to do anything different?' He'd say, 'No! Just go the way you were going in and I'll fight it out.' "[6]

Thus, Serling and Houghton were generally able to maintain the high quality of the first two seasons. Still, some of Serling's colleagues could see that all wasn't entirely well.

"There was one incident I remember," Richard Matheson said. "Rod had this film society that Chuck Beaumont and I belonged to. One night, we were invited to Rod's house to watch *The Incredible Shrinking Man* while he was at a meeting [with CBS West Coast executives]. When he came back, he looked like death warmed over. He was incredibly worn out. I remember feeling sorry that he was living under such stress: the lot of the famous writer. 'You wouldn't believe the day I had,' he said to Carol.[7]

"I've always thought that Serling's life was shortened by the pressures he dealt with on *The Twilight Zone*."[8]

Encounters like these weren't easy for the network men either. "He was impossible," said Mike Dann, one of those whose job was to rein in Serling. "He could be suicidal with regards to his career." Still, Dann, unlike Aubrey, admired Serling immensely. "He *loved* television. He had a passion for this business. And he was a martinet as far as the show was concerned. He never brought it in late."[9]

William Self, one of the chief executives in CBS's Hollywood office with whom Serling dealt, described what a typical meeting with the increasingly mercurial host, head writer, and executive producer of *The Twilight Zone* was like: "He came into my office one day, and he told me a story for a *Twilight Zone* episode. He acted it out for me, in great detail. At the end, he said, 'How do you like it?' and I said, 'I don't like it.' And he kind of got angry for a minute, then he said, 'Okay, I'm never going to tell you another story—from now on, you'll have to read them!' It wasn't a temper, it was sort of a momentary explosion, then he was right back to being friendly."[10]

As Serling himself admitted, he was a "pop-off."

At one point during the prior season, after Serling and Houghton had been forced to economize by videotaping six episodes rather than filming them, Serling actually tendered his resignation from the show.

Of course, it had only been a bluff. As much as Serling disliked James Aubrey and his breed and was rapidly becoming disillusioned with both CBS and the television industry as a whole, he still loved putting on *The Twilight Zone*. "At least three or four days a month," Serling's friend Dick Berg remembered, "he would come to me with the joy of something that happened on the set that day, an actor whom he had worked with like Bob Redford [who appeared in the third season episode "Nothing In The Dark"], or a director who was new who had done something terrific. He adored the freshness of the milieu, each show was a new experience for him, new cast, new directors."[11]

Moreover, Serling couldn't afford to resign—at least, he didn't think he could afford to resign (which was the same thing). CBS might have been dissatisfied with its 60 percent share of the profits from *The Twilight Zone*, which allowed the network to do little more than break even on its investment. But the 40 percent of the show that Serling owned had already made him wealthy. In 1960 and 1961, Serling reported incomes of $100,000 and $130,000; with tax shelters taken into account, he was earning something in the area of a quarter of a million dollars per year—the equivalent of $700,000 or $800,000 today—making him one of the wealthiest writers in the country. And he liked that.

Furthermore, by that point, Serling's increasingly flamboyant lifestyle had begun to *require* that kind of money. How else was he supposed to pay the maintenance on his house and his pool and his tennis court and his three cars—including a purple 1936 Auburn Boatail Speedster, which beeped out the theme song from *Bridge on the River Kwai* when Serling pressed the horn—and the cottage on Cayuga and the new cabin cruiser he had just put on the lake? How else was he to pay his maid and two secretaries and the Dictaphone repairman and Jody's riding instructor? The Serlings—both of them—had bought into Hollywood with a vengeance, and television paid the bills. Or, as Serling himself candidly put it in an interview with the *Ithaca Journal*, "Television is my bridge to affluence."[12] *The Twilight Zone* paid the toll.

Increasingly, Serling was falling into the same trap that Ernie Pandish, the protagonist of "The Velvet Alley," had been warned about. "You know how they do it," warns one of Ernie's directors when the writer arrives in Hollywood. "They give you a thousand dollars a week, and they keep giving it to you until you can't live without it. Then they start to talk about taking it away, and there isn't anything you won't do to keep that thousand dollars a week."[13]

Some of Serling's old acquaintances from Cincinnati and Westport, like the Marmers, already felt that Serling had "gone Hollywood." Another friend who felt this way was former Westport neighbor Robert Wise, who was chagrined when he could not get to visit his old friend on a visit to Los Angeles. "I had maintained phone contact," Wise remembered, "and each time I was out there, I tried to see Rod, but I could never get to see him."[14]

> Finally, the last time, I had said to my wife, 'You have to meet Rod, he's the most delightful person you'll ever meet, he'll leave a lasting impression on you.' She was really looking forward to it. I called him at the studio, at his office. I told his secretary who it was, and she came back on the phone and said, 'Mr. Wise, Mr. Serling is very busy, but there'll be two free tickets for you to Television City.' I said something like, 'Can you tell Rod, for me, that he can stick the tickets.' I became very angry. I mean, this was not the Rod Serling I knew. I had thought he could never go Hollywood, but he did. I never had any further contact with Rod after that phone call.[15]

"I only met him once, in 1961," said writer Loring Mandel. "In that meeting, I sensed someone who had retained the values of New York, aesthetically, but who had certainly made the compromises he felt he had to make in order to play the game out there. I thought he played the game very well."[16]

Serling was aware that Hollywood and television had changed him, according to Del Reisman. "I believe that that concerned him all of the time."

Serling, who prided himself on being a man of traditional—nay, biblical—values, also felt guilty about his continuing relationship with former women's tennis pro Alice Marble, a liaison that had grown into an affair a few years earlier. Nevertheless, he was sufficiently at ease about the romance to escort Marble to Hollywood parties. This did not ensure a happy countenance. "Ulcers made him perpetually grim-faced," Marble wrote in her autobiography. "Rod would sometimes sit all evening at a party and not say a word. Yet he loved [his work] with a passion, and the crew on his show thought highly of him. So did I. He had a marvelous mind, and we got along well. I often typed his scripts for him, and if I changed one comma he would notice and tell me he didn't need an editor."[17]

Inevitably, Serling's growing daughters felt that they were being cheated of their father's time and love, but, following their mother's lead, they kept their frustration locked up inside.

Nevertheless by the winter of 1960, Serling recognized that his life was seriously askew. He didn't want to quit television altogether. But he knew he needed to regain his bearings. So, in December, the harried writer-producer wrote to officials at Antioch College requesting that they consider taking him on as a sort of writer-in-residence during the 1962–63 academic year, by which time he hoped to be free enough of his contractual obligations to CBS and *The Twilight Zone* to effect such escape.

Flattered, Antioch officials readily accepted Serling's offer. They could only pay him three thousand dollars, they warned, but he was welcome to come back to Yellow Springs and teach.

Beginning in 1961, Serling also began putting other irons in the fire, partly out of distraction, partly to broaden his professional horizons, partly for the money.

He signed up with NBC to write a ninety-minute special adaptation of Somerset Maugham's play *Rain* for Marilyn Monroe and Fredric March that was to have marked Monroe's debut on television. "I went back to the Maugham story ['Miss Thompson'], never looked at the play," an enthusiastic Serling told his friend columnist Cecil Smith of the *Los Angeles Times*. "But my Sadie Thompson is not exactly Maugham's—she's a beautiful, lost woman; she's Monroe."[18] Unfortunately, the unstable actress's deteriorating mental health forced a cancellation of his brief collaboration with Hollywood's greatest sex symbol. Serling later called Monroe "a warm, friendly, beautiful, but odd girl."[19]

He also invested more and more of his time in preparing "Requiem for a Heavyweight" for the big screen. At one time, it had been Serling's hope to successfully adapt his still-famous *Playhouse 90* script for the Broadway stage. However, his partners in the project, David Susskind, Serling's comrade from the live television days, and Ralph Nelson, who had directed the teleplay, decided that the property would work better as a film, especially if they could get Anthony Quinn, who had been Serling's first choice for the Mountain McClintock role, for the lead.

To Serling's delight, Susskind and Nelson were able to collar Quinn. He attacked the screenplay forthwith, not being satisfied until he had produced four drafts.

Still smarting from the critical and commercial failure of his previous screenwriting efforts, and conscious of his relatively low place on the Hollywood totem pole, Serling hoped that *Requiem* would finally establish him in the movie industry for good.

Sydney Pollack described how the status-conscious media-industry town was constituted at the time:

> There was a first wave that came in from live television, which [Arthur] Penn was a part of, John Frankenheimer, Sidney Lumet, and Rod. Then in the late fifties, television made the transition to film. By the time I became a director in nineteen sixty, all of the shows were on film. Although some shows continued to work on tape, the bulk of the shows, even anthology shows, were done on film.[20]
>
> The first wave came out of multi-camera television. When the second wave came in, all of us came out of filmed television. There was no question that television in those days was something you went through, a rite of passage to get to a film career. In the pecking order, you would say that the film people were a bit more respected in the community, and most of the people who really shone in television moved rapidly into film.[21]

Although he still felt comfortable with television, Serling was anxious to move up the ladder. *Requiem* seemed to be the ticket.

Significantly, Serling installed his original ending in the film version, which had Mountain McClintock (renamed Rivera) selling out and becoming a wrestler. This non-Hollywood, more realistic ending made the message of the film—that money *does* have the power to rob a person's dignity—much more powerful. Most of the original scenes from the video version were kept. Ill at ease with all of the extra screen time on his hands, Serling also chose to pad the script with a number of unnecessary and unbelievable characters, including "Ma," a female gangster.

Filming got under way in the fall of 1961, with Jackie Gleason, on his own sabbatical from television, playing Maish, and Mickey Rooney in the role of Army—and a nervous, puffing, coffee-slurping Serling hovering nearby.

Behaving with increasing impetuosity and, apparently without much direction from his handlers at Ashley-Steiner, Serling took advantage of new opportunities to exploit his growing popularity. If *The Twilight Zone* had become an institution, Serling had become, for better or for worse, an icon. His visage, like that of Alfred Hitchcock, had become synonymous in the public's mind with the fantastic and the weird. And Serling, like Hitchcock, decided to roll with it.

"Another startling pack of weirdies out of that wonderful place!" announced the cover page of *New Stories from the Twilight Zone*, an instant collection of adapted *Twilight Zone* scripts, published in 1962. Below the headline was a large likeness of Serling's famous countenance, split open and spilling over with Hieronymus Bosch-like characters.[22] The first of five such anthologies, the Serling *Stories* would eventually sell over a million copies to hardcore "Zonies" (as the show's aficionados came to be called).

Serling also began receiving—and accepting—invitations to parody himself and his *Twilight Zone* persona on other television shows. In January 1962, he guest-starred on *The Jack Benny Show*, where he played straight man in a sketch pairing Benny as his usual skinflint with a certain "Mr. Twi."

He also made a surprise appearance in a similar *Zone* send-up on *The Garry Moore Show*. Carol Burnett, who played opposite Serling in the piece, vividly recalled the occasion. "He did exactly what he did on *The Twilight Zone*—all of that jargon that he would do when introducing a story of his own. This particular one had Durwood Kirby and I doing a takeoff of his own. Fortunately, Rod had the good humor to put himself on and do the introduction."

"*The Twilight Zone* was a major show—otherwise a variety show like Garry's wouldn't have been doing a takeoff on it. I remember when he walked out of the fog, at the beginning of the sketch, he hadn't been announced as a guest star at the top of the show, and the audience went crazy.[23]

"After we taped Garry's show, we went out and got a burger and went bowling, I think," the comedienne said. "Then Rod asked if I would do a guest appearance on his show. Of course, I was delighted to do it."[24]

The result was "Cavender Is Coming," a third-season teleplay directed by Chris Nyby, about a bumbling guardian angel (Jesse White) and his attempts to make a klutzy woman (Burnett) happy. Like several of Serling's other attempts to inject humor into *The Twilight Zone*, and to tailor scripts specifically for certain stars like

Burnett and Ed Wynn (for whom Serling had penned "One for the Angels" in the first season), it was not very effective. Serling the self-satirizing actor proved funnier than Serling the comic writer.

Encouraged by the reception of his walk-ons, Serling made a stab at starting a non-*Twilight Zone* acting career, with a starring appearance on "Ichabod and Me," a CBS comedy about a famous writer who moves to a small Vermont town and tries to stay incommunicado, to the chagrin of the editor of the local paper. The show was telecast on March 20, 1962, to the amusement and befuddlement of millions of Rod Serling fans. Of his short-lived acting career, on which he received unanimously poor reviews, Serling said, "I decided to quit while I was behind."[25] He was far more effective playing himself in "The Man in the Funny Suit," a drama about the behind-the-scenes drama of Ed Wynn's performance in the teleplay of "Requiem," written and directed by Ralph Nelson.

Still mindful of his reputation as the television industry's "chief critic" (according to a 1961 issue of *Television Age*), Serling also made time to participate in a printed *TV Guide* discussion with Reginald Rose over the question, "Can a TV Writer Keep His Integrity?"

Yes, he could, declared Rose, pointing to the success of his own controversy-based, top-rated drama, *The Defenders*.

"No," started Serling. "As writers, we have to work within the limits of—"

"Speak for yourself," Rose interrupted. "Personally, I have integrity. In all my work, my main purpose has always been to project my own view of good and evil—and this is the *essence* of controversy. What is your purpose?"

"If I have a preoccupation," replied Serling, "it is with conflict rather than with morality—the conflict of age versus youth, the lonely versus the mob. Too often when I've gone after moral themes with both hands—such as prejudice, which I abhor more than anything in the world—what I've wrought is not entertainment but pamphleteering. I am not disciplined enough to handle objectively and validly ideas that I have violently strong feelings about. I usually shy away from themes of good and evil."[26]

In spite of his appearances elsewhere, Serling was still anxious for *The Twilight Zone* to stay on the air, so much so that in another seemingly contradictory move, Serling broke one of his old rules and agreed to take on the additional role of commercial spokesman for Oasis cigarettes, the show's sponsor at the time. Well, didn't Mike Wallace do the commercials for his show, he rationalized? Why couldn't he? As always, Serling couldn't say no.

However, as always, Serling's most effective soapbox remained *The Twilight Zone.* In retrospect, probably the most striking quality about the scripts he wrote for the third season was the way they closely reflected current events and personalities about which the creator felt strongly. In this respect, *The Twilight Zone*, when decoded, becomes a script for the liberal conscience of the early 1960s.

Serling's increasingly scattered and grim mind-set was reflected in the scripts he wrote that season, which included two more episodes devoted to nuclear paranoia, a favorite theme of his.

"The Shelter" (directed by Lamont Johnson) was inspired by the then highly topical atom bomb shelter craze, and one cleric's comment that Americans would be justified in keeping their neighbors out of their shelter during an actual atomic attack. In the show, a radio announces to a small group of neighbors gathered for a party to honor their neighborhood doctor that UFOs have been sighted and everyone should run for their shelters. Doc Stockton (Larry Gates) locks his family in their shelter, but his neighbors are unprepared: they plead with Stockton for entry, but are refused. Their anger boils to the point where they break down the shelter door—just as the radio announces that the UFO sightings were a false alarm. Doc knows, however, that the experience has served to destroy them by revealing the ape within us all.

"No moral, no message, no prophetic tract," Serling orated at the show's end. "Just a simple statement of fact: for civilization to survive, the human race has to remain civilized. Tonight's very small exercise in logic from the Twilight Zone."[27]

Serling also used Armageddon as an element of revenge in "One More Pallbearer," also directed by Lamont Johnson, starring Joseph Wiseman as a bitter man who devises an elaborate scheme—including faking a nuclear holocaust—to force three people into apologizing for humiliating him at earlier points in his life.

Serling meted out nightmarish justice of a worse kind in "Deaths-head Revisited" (directed by Don Medford), Serling's statement on the Holocaust, written in reaction to the then-ongoing Eichmann trial, in which a former Nazi, played by Oscar Beregi, on a nostalgic visit to Dachau, is haunted and ultimately driven insane by the ghosts of inmates he had killed there during the war. There were a lot of people going mad on *The Twilight Zone* that year.

"All the Dachaus must remain standing," Serling sermonized. "They must remain standing because they are a monument to a moment in time when some men decided to turn the Earth into a graveyard." As a minor form of memorial, Serling scripted the only epilogue that didn't end with the words "the Twilight Zone": "And the moment we forget this, the moment we cease to be haunted by its remembrance, then we become gravediggers. Something to dwell on not only in the Twilight Zone, but wherever men walk God's Earth."[28]

Serling's morbidity was also reflected in two of the scariest scripts he ever wrote, "To Serve Man" and "It's a Good Life." The former, directed by Richard Bare and loosely based on a short story by Damon Knight, concerns the arrival on earth of the Kanamits, seven-foot aliens who promise prosperity and peace to all the people of the world. Soon, many earthlings are on their way to the Kanamits' home planet, including Chambers (Lloyd Bochner), a language specialist who has tried to decode a Kanamit book, *To Serve Man*. Just as he is boarding the spacecraft, his horrified assistant yells to him: the book is a cookbook, and man is the main course!

"It's a Good Life," directed by James Sheldon and based on a short story by Jerome Bixby, is one of the series' most chilling and best-remembered episodes. In the program, the residents of Peaksville, Ohio, are in terror because of the powers of a "monster" that resides there—six-year-old Anthony Fremont (Billy Mumy), a wide-eyed boy who can control nature and frequently turns people he doesn't like into grotesque creatures or "wishes them away to the cornfield." At a surprise party for neighbor Dan Hollis (Don Keefer), Anthony controls the entertainment and refuses to let an increasingly drunk Hollis listen to a Perry Como record—his sole birthday present. While distracting Anthony with his antics, Hollis pleads with the others to sneak up behind the boy and kill him—but they are petrified with fear. Hollis is turned into a jack-in-the-box. That evening, Anthony makes it snow, destroying his family's crops. His father (John Larch) doesn't get upset, however: "It's good you're making it snow, Anthony, real good," he says, almost in hysteria, as he looks out at the destruction his child has wrought. "And tomorrow's gonna be a *real good day!!!*"[29]

* * *

In retrospect, the end of the third season would have been a good time for Serling to take a permanent leave—not merely a sabbatical—from *The Twilight Zone*.

The opportunity to make a graceful exit from the series appeared in the spring of 1962 when the show was late in getting a sponsor and was edged off the fall schedule by another program, *Fair Exchange*, a family-oriented situation comedy in the Aubrey mold. Without a sponsor, Serling was unable to make a commitment to his crew for another season's work, with the result that he lost his key producer and collaborator, Buck Houghton.

Ironically, it was Serling's former patron, Hubbell Robinson, recently returned to CBS (after reportedly begging for his job back), who persuaded Serling to keep *The Twilight Zone* going by filming a series of one-hour episodes to be used as a replacement series in the spring of 1963.

"I begged him not to go to an hour," said Houghton, who went on to work for *The Richard Boone Show*. "I felt that the hour show was a bad idea. The problem was that suspension of disbelief—how long? And while they made some good ones, they made some very bad ones because of their inability to hold that belief. They had to have two miracles in the same show, and that the audience won't stand for. That was my position, and I begged them not to go to an hour because I thought they could not be done well. Rod wanted *The Twilight Zone* to keep going."[30]

"I didn't realize how tired he was," said Houghton, "but I was tired and he was tired. But he wanted *The Twilight Zone* to go on in any form it could."[31]

And so Serling spent the summer of 1962 producing a series of hour-long shows for producer Herbert Hirschmann, shows that would ultimately become the content of *The Twilight Zone*'s fourth season.

Serling's appearance at the 1962 Emmy Awards, his eighth appearance in nine years, and his third straight for *The Twilight Zone*, ought to have been at least a pleasant one—even though he wound up losing to Reginald Rose. Instead, it provided the scene for one of the most embarrassing moments of his career.

In deference to Serling's stature, the National Academy had asked Serling to act as one of the presenters. At the same time, Schlitz, one of the sponsors for the Emmys, offered Serling three thousand dollars to do a series of beer commercials.

Early on in the ceremonies, after the show's rousing opening number, the announcer's voice boomed out, "Ladies and gentlemen, the winner of five Emmy Awards, Mr. Rod Serling!" And there Serling was, nattily attired in a tuxedo, holding a frothy mug of Schlitz, inviting the audience to enjoy the show courtesy of the Joseph Schlitz company. There were two other spots throughout the presentation, each of which began with an introduction by television's most honored writer—and ended with Serling plugging the monster-sized brew.

"When the show was over," clucked an article shortly afterward in the *Dayton Daily News*, "Rod grabbed his wife and beat the well-known hasty retreat into the night."[32] For the moment, the overexposed writer was thankfully off TV. But he would be back.

13
SLOW FADE TO BLACK
(1962 – 64)

"It's a different kind of pleasure," he explained. "And, to me, a more acceptable one. I'm on the line back there, too. Those kids look at me and say: 'You're a big time Hollywood writer. Why?' "
—from an interview in the *Binghamton Press*, December 12, 1962

Serling was still the star of his own inner drama when he arrived in Yellow Springs on Labor Day, 1962, as Antioch's newest writer-in-residence, and publicly announced the reasons for his momentous return to academia.

"I'm doing this for three reasons," the thirty-seven-year-old told the press. "To regain my perspective, to do a little work, and to spend the rest of my time getting acquainted with my wife and children."[1] Unfortunately, Serling's very public inner drama was about to enter its last disillusioning act.

Serling's relatively light teaching load allowed him to accomplish his laudable objectives. He taught three courses a week: "Mass Media," a survey course about the "social and historical implications of the media," and "Writing in Dramatic Form," both for undergraduates; and "Drama and Mass Media" for adults. He was paid the less than grand sum of three thousand dollars—the equivalent, he frequently joked, of what he had received for doing those now-infamous Schlitz commercials. The rest of the time he was free to do whatever he wanted.

Serling had looked forward to mixing it up with the current crop of Antiochans. He numbered college students among his most avid

185

fans and naturally expected an enthusiastic reception from the newest Antiochans. He didn't get it. Antioch was still nonconformist Antioch. Serling's much-touted success in "the real world" worked against him: now he was seen as part of the Establishment, even if he *had* gone to Antioch once.

Instead of the deferential welcome he apparently expected, the novice teacher frequently found himself being "baited" by his younger students, according to his old teacher and friend Nolan Miller.

Publicly, Serling claimed to find his students' skepticism bracing. "A guy's reputation means nothing to these kids," he declared in a CBS press release from Yellow Springs. "You have to prove yourself every step of the way in the crucible of intellectual combat."[2] Privately, the harried writer-teacher was despondent about his inability to communicate with the younger generation. Already plagued with insecurity about his artistic status, he was particularly stung by the caustic, occasionally sneering reaction to his work. After he showed "Walking Distance" to his class, one of the students typically accused him of tacking on a "trick ending."[3] (Serling was so anxious to get in touch with his students that he reportedly took LSD with one group of Antiochans and went "tripping" in the Glen.)

The alienated writer found a more sympathetic audience in his older, adult students. Serling was especially delighted to discover that one of these was his former mentor, Pearl Bentel, who had come from Pittsburgh to learn about television writing from her former prodigy. Bentel noticed the world-weariness behind the traditional Serling bonhomie. After one class, Serling accompanied his students to a showing of *Da Vinci*, a documentary about the Italian master that was then playing at the Little Art Theater in Yellow Springs.

Afterward, walking home, as Bentel sadly recalled in her diary, Serling kept repeating da Vinci's dying, self-admonitory words, as though he felt they applied to him: "May God forgive me for not having used my talents."[4]

Serling's hopes for a new, improved home life were also unmet. He had hoped being back on campus would rekindle his love for Carol, and she surely did, too. Instead, it emphasized how far apart they had grown.

There was also less privacy. Now, unlike in Pacific Palisades, people could *hear* their arguments. A local poet, Judson Jerome, was one of those who witnessed the marital tension between the Serlings. Jerome remembered arriving at the Serlings' rented home in Yellow Springs one evening and walking into a crossfire of "loud, harsh words" between Rod and Carol.

The Serlings were annoyed by the constant celebrity treatment they got when they walked around town. "When we walk into the soda fountain and I am asked for autographs," Serling told one reporter, "my daughter says, 'I don't want to come anymore. I can't have a soda without people watching me.'"[5]

Serling had hoped while at Antioch to spend more time with his daughters, seven-year-old Nan and ten-year-old Jody. He didn't succeed in this effort, either. The breach between the celebrity father and his children widened, exacerbated by the former's patent disappointment in their apparent lack of literary prowess. "He'd like them to be writers," reported the *New York Journal-American*. "But so far there's no indication that they were born talented," the paper noted. "'Course,'" Serling told his interviewer, "'it's too early to tell, but I want them to do what they've got the talent for. Right now, they're only interested in horses, which isn't too bad. So maybe they'll be bookies?'"[6] (In fact, Nan would eventually become a gifted writer, although she mostly wrote for herself. Twelve years later, it was she who delivered the moving eulogy to her father at his gravesite.)

Perhaps the aspect of his sabbatical that he enjoyed most was a side job with Columbus TV station WBNS, as host and commentator for a Saturday night movie showcase, *WBNS Ten O'Clock Theatre*.

"You've been watching *Rebel Without a Cause*," ran one of Serling's typical, offbeat, on-camera sign-offs. "Violence, adolescence, and Jimmy Dean. The late Jimmy Dean has to depart the premises with at least one comment. He was an unusual guy and a skilled performer. He was also a deeply disturbed youngster whose life was chopped off with tragic prematureness. He *worked for me twice* [author's emphasis: Dean never actually worked for Serling —he did appear in one of his teleplays] in the days of the old *Kraft Theatre*. . . ."[7]

Serling was ultimately disappointed by the lukewarm reaction to the release of his own *Requiem for a Heavyweight*, which he now introduced to an appreciative audience in Yellow Springs. As with the video version, he had hoped for a knockout. He didn't quite get it, as A. H. Weiler wrote in the *New York Times*: "No knockout, this new film version . . . is a serious incisive drama that pulls no punches in its low-keyed exposure of its pitiable has-been hero and the sleazy, harried sidekicks who share his sweat-stained and blood-stained world."[8] Serling confirmed his disappointment with the finished product after a screening at the Little Art Theater in Yellow Springs. Popping up after the lights went on, the writer somewhat disingenuously blamed the film's producers for *Requiem*'s not entirely successful transition to film, particularly the romance between Quinn and the social worker (now played by Julie Harris) which the producers had insisted on. He vowed to exercise greater creative control over his future films.

Serling compensated for his mixed showing with *Requiem* by investing a great deal of his time working on the screenplay version of *Seven Days in May*, the best-selling novel by Fletcher Knebel and Charles Bailey II, the Washington–based reporters for the *Des Moines Register*, about a hypothetical American coup d'etat. "I think it's some of the best writing I've done in seven or eight years," the upbeat author told the *Los Angeles Times*.[9]

In many respects, the project, inspired by the criticism that the Kennedy Administration had been getting from the military over the proposed nuclear disarmament treaty, was tailormade for Serling. For one, he was working with director John Frankenheimer. For another, it was about two of his favorite subjects, the power of the military and nuclear disarmament (like Kennedy, the president in Knebel and Bailey's book is accused of weakness because of his support of disarmament).

This time, the dialogue—as in the climactic confrontation between liberal President Jordan Lyman (Fredric March) and the head of the conspiracy, General Scott (Burt Lancaster)—seemed to work, with so much tension crackling when the two actors played the scene that they had difficulty playing it through.

When the film was finally shown in February 1964, many critics, including Bosley Crowther of the *New York Times*, applauded Serling's work, especially his "vivid and trenchant dialogue . . . the President sadly notes the cause of such a move towards upheaval is not one's lust for power but the consequence of a concentration of fear and anxiety. The enemy is not the general, he says, it is the nuclear age. 'It happens to have killed man's faith in his ability to influence what happens to him,' he says.[10]

"If for no more than this statement, the film is worth its salt." Crowther also, rightly, gave credit for the film's success to John Frankenheimer's direction, which deftly lifts some of the tricks of pictorial and musical emphasis from the old Nazi "blitzkrieg" films. The authors of the original work were also pleased, although they had originally objected to the enhanced antimilitary slant they felt Serling gave the treatment.[11]

To Frankenheimer's and Serling's disappointment, both they and the film were passed over at Oscar time, although Edmond O'Brien did garner a much-deserved nomination for his work in the pivotal role of a boozing senator from Georgia and friend of the President's, who risks his life to prevent the government from being taken over.

Perhaps, coming so soon after the Kennedy assassination, it was too searing for the Academy of Motion Picture Arts and Sciences' tastes. Instead, *Zorba the Greek* and *My Fair Lady* walked away with most of the cinematic honors that year. Nevertheless, *Seven Days* remains one of the best serious entertainments made in the early 1960s. It may have been director Frankenheimer's finest work (*The Manchurian Candidate* possibly excepted). It certainly was Serling's outstanding screenplay.

In June, Serling returned to Binghamton for the twentieth reunion of the Binghamton Central Class of 1943.

Serling was particularly moved when he was led to the place behind the auditorium where, as a mischievous teenager, he had carved his initials, which had become something of a BCHS landmark. Carol, who seemed to associate Binghamton with Esther's disapproval of her, went along, but according to a friend decided at the last moment to stay in the car.[12]

Four months later, during the traditional *Twilight Zone* production break, Serling made another pilgrimage to the past, this one of a more wrenching kind. Early in 1963, the Kennedy Administration's culture-conscious State Department, which had eagerly been recruiting various kinds of artists to act as cultural goodwill ambassadors, had asked Serling to make a tour of Australia and the South Pacific to conduct seminars on television writing and generally to spread the good word about America and American broadcasting—much as Louis Armstrong, the most noted such ambassador, had done for American music by touring behind the Iron Curtain with his horn. With *The Twilight Zone* seen in syndication throughout the world, and his dynamic voice and presence, Serling seemed the perfect choice to act as video Satchmo.

"I've wanted to find the time for this for years and now we're going," Serling told a reporter before leaving Los Angeles on his grand tour of the East. "I'm going back to every place where the enemy shot at Old Rod, and I don't exactly know what's going to happen, but I want to go."[13]

First, the Serlings visited Australia, where *The Twilight Zone* had been showing for two years, and where Serling was surprised (and of course delighted) that he was nearly as famous as in the United States. An even more enthusiastic reception awaited the Serlings in the Philippines. Thanks to advance (and exaggerated) word about Serling's Philippine exploits—which had him all but liberating Manila single-handed—Serling, overcome with emotion, was accompanied by joyous crowds of Filipinos when he visited Tagaytay Ridge, the site of his one combat jump.

The trip did get his creative juices flowing. By the time he and Carol flew to Hong Kong, their next (and next-to-last) stop, Serling, re-obsessed with his wartime experiences, was firing off memos to CBS and Ashley-Steiner with ideas for various series and documentaries, using the still-war-scarred Philippine landscape for a documentary about Corregidor set in the Philippines and the Orient, as well as a dramatic series like the concurrent *Combat* and *Gallant Men*, set in Bataan.

He also concocted an idea for a kind of American James Bond series, to be set in various exotic locales and called *The Chase*.

Serling was in a cynical mood when he returned to Los Angeles from his sabbatical. He had done some work—some good work—but Serling, always age-conscious, now felt even older as he began to prepare for the fifth season of *The Twilight Zone*.

Buck Houghton had been right. The fourth season of *The Twilight Zone* had not worked in hour-long form. Most of the hour-long shows, which appeared during the spring and summer of 1963, came off as padded and ponderous.

However, in several memorable cases, the continued fine performances that Serling's scripts drew from the actors helped pull off the switch. A remarkable one by James Whitmore helped save a

Serling morality play, "On Thursday We Leave for Home" (directed by Buzz Kulik), which was about rescued survivors of a failed space colony who suddenly must choose between returning to Earth or staying behind with their power-addicted leader (Whitmore).

Serling also wrote one funny episode, "The Bard," directed by David Butler, about a frustrated writer (Jack Weston)—ostensibly about Serling himself—who can't sell any of his many WLW-vintage ideas. Little wonder: they include a story about a girl who unwittingly marries a zombie; a love story where a woman scientist falls for a robot; a Western with Belle Starr as president of the Western Pacific Railroad; a weekly boy-meets-girl series ("Every week we have a different boy and a different girl!"); and *The Millionaire* recast as a hour-long show and called *The Multi-Millionaire*. The frustrated writer then somehow summons up William Shakespeare (John Williams), who becomes his, well, ghostwriter, and an amazingly successful one at that—until sponsors, network executives, and a temperamental Method actor (Burt Reynolds) begin to interfere with the Bard's work.[14]

Nevertheless, Serling was quick to call the experiment a failure. So were his fans, who, like addicts deprived of their fix of Serling's patented "twist endings," hankered for a return to the half-hour form.

And so, with considerable misapprehension, Rod Serling returned to doing what he knew best: writing half-hour *Twilight Zone*s.

If Serling and CBS were hoping the return to *The Twilight Zone*'s original half-hour form would revitalize the series when it returned to the air in the fall of 1963, both he and the network were quickly disappointed. Of necessity, most television series—if they survive that long—begin cannibalizing themselves after four or five years, and *The Twilight Zone*, in spite of its anthology format, was no exception.

The show looked tired. So did Serling. Actor Martin Landau was quick to notice the change in the once ebullient writer-producer's attitude and demeanor when he reported to Cayuga Productions for his first appearance on *The Twilight Zone* in four years, in the Serling-written episode "The Jeopardy Room." "He was less talkative than he had been before," Landau said, "more meat and potatoes, more perfunctory." The familiar Serling zing was gone.[15]

Fortunately, Landau and the other directing and acting noteworthies who continued to flock to the show hadn't lost their zing. Landau, ably directed by Richard Donner, turned in an excellent performance as the defiant defector caught in a hotel room in a deadly cat-and-mouse game with a clever KGB commissar. Thanks to a *Zone*-esque hunch, Landau's character manages to escape his pursuers' trap (a bomb hidden in a phone)—and catch them in it instead. Also that season, in "Last Night of a Jockey," Mickey Rooney, playing a corrupt jockey whose only wish is "to be big" (and whose wish comes true), excelled in a similar tour de force, set once again in another dingy hotel room, which was good enough to make viewers forget that the script was essentially recycled from "Nervous Man in a Four-Dollar Room."

Even at its most predictable, however, *The Twilight Zone* remained one of the most watchable dramatic programs on the air. There was even a slight improvement in the show's ratings, though not enough to stave off its inevitable doom.

To add to his misery, Serling was hit with charges by various science fiction writers that he had stolen their stories for *The Twilight Zone*, charges that he vehemently denied.

Buck Houghton, like Johnson, ascribed the plagiarism charges to the narrowness of the science-fiction field. "The field of imaginative fiction is very small, and it's very easy to step on someone else's toes. We were sued very often, the reason being that there are very few premises for a 'What If?' story.

"If you were to write a book of twenty short 'What If?' stories, without reading any more, I'd guarantee you that you'd light on the same cube of sugar that somebody else has. If you can find yourself a story about modern high school students in the big city, you are going to steal from somebody, because there aren't that many stories to tell."[16]

To be sure, there was a good deal of professional jealousy behind the plagiarism accusations, especially on the part of Ray Bradbury, with whom Serling was still feuding after their falling out during the first year of the show.

"I was at a dinner party with Ray Bradbury," writer Malvin Wald recounted. "*The Twilight Zone* had just started. Bradbury said that all of the science fiction writers in Hollywood were furious because, they said, Serling wasn't a true science fiction writer like they were, and he was stealing all of their plots. They were going to boycott his program. Bradbury felt that Rod became world-famous by taking the work of all of these people, in an area that these people had struggled in for so long. . . . They were jealous because he was not a part of that world."[17]

Serling insisted that he had never intentionally stolen another writer's line, theme, dialogue, mood, or concept; nevertheless the charges persisted, and after several unsuccessful suits, late in 1963 they finally stuck when Serling, on the advice of his attorney, settled a suit over the fourth-season episode "The Parallel" by paying the putative original author the sum of sixty-five hundred dollars.

Serling was stricken about the price he had paid for his fame, and he expressed his feelings about this in a column for *Seventeen* magazine that was published that year. Although meant to be inspiring, the article ended up making fairly depressing reading. "Don't pay too high a price for the status of popularity," he cautioned his young readers. "Don't succumb to this itch [of rebellion and wanderlust], but don't deny it either. . . . Believe in truth . . . in that formless amorphous thing called honor . . . in courage. . . . Have a ball!"[18]

The assassination of John Kennedy in November 1963 jolted Serling as it did all Americans, but he had little time to grieve. The day after the tragedy, there was another governmental summons from the United States Information Agency, to prepare a documentary for international distribution about Kennedy's as-yet little-known successor, Lyndon B. Johnson. While most Americans were crouched in front of their television sets watching Kennedy's funeral cortege slowly move down Pennsylvania Avenue, Serling was sequestered at the agency headquarters, watching (in his own estimation) 8 million feet of newsreel footage about LBJ.

Serling threw himself into the documentary assignment, coming up with a stirring film that he and producer William Froug called "Let Us Continue." "One does not cry in English, or in Spanish, or in Russian, or in Egyptian, or in Italian," Serling's opening narration intoned over clips of the funeral procession moving past weeping Washingtonians, "one only cries." Johnson and the USIA, genuinely pleased at the result, offered Serling and Froug their profound thanks.

The film ended with an injunction for the future which sounded like a *Zone* sign-off (in fact, much like the one he wrote for "Monsters Are Due on Maple Street"):

To the Leftists and the Rightists, to the Absolutists, to the men of little faith but strong hate, and to all of us who have helped plant this ugly and loathsome seed that blossomed forth in Dallas last Friday—this is the only dictum we can heed now. For civilization to survive it must remain civilized. And if there is to be any hope for our children and theirs—we must never again allow violence to offer itself as an excuse for our insecurities, our own weaknesses and our own fears. This is not an arguable doctrine for simply a better life. It is a condition for our continued existence.[19]

However, once again Serling's flair for controversy got him in trouble—again with the Jewish community. In a press interview about the making of the film, the writer-narrator related how he and Froug had been asked not to use a photo of a rabbi so as to smooth the film's reception in the Arab world. Accusations ensued that he had condoned anti-Semitism.

Serling thought the controversy overblown. "We were told quite informally that using a rabbi in the film would make it hard to peddle in the Arab countries," said Serling, insisting that he had not been censored. "We figured out a better way of getting him [the rabbi] into the film. I don't even *know* any Arabs. And of course, with my background, I have a lot of sympathy for the Arabs. Actually," he cracked, "it was my idea to run *Exodus* backwards so the Arabs would win."[20]

But Serling himself wasn't laughing much in 1963.

The Serling touch was more in evidence in the scripts he wrote that summer and fall for *Bob Hope Presents the Chrysler Theater* on NBC, a combination comedy-dramatic anthology show somewhat similar to the old *Westinghouse Desilu Theater*. One of these scripts was an adaptation of the celebrated John O'Hara short story "It's Mental Work" (broadcast on December 20, 1963), whose plot line perfectly suited Serling's increasingly nostalgic mood. The story, about an ambitious young man who longs to take over a failing bar from its aging owner at the expense of their relationship, would earn Serling his sixth and last Emmy.

In January 1964, several weeks after his thirty-ninth birthday, Serling was given the word: *The Twilight Zone* would not be renewed for the following season. The cancellation, though not entirely unwelcome, deepened Serling's gloom.

*   *   *

Serling gave more eloquent, albeit oblique, expression to his mid-life crisis in "Slow Fade to Black," a teleplay broadcast March 27, 1964, on *Bob Hope Presents the Chrysler Theater*.

In "Slow Fade to Black," veteran film producer Michael Kirsch (Rod Steiger), one of the last remaining moguls of the silver screen's golden age, finds himself presiding over a failing studio with young talent he cannot relate to and a group of executives who are thinking about replacing him with his young protégé, Peter Purgatch (Robert Culp). Kirsch will not relent, convinced that one good picture, "a picture that has mother in it, has the American flag and ice cream cones, not the agony you see today," will save his job. But his ideas are out-of-date and the executives begin to assemble their stocks to take control of the studio away from him.

Desperate, Kirsch turns to his estranged daughter, Jeri (Sally Kellerman), for the stock he gave her for her first wedding. She is unsympathetic, however, and has never forgiven her father for ruining her life by not loving her. Spitefully, she sells her stock—and any hope Kirsch has of running the studio—to the other side. Knowing he is beat, Kirsch—ironically, as he is receiving an award for "Producer of the Year"—makes a moving speech in which he berates the up-and-coming generation of executives for not respecting the medium's history and its founders:

> To all you Johnny-come-latelies out there, you who had this business handed to you like an inheritance and a legacy, all of you, you who never had to scramble or bleed to give birth to it or keep it alive, let me say this:
>
> There were a lot of people who couldn't speak English so good, that paved the way for you. And they broke their backs, and they did it in cellars, and they did it in attics trying to figure out which way to aim the camera so all of you "Angry Young Men" could say that you were part of an art form.
>
> Now I'm speaking of people like Jesse Lasky, D. W. Griffith, Mack Sennett, and let us not forget a funny little man with baggy trousers and a Nazi mustache. They had talent. They loved what they were doing, and people loved them for doing it. But you don't love to make movies, and that is a shame. Because you don't know what you're missing.[21]

For Serling—as for Kirsch, with whom the author clearly identified—the era of television was past. This seemed to be confirmed when, in short order, both CBS and ABC halted negotiations with Serling for follow-up shows to *The Twilight Zone*. First, Aubrey and the powers-that-be at CBS nixed Serling's proposed budget for *The Chase*, now retitled *Jeopardy Run*. "I would have done it if they had let us go to Hong Kong as we'd planned," the dejected writer told the *Binghamton Press*.[22]

Shortly afterward, preliminary negotiations with ABC to develop a horror series broke down after Serling criticized programming executive Tom Moore for seeking "Class C movie concepts" instead of backing his approach, which was "to deal with the occult in thoughtful pieces."[23]

On April 1, 1964, Rod Serling did something he hadn't done in nineteen years and had sworn he would never do again: he jumped out of an airplane. In uniform, no less.

Serling had at first dismissed the idea of parachuting again—in uniform or out—when William Lindau, an old friend and fellow "paraguy" from the 511th Parachute Infantry Regiment, had written Serling the previous year about the fun he'd recently had making *his* first jump since the war at Fort Bragg, just for the hell of it. "Thanks, but no thanks," Serling had replied when Lindau suggested that he join them for an encore.

But Serling was still a trooper at heart, a fact that he proudly acknowledged by wearing a wrist bracelet bearing the crossed parachute and wings insignia of the Army Airborne. And when he had toured the Philippines, the memories had come back, along with the impulse to go for it—to make the big one—one more time.

So, when a year later Lindau asked Serling about jumping again—this time backed up enthusiastically by the information officer for the 82nd Airborne Division based at Fort Bragg—again he capitulated and said yes.

Puckishly he set April Fool's Day as the date for the stunt—so that if anything untoward *did* take place while the photographers assembled by the army for the celebrity stunt snapped away, the joke would be on Rod Serling—and Uncle Sam.

And so there Serling was at the Fort Bragg field on the appointed foolish morning, fresh from an intensive six-hour refresher course on the basics of jumping and landing, waiting around with his chute strapped on for the twenty-five-mile-per-hour winds to subside so that he and the rest of his gung-ho thirty-six-man "stick" of volunteer paratroopers could board the C-124 waiting to take them to their drop zone. There was a sheepish grin on his face. Lindau looked on from afar, trying to offer encouragement; he had backed out at the last minute. Serling forgave him: this was *his* stunt.

And suddenly they were off, and he was back *there* again, looking at the all-too-familiar faces lined up before him—the faces of war.

"You hear the old engines roaring," he said, "and you sit there in those bucket seats, and you look at the faces of the men and the years drift away. . . ."[24]

The jump was a success. Serling landed on target without injury. He had done it: he was still a man.

Now Serling had to figure out what to do with the rest of his life.

14
THE LONER
(1964 – 69)

Talking to me is like dredging up the past glory of a major league pitcher who won the Most Valuable Player award twenty years ago.
　—Serling in an interview with the *Los Angeles Times*, June 25, 1967

Unfortunately, Rod Serling never did really figure out what he wanted to do with his life following the demise of *The Twilight Zone*. Inarguably, the drive was still there; so was the talent. But the focus was gone. The list of television and screenwriting assignments, game show invitations, lecture dates, and commercial voice-over requests that Serling took on after 1964 is dizzying. Clearly, his critical judgment had left him. His agents didn't evince much either.

Of course, *The Twilight Zone* was a difficult act to follow—for a writer or a "TV personality." "*The Twilight Zone* experience conditioned him to turn out an infinite number of pages every week," said Dick Berg. "From the time it was canceled forward, I think, he felt frustrated. Although he had many assignments, he was never able to fill the day as a writer as fully as he had during *The Twilight Zone*. After the demise of the show, he found himself at sixes and sevens by his criteria, which had been set by the *Twilight Zone* experience and were so unique."[1]

"He had had enormous freedom, and that had to diminish anything that came afterwards," said Martin Landau.[2]

Besides freedom, *The Twilight Zone* had also conditioned Serling to receiving a national celebrity's attention and applause, as well as a lot of money. He didn't want that to stop either. That at least helps explain such abominations as *Rod Serling's Liar's Club*, a short-lived game show that Serling hosted in the late 1960s, and the advertisements for Famous Writers School which featured Serling "talking" about the correspondence school while sitting by his swimming pool, bought and paid for with his famous-writer earnings.

One of the reasons Serling was anxious about money was that he was fearful he would die at a relatively young age—as unfortunately he would—and he wanted to ensure that his family was provided for. To be sure, the nation was having its own midlife crisis at the time; still, it is hard to believe a lot of the things that Serling did in the sixties.

Here are some of the things that Serling did in a one-month period in 1964: On New Year's Day, he flew to Columbus from Los Angeles to tape several lead-ins for *Ten O'Clock Theater* and to discuss syndicating *The Twilight Zone* on a regional four-city basis with the manager of WBNS. Five days later, he galloped back to the College of the Desert in Palm Springs to participate in a symposium on television, where he was the featured speaker for three days. Next, Serling was off to Detroit, where he was the principal speaker at the Detroit Advertising Club. The next day he touched down in Honolulu, on the first leg of his second government-sponsored goodwill trip to the East.

From Honolulu, Serling flew to Manila for lectures and appearances. Still fixated on the war, he did research there for an autobiographical film about a neurotic veteran's return to Corregidor, *The Long Retreat*. (The film was never produced.) He and Carol revisited Tagaytay Ridge and retraced the 511th's hellish assault on the Filipino capital. Soon after, the State Department asked Serling if he wouldn't mind visiting Hong Kong as well. Of course Serling said yes.

Although Serling did not have much clout left with the networks, there was still a great reservoir of goodwill toward him in other areas of the television industry. This was borne out by his election in May 1964 to the presidency of the National Academy of Television Arts and Sciences, a post that he would hold for two years. Evidently, Serling's peers felt that it was time for a reformer like

Serling to take hold of the reins and regain some of the medium's lost luster, as well as to bolster the academy's fragile support within the industry itself. Surprised and gratified by his election, Serling gladly accepted the post, which had been previously held by Walter Cronkite. He applied himself to the task of reforming the academy, which was seeking to make itself the aesthetic and institutional equivalent of the film industry's Academy of Motion Picture Arts and Sciences. The urgency of Serling's task was underlined on May 18, 1964, a month before Serling took office, when both ABC and CBS withdrew from the academy's annual Emmy Awards show because of their unhappiness over the increasingly complicated procedures for choosing winners. Serling jumped into the fray with characteristic aplomb, skirmishing in the press with Fred W. Friendly, Edward R. Murrow's old producer and now head of CBS News, who had his own ideas about how the Emmys should be awarded. "If we listened to Fred Friendly's ideas we would wind up with 900 categories and need eight days and eight nights [to present the awards]," Serling told the *New York Times*.[3] With Cronkite's support, Serling eagerly went to work on a new awards system, whereby Emmys would be awarded by craft rather than by program, so that all deserving programs and individuals would be rewarded. Unfortunately, Friendly and many others didn't go for it, and after Serling's tenure as president, the academy returned to the old competitive system of handing out a seemingly endless number of awards. "The television industry, like any other, loves to give awards to itself," recalled Cronkite. "We were bound to lose."[4]

Serling also made a limited attempt to use his presidency to spotlight other industry shortcomings, including the blacklist. This, too, raised hackles. Serling's impatience and confrontational manner didn't help matters. His presidential zeal was short-lived.

Serling's frustration was evident in the memorable introduction he gave at the 1965 Emmy Award ceremonies:

> Ours is a medium whose potential to entertain, to enlighten, is without parallel and should be without limit. Unfortunately, this potential is too often invisible to the eye. We seem prone to let George do it. And apparently, over many a long viewing season, there are too few people in the Academy that answer to the name of George.
>
> The National Academy believes that it is time our industry

found a lot of Georges, and it's time we became not just an industry, but an art form. All of you out there who work in television, and all of you who are the American public, deserve it.[5]

The audience applauded, but his appeal fell on deaf ears, as the industry continued to program for the lowest common denominator. The 20 million viewers who might have preferred an *Omnibus* or a *Playhouse 90* or a *Twilight Zone* were forgotten. The airwaves were now all but bereft of serious drama—only Reginald Rose's *The Defenders, Alfred Hitchcock Presents*, and, to some extent, *The Fugitive,* and *The Outer Limits* attempted to maintain the higher quality of television's not-so-distant golden age. More typical of the era were some of the other shows making their debuts in 1964 and 1965: *Gilligan's Island, Gomer Pyle U.S.M.C., The Munsters*. James Aubrey himself was gone from the scene, cashiered by William Paley because of his bizarre after-hours life. But the Aubrey dictum lived on.

Meanwhile, Serling's friends' and family's fears about the toll the frenetic pace was taking on his health had been confirmed in March when Serling was in Washington to make a speech before that city's chapter of the National Academy.

One of those in the audience was Mark Olshaker, a young writer who was to remain friendly with Serling for the remaining years of his life. He and Serling struck up a conversation before the speech: "We talked for a long time, fifteen or twenty minutes, until it was time for the speech to start. He was really interested in what I was doing. Then, as soon as the speech was over and he had answered questions from the audience, I assumed he would stay around and talk to people for a while. But he just walked right out."[6]

Just off stage, Serling ran to his brother, Robert, complaining of chest pains. "He later told me he thought he was going to die," Olshaker said. The Serling brothers rushed to Washington Hospital Center, where Robert's physician was waiting.

It turned out that Serling was suffering from exhaustion and gastritis, serious enough in itself. However, a tipster at the hospital had called the *Washington Post* with an exaggerated report of Serling's condition. The Associated Press picked up the story the next morning and spread the word that Serling had suffered a coronary.

Bob was in his brother's hospital room with him when Alden Schwimmer, his agent from Ashley-Steiner, called from Los Angeles, unaware that it had been a false alarm. According to Robert, the conversation went something like this:

"Rod, I'm stunned, absolutely stunned. How are you feeling?"

"Well, buddy," the inveterate joker replied in a deadly serious tone, "I've got good news and bad news. The bad news is that they give me only six weeks to live. The good news is that I'll have enough time to finish that screenplay."[7]

Serling slowed his pace a little as a result of the attack, but not for long.

To be sure, Serling had become so disillusioned with television and where television seemed to be going that he officially switched his "allegiance" to the movie industry while he was still academy president. "Television has left me tired, frustrated," he told the *New York Times* in November 1964, shortly after the Emmy debacle. "Television doesn't want to knock television too much. Television gave me an identity as a writer, you can't knock that. It's just that now I like movies better."[8]

Hastening Serling's departure for the other medium was the storm cloud created by his teleplay for "A Carol for Christmas," a Xerox-sponsored special designed to promote the United Nations. Based on the Dickens story, Serling's morality play featured a missile-rattling, UN-hating Scrooge named Grudge (played nimbly by actor-comic Peter Sellers), who thinks human security depends on mastering an international game of "chicken" until he is mellowed by the ghosts of Christmases past, present, and future. The show triggered a blizzard of protest and hate letters from right-wing groups. At one time, Serling would have relished the controversy. But now it only wearied him more.

His preference for film was based in part on the enthusiastic reception he had received for *Seven Days in May*. Unfortunately, it turned out, the movies didn't like *him* any better. Serling's cinema work in the 1960s followed a general pattern: initial excitement, increasing frustration, followed by abandonment, or, in several cases, outright dismissal.

For example, in 1964, Serling was engaged by producer Arthur P. Jacobs to write the screenplay for a film entitled *A Time of Glory*. The film, a fictional account of how the Air Force was born with a group of gung-ho volunteers in World War I, was to be director Sydney Pollack's first feature assignment. However, Jacobs wasn't happy with Serling's work and pulled him off the project, and the film was never made.

Pollack recalled that Serling was "very cheerful in defeat. I remember a note that he left me on my desk at MGM just after he was pulled off the picture. It was a cheery, funny note, something about going down in flames himself, just like the fliers in the picture."[9]

Serling would not be so cheerful after subsequent cinematic failures. *Assault on a Queen*, a 1966 adaptation of a novel by Jack Finney, about a bunch of drifters (led by Frank Sinatra, who had hired Serling to write the script) who attempt to hijack the *Queen Elizabeth* with a renovated World War II submarine, *did* make it to the screen, much to Serling's chagrin. (The *New York Times* called it a "celluloid duck . . . with dialogue ranging from flip to banal.")[10] *Bodo*, based on the novel *The Shamir of Dachau* by Christopher Davis, about two concentration camp survivors who discover their Nazi tormentor alive and set out for revenge, was not produced. *Gresham's People*, later retitled *The 'R' Project*, a *Frankenstein*-like story about a military man who invents a race of robots in an attempt to end war, was eventually assigned to Richard Matheson, to Serling's dismay. *The Devil in Paradise*, a Western-*cum*-Satan story that was based on *Shadow of Thunder* by Max Evans and was to star Gregory Peck, was also shelved.

Perhaps Serling's most painful failure was *Children's Crusade*, a 1968 screenplay about the unfolding student movement that producer-director Stanley Kramer asked Serling to write. He went to great lengths to research the subject, visiting numerous Eastern campuses and hanging out with students, only to be fired by Kramer and replaced by Erich Segal (of *Love Story* fame). Segal rewrote the script entirely, and the film was retitled *R.P.M.* and released in 1970 without a word of Serling dialogue. "I think that took a lot out of Rod," said Del Reisman, one of the few members of *The Twilight Zone* crew who kept in touch with Serling during this increasingly troubled period. "I think he spent so much time on that script in research, traveling around the country, and I think it depressed him.[11]

Serling saw a little more come out of his work on another movie project he initially had high hopes for: the movie adaptation of

Pierre Boulle's futuristic novel *Planet of the Apes*, about a group of human astronauts, imprisoned by a race of apes, who escape their chains with the aid of some sympathetic gorillas. Here, too, Serling's initial scripts proved too elaborate, and he ended up sharing screenwriting credit with Michael Wilson, who revamped the setting and action to make the film more financially feasible. Serling did, however, turn Boulle's *Zone*-esque trick ending (where the escaped astronauts discover that they are really on Earth, several thousand years into the future) into one of the most visually powerful scenes in science-fiction cinema: Charlton Heston escapes into forbidden territory only to discover the remains of the head of the Statue of Liberty washed up on the beach; "You fools!" he shouts. "You had to do it!"

"I think he was a little bitter about not becoming a big movie writer," said Ethel Wynant. "He never wrote *the* great movie, and that must have hurt him. He'd been a major star in television, but he was a nonentity in the film industry."[12]

Why couldn't Serling make that transition to the big screen—as Paddy Chayefsky had—in a more powerful and demonstrative fashion? Director Sydney Pollack said, quite simply, that the two media are very different, and success in one doesn't insure success in the other. "The film form is different, the concerns are different. It's quite different to do a one-hour piece that contains forty-eight minutes of story, and twelve minutes of commercials, than to do two hours. It's like the difference between doing a novella and a novel."[13]

"After all," he continued, "why didn't Sterling Silliphant [the writer-producer of *Naked City*] become a big screenwriter? There are certain people whose gift is the shorter form."[14]

Buzz Kulik, who directed one of Serling's cinematic misfires, the 1963 Pat Boone thriller *The Yellow Canary*, felt that Serling didn't have the patience essential for movie writing. He recalled that Serling, used to using his own first drafts on *The Twilight Zone*, hated the rewriting process on *Canary*: "We worked on *Yellow Canary* when he was teaching at Antioch, and I'd call him and say, 'Rod, we really need to work on this.' And he'd say, 'Yeah, yeah, yeah, okay.' And I'd call him again and he'd finally say, 'What's the problem?' and I would tell him on the phone and he'd say, 'Okay, let me think about it.' It never worked, you know? And in the television medium it always worked. We would get together and it would work."[15]

William Self, who attempted to get Serling to write one of the *Planet of the Apes* sequels, agreed: "I think he had the talent, but I think in a way he spread himself too thin on the things that he worked on. He couldn't say no. I remember when I called him up for this *Planet of the Apes* sequel, he said, 'Well, Bill, I'm just about to go on vacation.' I said, 'I don't want to spoil that, Rod.' And he said, 'What the hell, I'll do it.' He took a vacation and wrote a script for me at the same time because he didn't want to say no. He was a nice man that way, but I think he didn't really take enough time for feature work, he was just used to working so fast and so quickly."[16]

Inevitably, all roads for Serling led back to the medium he loved to hate.

Ironically, it was a call from Self, who had produced the pilot for *The Twilight Zone*, that got the avowedly TV-proof writer involved with series television again in 1965.

Five years earlier, when he had been at the helm of *The Twilight Zone*, television Westerns were somewhat in vogue, and Serling had circulated a proposal for a program called *The Loner*, a kind of existential Western about a disillusioned Civil War veteran searching for meaning and meeting up with adventure riding around the West in the late 1860s. As had earlier been the case with *The Twilight Zone*, at first CBS hadn't been interested, and the proposal was shelved.

Now Self stepped in. "When I became a production manager at Twentieth Century-Fox Television after having left CBS, I was looking for a Western, and I called up Rod and said, 'What did you ever do with *The Loner*?' "[17] Would Serling be interested, Self wondered, in attempting the series now?

As with *The Twilight Zone*, Serling was initially very excited about *The Loner*, seeing it as an opportunity to use an established form, the Western, as an instrument with which to make a statement about war and its aftermath.

Serling did use the program this way in some of the better episodes. In "One of the Wounded," the hero, Colton (played by Lloyd Bridges), wanders upon the farm of a woman (Anne Baxter) whose husband is completely catatonic after the horrors of the war. In "The Vespers," Jack Lord plays an old war buddy of Colton's who has become a minister, and whose adamant passive resistance begins to threaten his own life and the future of his young, pregnant wife.

The look of *The Loner*, like that of *The Twilight Zone*, was unique, a cross between Westerns and Hitchcock. The show was one of the only Western series to make extensive use of the close-up, the zoom, and voice-over narration. Unfortunately, these innovations were lost on most television critics. Though Serling had once been the darling of the press, his reputation had sunk to the point where leading critics seemed to enjoy taking potshots at him. Thus, Richard Schickel of *Life*, in his review of *The Loner*, disparaged it as "another example of Rod Serling's colossal nerve."[18]

The Loner wasn't popular with CBS management, either, which urged Serling to inject more *action* into the series.

Serling, ever the network rebel, made the mistake of airing his grievance with CBS in public, embarrassing Dann in an interview with a reporter friend, Harry Harris of the *Philadelphia Bulletin*. "I told Dann that if the network wanted a conventional Western with an emphasis on violence and action, it should have hired a conventional Western writer."[19]

Dann, infuriated, reacted by showing Serling the door. "He often took it to the press," Dann said, "which isn't the best place in a bureaucracy to run to. He did run that line constantly and that was suicidal."[20]

Serling wrote an effusive letter of apology, but it was too late. He had publicly embarrassed the network. *The Loner* was canceled after only thirteen episodes, and Serling had succeeded in making himself *persona non grata* at CBS. He wasn't completely locked out of the world of television; but most of the projects he did get involved with during the rest of the decade came to disaster.

The most notorious case in point was his ill-starred made-for-television movie *Doomsday Flight*, which he wrote for NBC in 1966. The film, one of the first made-for-television movies, was a thriller about a disgruntled airline employee (Edmond O'Brien) who attempts to extort money from his former employer by placing an altitude-sensitive bomb aboard a passenger plane. Once the plane dipped below four thousand feet, the bomb would go off. Inspired by a real-life incident that Serling's brother, Bob, had related to him while working as aviation editor at United Press International, *Doomsday Flight* aired on December 13, 1966, and was the second-highest-rated program of the season.

Unfortunately, the teleplay described the crime in such detail that it inspired eight "copycat" bomb threats in the one week following the show—including one successful hijacking in Australia. "I wish to Christ I had written a stagecoach drama starring John Wayne," a devastated Serling told the press. "I wish I'd never been born."[21]

Serling also had high hopes for a 1968 teleplay he wrote for an NBC live broadcast. Entitled "Certain Honorable Men," it was based partially on the case of Senator Dodd, and concerned a congressman (Van Heflin) who is exposed by his protégé (Peter Fonda) for being corrupt. It seemed like an appropriate Serling vehicle, and NBC touted it as "a penetrating look at national politics."[22]

Again, the critics begged to differ. Decrying the compromise ending Serling had tacked on, Jack Gould wrote in the New York Times: "A braver voice than Mr. Serling's might have argued the hypocrisy of a procedure that allows a man found to have abused the trust of public office to continue in that office and indeed even aspire to re-election."[23]

The following season, Serling was approached by producer Aaron Spelling to write the pilot episode for a new series he was developing called The New People, about an assorted group of sixties children who are stranded on a desert island. Serling gave the project only a half-hearted endorsement: "That's Aaron Spelling's show," he told Cecil Smith. "I have nothing to do with it. The show is somewhere between Gilligan's Island and San Francisco State. It may work, but not with me."[24]

Serling's pilot was predictably combative and talky and demonstrated how out of touch he had become with the younger generation. It was, ironically, Richard Kiley, star of Serling's first television hit, "Patterns," who played the only adult role in this, one of Serling's more dismal efforts. "It was lightweight entertainment as far as I was concerned," said Kiley. "It was no 'Patterns.' "[25]

With racial and generational tensions—two themes that Serling had long felt passionate about—flaring up around the country, he felt frustrated at the lack of a video forum to address those and other relevant issues.

"I can't sit on a fence and let carbuncles form," he complained to a Los Angeles Times reporter in 1967. "I happen to think that the singular evil of our time is prejudice. It is from this evil that all other evils grow and multiply. In almost everything I've written, there is a thread of this: man's seemingly palpable need to dislike someone other than himself."[26]

Serling also spoke out against the increasing American involvement in Vietnam. "I'm hung up on the Vietnam thing. I want all men to have freedom . . . but I see no beckoning hand of a free people or a would-be free people asking us for help. If Americans must die for free speech, I'd like to make damned certain that the governments we will support will guarantee that free speech. I reject in principle this business of a massive blood-letting simply because the opponent is a Communist. There are some other evils extant which are just as bad as denying of freedom."[27]

Serling's opposition to the war would lead him to campaign actively for the antiwar presidential candidate, Senator Eugene McCarthy. One of those who joined Serling on the campaign trail was his old hero, Norman Corwin.

Deprived of his video bully pulpit, Serling, the former angry man of television, took to the lecture circuit to expound his views on Vietnam, television, government, the generation gap, and other subjects that bothered him.

He spoke of the war in Vietnam and his opposition to it during a speech he delivered to the BCHS graduating class of January 1968. "Are you tough enough to try and build a world in which young men can live out their lives in fruitful pursuit of a decent, enriching consummation of both their talents and hopes?" he asked. "If survival calls for the bearing of arms, bear them you must," the former paratrooper said. "But the most important part of the challenge is for you to find another means that does not come with the killing of your fellow men."[28]

Serling was particularly popular on college campuses, where reruns of *The Twilight Zone* had already become a television room standby.

However, Serling had mixed feelings about the show's continued popularity, reminding him as it did of his original decision to sell away the syndication rights in 1966. According to Carol Serling, her husband sold the rights to the show because he "wanted to put it behind him, never dreaming that it would continue to have a life of its own." Nevertheless, its creator was constantly irked by the idea that CBS was making millions from the reruns.

Adding insult to injury was the common practice of cutting a minute or two from the original episodes for syndication, making them almost unbearable for their progenitor to watch. "When you cut a minute out of a 23-minute drama," Serling lamented in an interview, "not much is left. . . . It all seems like a bad dream."[29]

To be sure, Serling still owned the rights to his nationally famous face and voice, which he began to promote mercilessly, agreeing to do all kinds of commercials and ads. Serling's colleagues were shocked at his willingness, even eagerness, to become a shill.

The low point of Serling's career may have been when he was asked, and agreed, to narrate a Procter & Gamble ad for Echo house wax:

> I'm Rod Serling. And this is woman. Her laundry and kitchen *invaded* by amazing new technologies . . . only her *floor* remains an oasis of tradition.
>
> Tradition that says it must be washed and cleaned and waxed to be clean . . . and shining! But, what if there were an *incredible* new formula, called Echo . . .
>
> That washed *and* waxed the floor at the same time . . . and did it *better* than two separate products?[30]

Other products that Serling did either on- or off-camera narration for included Anacin, Crest, and Z-Best rustproofing.

Said his estranged friend from Westport, Robert Wise, "I felt every time I watched him do a commercial with that beautiful voice, that either he was laughing while he was gobbling up this money, or he was crying inside."[31]

By the end of the decade, Serling's reputation as a commercial spokesman eclipsed his reputation as a writer, at least in some circles.

Buzz Berger, the former partner of producer Herbert Brodkin, remembered getting a call from a friend at an ad agency who wanted to know Berger's opinion of an announcer who was up for a job by the name of Serling.

"Rod Serling isn't an announcer, he's a writer!!" Berger exclaimed.

"No," the agency man insisted, "he's an announcer."

"No! He's a writer!!!"

"No, I'm telling you, he's an announcer."[32]

15
ZERO HOUR
(1969 – 75)

His mood is heavily nostalgic these days. "I have a desperate desire for serene summer nights, merry-go-rounds, and nickel ice cream cones," he says.
—from an interview with Serling in *TV Guide*, June 3, 1972

In 1970 Serling reluctantly went back on his frequently broken promise never to do another series when he appeared as the host of the NBC thriller series *Night Gallery*.

The show was based on a made-for-television movie that appeared on NBC on December 13, 1969, which itself had been adapted from *The Season to Be Wary*, a group of three short stories about the supernatural, which Serling published earlier in the year. The collection only sold five thousand copies, somewhat to Serling's chagrin (he blamed Random House for not doing enough to promote the book), but—somewhat ironically—it managed to arouse the interest of Universal. Somehow, no matter what he did, all roads still led Serling back to television. The movie that was ultimately made—really three thirty-minute stories—was produced for Universal by veteran television producer William Sackheim, who had asked Serling to do the adaptations and help oversee the project. Serling agreed, little thinking that it would lead to another series job.

The centerpiece of the original film, which still plays on late-night TV, was "Eyes," a story of a wealthy blind woman (Joan Crawford, in her last dramatic appearance) who blackmails a doctor into giving her an eye transplant that will allow her to see for a period of twelve hours. A donor is found—a pathetic bum (Tom Bosley)—who needs the paltry fee to pay off gambling debts. The operation is successful, but there is a power failure right afterward: the confused woman, alone, blind again, is robbed of her temporary eyesight and falls to her death. The episode was superbly directed by a nineteen-year-old filmmaker named Steven Spielberg, who had wangled his way into a Universal contract. The temperamental Crawford was nervous about being directed by a youngster, and it was only because of Serling's intervention that Spielberg kept the job.[1]

The movie drew tremendous ratings, and Serling won a special Edgar award, given out by the Mystery Writers of America, for his scripts. As a result, NBC gave the go-ahead for a series to be spun off from the TV movie.

The premise behind *Rod Serling's Night Gallery*, as it was now called, revolved around a roomful of bizarre paintings, with Serling once again acting as host, introducing each episode in a decidedly *Zone*-esque manner, and, at least at the onset, contributing his share of scripts.[2]

Serling initially liked the *Gallery* concept of treating the supernatural in a nonformulaic way. "My impression was," said Serling's friend Mark Olshaker, "that he hoped at first that it would be another *Twilight Zone*, and kind of bring him back to his peak.[3]

"I think what sold him the most of all was the idea that he would be host, to tie it all together. He really enjoyed being on camera," said Olshaker. William Sackheim proved unavailable to produce the series; the role of producer went to Jack Laird.[4]

Night Gallery debuted on December 14, 1970. "A poor man's Hitchcock," the host disparagingly called himself in the introduction, during which he walked into an eerily lit gallery full of paintings especially done for the show and proceeded to give his trademark lead-in. The series achieved respectable ratings, enough for NBC to keep it on the air for three years—by the end of which time Serling's interest in it had long flagged.

Shortly after the *Night Gallery* movie aired, Serling had also scored something of an artistic triumph, and a commentative bull's-eye, with "A Storm in Summer," an hour-long script he wrote for *Hallmark Hall of Fame*. The story, about an unlikely friendship between a small black boy from the ghetto (N'Gai Dixon) and an elderly Jewish butcher (Peter Ustinov)—partly modeled on his father—was a bit on the sentimental side, but Serling's honest and touching script, along with a wonderful performance by Ustinov, made the show a moderate success when it aired on February 6, 1970. The following year, the show and Ustinov each won Emmys. Serling was also nominated, but lost.

Several of the scripts Serling wrote for *Night Gallery* were also good enough to garner Emmy nominations. Once again, as with the best of his *Twilight Zone* scripts, Serling's strongest work went back to the autobiographical.

"They're Tearing Down Tim Riley's Bar," for example, which aired January 20, 1971. Harried businessman Randolph Lane (brilliantly played by William Windom) knows he is at the end of his rope—that the "new guy" (Bert Convy) is poised to take his job, and that he will be forced to retire shortly. He seeks solace in his old business luncheon hangout, Tim Riley's, a place that has been condemned but still holds, for Lane, a vital link to a better past. Helping to prop him up, as always, is his gentle, supportive secretary. His wife, whose harsh, controlling voice echoes back to him when he revisits their old house, has already died.

Lane is Serling come full circle: he is Fred Staples on "Patterns," who, thirty years ago or so, was the "new guy"; he is Martin Sloan, who suffered his first attack of nostalgia just a few years back in "Walking Distance"; now, it is *he* who must get out of the way and make room for the next generation.

Serling also won kudos for his script "The Messiah on Mott Street," in which a young boy (Ricky Powell) goes to Chinatown to save his ailing grandfather (Edward G. Robinson). Finally, in one of his last scripts for the show, Serling turned Oscar Cook's short story "The Boomerang" into "The Caterpillar," about a man (Laurence Harvey) who suffers the excruciating pain of having a bug eat through his brain, as well as the aftershock of discovering that the bug was female—and laid millions of eggs inside his head. Horror novelist Stephen King, in his book *Danse Macabre*, said this episode was one of the single most frightening and effective things ever presented on television.

But *Night Gallery* did not prove to be the comeback Serling had hoped for. His enthusiasm for the series waned as it descended into formula horror and as his ideas diverged more and more from those of producer Jack Laird. Naively, he had waived creative control. He also realized that, unlike on *The Twilight Zone*, where he had executive producer control, there was very little he could do about it.

"I think Rod realized very quickly that it wasn't going to be what he thought," Mark Olshaker recalled. "He didn't have the control that he wanted, and he sort of felt like he was just a front man and they were going more for gimmicks and cheap thrills than they were for serious stories.

"I know he didn't like showing up. I remember once I was out in California and I wanted to see him. . . . I told him I'd meet him at Universal, and he said, 'No, I don't want to spend any more time there than I have to, I'll meet you at my house.' He really didn't want to have anything more to do with the show than he needed to. . . . It was sort of a take-the-money-and-run situation."[5]

In 1971, the second season of the show, Serling, as had often been his wont, went public with his objections, saying that Laird and Universal wanted a "*Mannix* in a cemetery" (referring to the show's major competition: a formulaic detective show). Del Reisman noted, "He knew he was hired by Universal to do the show on the basis of his *Twilight Zone* image, and bring that kind of charisma to the show. It wasn't even his show." "I'm staying on as announcer," Serling said bitterly, "a short book of gristle. It's not mine at all. It's another species of formula series drama."[6]

Night Gallery ran until 1973, but by that time, Serling had long stopped taking any kind of satisfaction in it.

Meanwhile, Serling had decided to spend more time at Lake Cayuga and in Ithaca, in order to devote more time to teaching at Ithaca College, and from 1972 on he lived half of each year in the area.

It was teaching more than anything else that gave Serling the greatest pleasure during the last few years of his life.

Serling was a popular figure at the college, where he would schedule special evening sessions to show his films and talk about show business. He was also popular in town. According to the *Ithaca Journal*, Ithacans were "pleased to find that the famous Rod Serling was down-to-earth enough to like flea markets, local fairs and shops, and antiques, and one could chat with him as with other neighbors at these places."[7]

He was at his happiest when relaxing on the lake with his friends, including Dr. Ed Hart, a local optometrist. "We'd go to the occasional football game, or we'd go to the restaurant," said Hart. "Most of the time we'd get together at someone's house and cook a steak. He didn't talk about his successes much because that wasn't the basis of our friendship. It was a very pleasant time because we didn't have any conflict at all, we avoided it by just enjoying each other and being friends."[8]

The move away from Hollywood also helped restore some much-needed tranquility to Serling's home life, as he quit his philandering and reconciled with his wife. He also spent more time with his two daughters. Jody, his first child, remained his apparent favorite, even while she veered from one school to another. As a child of the sixties and the firstborn of Rod Serling, the striking blonde was probably bound to be a little different from her peers. An animal lover who used to ride horseback with Patty Reagan in Pacific Palisades, she was fixated on becoming a veterinarian. She eventually became a registered nurse.

Nan, the less temperamental one, resembled her mother more; prim, self-controlled, discriminating, she married an Ithaca architect. It was Nan who tried to follow in her father's shoes, dabbling in writing verse and short stories.

At one time the daughters had resented their father's inattention to them. "They were both very darling, attractive girls," family friend Ann Goodman remembered. "But they felt that somehow or other they were pushed into the background by their father's fame." But by the 1970s, they had forgiven him and were able to see and accept their father for the man-child he was. As Goodman liked to say, "He was just my little boy, that's all. Rod was my little boy and he never grew up."[9] Serling had also drawn closer to his brother, Robert, who in 1968 had finally scored a commercial success of his own with his best-selling novel, *The President's Plane Is Missing*.

In addition to his duties in Ithaca, Serling also taught classes at the Sherman Oaks Experimental College during his still-frequent stays in Southern California. "It was very loose," said Benjamin Krepack, a student at the school, recalling the atmosphere of a Serling classroom. "He let people discuss anything they wanted. He was such a funny, good-humored man. He made people laugh and he loved to laugh. He had a nice rapport with people and was very warm and gregarious."[10]

The increasingly nostalgic writer seemed proudest of "Requiem for a Heavyweight." "He felt it was one of his best pieces of work, and sort of legitimized him that much more in the eyes of the people who always drew that line between television and film writing," Krepack recalled. "He felt everything fell into place there just right, the actors he chose, the art direction, and everything else."[11]

"If it's never been done before, do it," he advised his students. "If it's never been shot before, by all means shoot it." "Rod was coaching us with values by which he himself was never able to exist in the world of network television," one of his students recalled.[12]

Still, the same student wondered: "What was a talented man like Serling doing spending his last years as a devil's advocate of broadcasting for an upstate New York college? He should have been working in television drama just as he was twenty years before."[13]

Serling was asked to contribute to *ABC Playhouse* by Herbert Brodkin, with whom Serling had worked on *Playhouse 90*, and he even drove into New York to discuss the matter with his old friend and producer. Buzz Berger, Brodkin's partner, said that Brodkin "gave Rod hell about not writing for television anymore," but in the end, Serling decided it wasn't worth it. Perhaps if more of Serling's old friends had been as tough on him, he might have made a real comeback. Thanks to Norman Lear, who had begun his program reign, serious issues were once again being treated in television: certainly, there should have been room for someone like Serling, if he still cared.[14]

The last major project that came to Serling was an adaptation of *The Man*, Irving Wallace's novel about a black man who becomes president. Originally written for television, it was theatrically released in 1972 starring James Earl Jones, to mixed reviews. "That taught me not to write about people who don't go to the bathroom," Serling later said of the project.[15] After it, he continued to work as a theatrical narrator, signing on to do the voice-over for Jacques Cousteau's underwater specials and other documentaries. He also returned to his radio-land roots and served as the host of a syndicated anthology program, *The Zero Hour*.

Serling's students also couldn't help noticing and worrying about how much he smoked. "The thing that bothered me about his appearance was that he always had a cigarette in his hand," said Krepack. "He was always smoking, basically chain-smoking one right after another. As a nonsmoker, it was something very notice-able to me."[16]

Carol did her best to stop him, forbidding him to have cigarettes in the house, but Serling generally found a way of avoiding her searching eye. After Rod's death, Carol would find cigarettes hidden in dozens of nooks and crannies around the house.

His drinking also increased. One Cornell professor recalled seeing Serling sitting by himself in a local bar "getting stewed."

Serling continued to do some writing every day, more for ther-apeutic reasons than anything else.

Still, he had a lot of time on his hands, too much time. His increasing frustration was evident in the final interview he gave for *TV Guide* in June of 1972:

> If Rod's fire seems not to burn so brightly as it once did, he keeps busy. "I function well," he says. "I've my moments of depression. But I guess you'd say I'm a pretty contented guy."
>
> Still, one suspects there is another voice inside him echoing the words of Maish, Mountain McClintock's manager . . . in which he suggests a career as a wrestler, thus stripping away the last shred of dignity from his hulking, washed-up prize-fighter.
>
> "We could make him something like Gorgeous George and the Mad Baron," Maish says. "He'd be Mountain McClintock the Mountaineer. We could dress him up in a coonskin hat and . . . a costume of some kind. . . . So what's wrong? It's money, ain't it?"[17]

One of the ways Serling fought off his growing gloom was with his funny bone. Many of his friends, when asked to recall his most salient quality, would recall his prankishness. How could you not like a man who greeted dinner guests with a paper bag over his head, as he was known to do, or who could entertain his fellow airline passengers by acting out all of the roles in *Stagecoach*?

Serling seemed to grow more withdrawn after *Night Gallery* went off the air. "I saw Rod about a half-dozen times during the last eighteen months of his life, and noticed him, at times, quite de-spondent," his friend Elliot Jay Novak wrote. "Although his warmth

216

and magnetism remained, he had become somewhat reclusive."[18]

George Grunbok was a fellow passenger on a cruise that Serling and his wife took to South America in 1973. "He was kind of temperamental," said Grunbok. "He'd be high and low in the same day. I'd see him in the morning, and he'd sit and cough, had coffee, and he'd smoke a cigarette, and he'd start doing his writing for an hour or so. Then he'd get up and leave without saying good-bye or anything.

"At other times," Grunbok continued, "he'd be very outgoing, very extroverted and buddy-buddy. And very intense. Drive, drive, drive." According to Grunbok, Carol stayed in her cabin and only appeared on deck with Rod once in ten days; Grunbok didn't even know she was aboard for the first three or four days.

When a woman on board became sick Serling snapped out of his funk and took charge, escorting the woman ashore and making sure she was taken care of.[19]

Presentiments of death began appearing in Serling's work. "One night, he mentioned he was working on a story he would share with us," according to Craig Curtner, another student of Serling's at Sherman Oaks Experimental College. "The story concerned a small town where everyone relied on one man to provide them with a secret potion that promised long life and maintained a more youthful appearance. But he had grown tired of keeping the townspeople going, and of living for so long, and decided he was ready to die. This sent shock waves through the community as each person had to finally come to grips with their [sic] mortality. Just from this one example, however, I could tell he was a consummate storyteller.[20]

"Less than a year later," Curtner recalled, "I heard of his first heart attack. I was shocked, but not surprised. I remember feeling he was tightly wound inside, extremely intense and very demanding of himself."[21]

The first attack occurred on May 3, 1975, while Serling was working in his garden by the cottage at Interlaken. After recuperating for two weeks at Tompkins County Community Hospital, he was released.

Delbert Mann remembered thinking, "It must have been the diamond" when he first heard the news of Serling's attack. Three months before, Mann had directed a documentary with Serling about the Hope Diamond and the legendary curse surrounding it. According to the curse, anyone who touches the diamond is fated to die shortly thereafter. Ever the joker, Serling had touched the diamond during the shoot.[22]

The second attack occurred two weeks later. "You can't kill this tough Jew," he defiantly wrote ex-*Zone* publicist Owen Comora from his hospital bed.

Across the country, Serling's myriad fans followed their hero's condition, which was widely reported in the news.

On June 28, 1975, while in the middle of open heart surgery, Serling suffered a third and fatal heart attack. He died at 2:15 P.M.

In Ohio, Don Scobel, like so many of Serling's old friends and acquaintances who hadn't seen him in years but had closely followed his career, cried when he heard the news.

Later, Serling was memorialized by an old friend, the Reverend John F. Hayward, director of religious studies at Southern Illinois University, during services at Sage Chapel of Cornell University. Hayward said that Serling should be remembered in the great land of storytellers. "His stories conveyed values that were closest to his heart, and conveyed fears and misgivings he had about himself, and those of the world at large that troubled him."[23] Nan read a story that she had written. There were tears. Later, Carol and the daughters listened to a tape Serling had secretly made for them while in the hospital, just in case. By his own request, Serling was cremated.

Harriet Van Horne, television critic of the *New York World Telegram*, delivered one of the most eloquent eulogies for Serling in her obituary the following Monday:

Rod Serling died this weekend at 50, too talented, too valuable a citizen to be cut down in his prime.

At the time of his death, Serling was earning his living as a professor. He should have been where he belonged, in the thick of television, turning out wise, touching and, occasionally, very spooky scripts. In a medium that produced few giants, Rod stood bold and tall. He was one of the first dramatists to cast a critical eye upon the social order. And, in time, the medium punished him with its displeasure. Like so many of his contemporaries, he finally had to depart the medium he loved, and for which he was much too good.

Rod Serling had a special fondness for the scene in which arguments for evil are advanced, colorfully, incisively, and then, abruptly toppled by a statement of blazing truth. In a world that needs truth tellers, Rod Serling will be greatly missed.[24]

EPILOGUE

As long as they talk about you, you're not really dead, as long as they speak your name, you continue. A legend doesn't die, just because the man dies.
   —from "A Game of Pool," by George Clayton Johnson, aired on *The Twilight Zone*, October 31, 1961[1]

"I just want them to remember that I was a writer a hundred years from now," Rod Serling said in his last interview, a few months before his death in June 1975. Alas, Serling himself didn't do very much in the last decade of his too short life to ensure that. His last scheduled job was to have been as master of ceremonies for an ABC summer replacement variety show with the unpromising title of *Keep On Truckin'*, in which he was to have flogged his *Zone* persona yet again, this time in the service of introducing a gaggle of young comics—a final indignity that both we, and he, were fortunately spared. But just as there are those who remember Orson Welles as the fat man in the Paul Masson wine commercials, there are still numerous people who think of Serling as the voice of Manufacturers Hanover Trust. Indeed, sadly, Serling's obituary in *Variety* identified him as both "writer" and "commercial spokesman."[2]

Happily, millions more associate Serling with the outstanding work he did in the former capacity, during the ten years when he was master of the medium he loved and helped create. *The Twilight Zone* continues to enjoy an astounding, multidimensional life in the "rerun zone." Twenty-seven years after it went off the air, it remains one of a handful of programs (*I Love Lucy*, *The Honeymooners*, *Star Trek*) to have remained in continuous circulation. In 1983,

Warner Brothers released *Twilight Zone—The Movie*, in which four directors (Steven Spielberg, John Landis, Joe Dante, and George Miller) paid homage to Serling. In 1985 CBS revived a version of the *Zone* that lasted only one season. And in 1989 MGM/UA launched a new *Twilight Zone*, which aired on independent TV stations and sometimes used original, unproduced Serling scripts as the basis for its episodes.

Meanwhile, the original and, it would seem, inimitable version continues to travel through other dimensions, or at the very least, other formats. In 1986, CBS Video Library began issuing videocassette versions of all 152 episodes. And Varese Sarabande has recently issued an album of *Twilight Zone* music, including the haunting, metronomic theme created by French composer Marius Constant. Every year Los Angeles station KTLA-TV devotes an entire day of programming to old *Zone*s, and New York station WPIX-TV has followed suit.

The phrase "the twilight zone" has entered the English language. The "twilight zone" concept—the idea that, as the Jefferson Airplane used to sing, there might be another side to this life—or as George Clayton Johnson put it, "the concept that there are things here that do not meet the eye . . . that the human being has a greater potential than anyone dreamed"—has entered our culture. Johnson believes that *The Twilight Zone* is "one of the greatest sources of expanded consciousness up until this point."[3]

The Twilight Zone was far more than entertainment, said Marc Scott Zicree, author of the best-selling *Twilight Zone Companion*. "Serling invited the viewer into a universe of wonder, magic, and delight. It is this sense of wonder, along with Serling's deep human concerns, that make his show timeless and universal."[4]

Then there are the indelible *Twilight Zone* images that Serling has contributed to our collective imagination, images that, particularly for those who were ontologically weaned on the show, serve as a kind of generational reference point: Henry Bemis sitting forlorn amidst the postnuclear wasteland in "Time Enough at Last"; the Chancellor being dragged to his death by his disillusioned subjects in "Obsolete Man"; the deformed—yet beautiful, in their world—doctors and nurses in "Eye of the Beholder"; the outer space Joe McCarthys congratulating themselves on the suburban mayhem they have created below in "Monsters Are Due on Maple Street"; Christian Horn straying into the 1960s, then running back through the desert to the 1840s with a police car in hot pursuit in "A Hundred Yards over the Rim"; Mr. Fremont hysterically congratulating his prodigy-master son for making it snow in "It's a Good Life."

Serling also would have been pleased with the continuing interest in the pre-*Twilight Zone* work. As Stephen King noted in *Danse Macabre*, "Serling's early teleplays—'Patterns,' 'The Comedian,' and 'Requiem for a Heavyweight'—form a large part of what television viewers mean when they speak of a 'golden age.' "[5] Indeed, the works that King mentioned were featured in a 1982 Public Broadcasting Service retrospective, *The Golden Age of Television*, as well as a major Museum of Broadcasting (now the Museum of Television and Radio) retrospective.

In 1982 Serling's "errant wish" (as he would have put it) of making it to Broadway was fulfilled when "Requiem for a Heavyweight" enjoyed a brief run as a stage play, with John Lithgow acting the part of Mountain McClintock and George Segal playing Maish. In 1989 "The Strike" was also adapted for the stage, and its off-Broadway production was well-received by the critics.

Nowhere is Serling more beloved than in his hometown of Binghamton, where the 150-member Rod Serling Memorial Foundation has gone to great pains to perpetuate the memory of Broome County's most famous son. Thanks to the efforts of the foundation, which is headed by Serling's former teacher Helen Foley, there is a Serling commemorative marker in front of Binghamton Central High, as well as a large star dedicated to Serling in the sidewalk downtown. The foundation also placed a marker on the floor of the gazebo in Recreation Park that helped inspire Serling to write "Walking Distance" (although it was so heavy it nearly destroyed the gazebo) and is currently lobbying for a United States postage stamp for Serling. The idea of his image winging its way to postal zones everywhere would doubtless have amused him greatly.

And if one looks around at the pillars of the gazebo, one will eventually find the initials that the young Rod Serling—like the young Martin Sloan—carefully carved on a summer evening in 1936.

APPENDIX A:
VIDEOGRAPHY

Rod Serling was a prolific writer, probably the most prolific writer in TV history. He is known to have written over 200 individual teleplays that were eventually produced. All of these, to the best of my knowledge, are listed below along with as much vital production information as my researchers and I were able to cull from bibliographic and oral sources. In some cases, particularly in the early 1950s, when producers and directors were often not even listed in the credits for shows, only the title and air date, if that, were available. Special attention has been given to the shows with which Serling was most involved, notably *Playhouse 90* and *The Twilight Zone*.

Future Serling scholars are invited to use this admittedly incomplete index as the basis for further efforts.

1950

Date unknown   "Grady Everett for the People." *Stars over Hollywood*, NBC

1951

THE STORM
(July 1951-February 1953)
(Series produced for WKRC-TV, Cincinnati: all episodes produced and directed by Robert Huber, associate producer: Robert McHandrix)

2/07/51	"The Last Waltz"
7/10/51	"The Keeper of the Chair"
11/20/51	"The Sands of Tom"
1/29/52	"No Gods to Serve"
4/52	"The Machine that Talks"
Date unknown	"The Tennessee Waltz"
"	"The Twilight Hounds"
"	"Aftermath"
"	"Law Nine Concerning Xmas"
"	"Phone Call from Louie"
"	"Sight Unseen"
"	"Vertical Deep"

1952

April 29
"The Sergeant." *Armstrong Circle Theater*, NBC. Producer: David Susskind.

June 23
"Welcome Home, Lefty." *Lux Video Theatre*, CBS. Producer: Dick McDonagh.

August 3
"The Carlson Legend." *Hallmark Hall of Fame*, NBC. Producer/Director: Albert McCleery.

August 17
"I Lift Up My Lamp." *Hallmark Hall of Fame*, NBC. Producer/Director: William Corrigan.

August 18
You Be the Bad Guy." *Lux Video Theatre*, CBS. Producer: Dick McDonagh.

October 5
"No Gods to Serve." *The Doctor*, NBC. Producer: Marion Parsonnet. Series directors: Rodney Amateau, Robert Aldrich, Don Siegel.

October 19
"Those Who Wait." *The Doctor*, NBC. Producer: Marion Parsonnet. Series directors: Rodney Amateau, Robert Aldrich, Don Siegel.

November 3
"The Face of Autumn." *Lux Video Theatre*, CBS. Producer: Dick McDonagh.

November 24
"The Hill." *Lux Video Theatre*, CBS. Producer: Dick McDonagh.

December 25	"The Happy Headline." *Campbell Soundstage, NBC*. Producer: Martin Harrell. Series directors: Gary Simpson, Don Appell.

1953

Date unknown	A Walk in the Night." Co-written with Verne Jay.
"	"Sole Victory."
"	"The Victory."
January 26	"The Inn of Eagles." *Lux Video Theatre, CBS*. Producer: Dick McDonagh.
March 2	A Time for Heroes." *Lux Video Theatre, CBS*. Producer: Dick McDonagh.
March 8	"Horace Mann's Miracle." *Hallmark Hall of Fame, NBC*. Producer/Director: Albert McCleery.
April 8	"Next of Kin." *Kraft Television Theatre, NBC*. Series alternate producer-directors: Maury Holland, Richard Dunlap, Harry Herrmann.
May 27	"The Twilight Rounds." *Kraft Television Theatre, NBC*. Series alternate producer-directors: Maury Holland, Richard Dunlap, Harry Herrmann.
August 5	"Old MacDonald Had a Curve." *Kraft Television Theatre, NBC*. Series alternate producer-directors: Maury Holland, Richard Dunlap, Harry Herrmann.
August 18	"Nightmare at Ground Zero." *Suspense, CBS*. Producer/Director: Bob Stevens.
August 22	"The Quiet Village." *Medallion Theatre, CBS*. Producer: William Spier. Director: Seymour Robbie.

August 26 "The Blues for Joey Menotti." *Kraft Television Theatre,* NBC. Series alternate producer-directors: Maury Holland, Richard Dunlap, Harry Herrmann.

November 11 "A Long Time Till Dawn." *Kraft Television Theatre,* NBC. Producer/Director: Richard Dunlap.

November 23 "Buffalo Bill Is Dead." *Studio One,* CBS. Producer: Felix Jackson. Director: Franklin J. Schaffner.

December 9 "Twenty-four Men to a Plane." *Medallion Theatre,* CBS. Producer: Mort Abrahams. Director: Don Medford.

December 15 "At Ease." *Motorola Television Hour,* ABC. Executive Producer: Herbert Brodkin.

December 26 "They Call Them the Meek." *Medallion Theatre,* CBS. Producer: William Spier. Director: Ralph Nelson.

1954

Date unknown "Taps Played on a Bugle."

" "Telltale Clue."

" "Knife in the Dark." Adaptation.

" "The Survivors."

" "The Pitch."

" "Save Me from Treason." *Armstrong Circle Theater,* NBC. Producer: David Susskind. Director: William Corrigan.

" "Mr. Finchley versus the Bomb." (halfhour). *Lux Video Theatre,* NBC.

" "Last Performance."

February 1	Herman Came by Bomber." *Studio One, CBS*. Producer: Felix Jackson. Director: Franklin J. Schaffner.
February 18	"A Walk in the Night." *Philip Morris Playhouse, CBS*.
February 23	"The Muldoon Matter." *Motorola Television Hour, ABC*. Executive Producer: Herbert Brodkin. Director: Donald Richardson.
June 7	"The Strike." *Studio One, CBS*. Producer: Felix Jackson. Director: Franklin J. Schaffner.
August 24	"The Worthy Opponent." *Center Stage, ABC*.
September 6	"U.F.O." *Studio One Summer Theater, CBS*. Producer: Alex March. Director: Mel Ferber.
September 14	"One for the Angels." *Danger, CBS*. Producer: Stanley Niss. Director: Byron Paul.
November 18	"The Summer Memory." *Ford Theater, NBC*. Producer/Director: Jules Bricken.

1955

Date unknown	"A Great Man Lay Dying." *Modern Romances, NBC*. Producer: Wilburg Stark/Jerry Layton. Director: James Sheldon.
January 12	"Patterns." *Kraft Television Theatre, ABC*. Producer/Director: Fielder Cook. Cast: Richard Kiley, Ed Begley, Everett Sloane.
March 21–25	"A Long Time Till Dawn." *Modern Romances, NBC*. Director: Tom Reynolds.
March 24	"Garrity's Sons." *Ford Theater, NBC*. Producer/Director: Jules Bricken.
March 31	"The Champion." *Climax, CBS*. Adaptation from Ring Lardner's short story. Producer: Martin Manulis. Director: Allen Reisner.

April 12   "The Rack." *The United States Steel Hour*, ABC. Producer: The Theatre Guild. Director: Alex Segal.

April 17   "The Fateful Pilgrimage." *Appointment with Adventure*, CBS. Executive Producer: David Susskind. Director: Robert Stevens.

May 15   "Man with a Vengeance." (formerly "The Quiet Village"). *General Electric Theater*, CBS.

June 16   "Strength of Steel." *Star Tonight*, ABC. Producer: Harry Herrmann.

June 25   "To Wake at Midnight." *Climax*, CBS. Producer: Martin Manulis. Director: John Frankenheimer.

September 13   "The Director." *Fireside Theater*, NBC. Producer: Frank Wisbar. Director: Herschel Daugherty.

November 23   "Incident in an Alley." *The United States Steel Hour*, CBS. Producer: The Theatre Guild. Series directors: Dan Petrie, Sidney Lumet or Norman Felton.

November 24   "Portrait in Celluloid." *Climax*, CBS. Producer: Martin Manulis. Director: John Frankenheimer.

November 28   "The Man Who Caught the Ball at Coogan's Bluff." *Studio One*, CBS. Producer: Felix Jackson. Director: Franklin J. Schaffner.

December 12   "O'Toole from Moscow." *Matinee Theater*, NBC. Producer: Albert McCleery.

1956

April 9   "The Arena." *Studio One*, CBS. Producer: Felix Jackson. Director: Franklin J. Schaffner.

April 15   "Beloved Outcasts." *Catholic Hour*, NBC. Religious series produced in cooperation with the National Council of Catholic Men.

April 25   "Noon on Doomsday." *The United States Steel Hour, CBS*. Producer: The Theatre Guild. Director: Daniel Petrie.

September 25   "Mr. Finchley versus the Bomb." *Kaiser Aluminum Hour, NBC*. Producer/Director: Fielder Cook.

October 4   "Forbidden Area." *Playhouse 90, CBS*. Producer: Martin Manulis. Director: John Frankenheimer. Based on the book by Pat Frank. Cast: Charlton Heston, Tab Hunter, Diana Lynn, Vincent Price, Jackie Coogan.

October 11   "Requiem for a Heavyweight." *Playhouse 90, CBS*. Producer: Martin Manulis. Director: Ralph Nelson. Cast: Jack Palance, Keenan Wynn, Kim Hunter, Ed Wynn.

1957

February 14   "The Comedian." *Playhouse 90, CBS*. Producer: Martin Manulis, Director: John Frankenheimer. Based on a short story by Ernest Lehman. Cast: Mickey Rooney, Edmond O'Brien, Mel Tormé.

September 19   "The Dark Side of the Earth." *Playhouse 90, CBS*. Producer: Martin Manulis. Director: Arthur Penn. Cast: Earl Holliman, Kim Hunter, Dean Jagger.

November 28   "Panic Button." *Playhouse 90, CBS*. Producer: Martin Manulis. Director: Franklin J. Schaffner. Cast: Robert Stack, Vera Miles, Leif Erickson, Marion Seldes, Lee J. Cobb.

1958

Date unknown   "The Cause."

May 22   "Bomber's Moon." *Playhouse 90, CBS.* Producer: Martin Manulis. Director: John Frankenheimer. Cast: Bob Cummings, Hazel Court, Martin Balsam, Rip Torn, Larry Gates.

June 19   "A Town Has Turned to Dust." *Playhouse 90, CBS.* Producer: Martin Manulis. Director: John Frankenheimer. Cast: Rod Steiger, William Shatner, Fay Spain, James Gregory.

November 24   "The Time Element." *Westinghouse-Desilu Playhouse, CBS.* Producer: Bert Granet. Director: Allan Reisner. Cast: William Bendix, Martin Balsam, Darryl Hickman, Jesse White.

1959

January 22   "The Velvet Alley." *Playhouse 90, CBS.* Producer: Herbert Brodkin. Director: Franklin J. Schaffner. Cast: Art Carney, Jack Klugman, Leslie Nielsen, Katherine Bard, Bonita Granville.

May 28   "The Rank and File." *Playhouse 90, CBS.* Producer: Herbert Brodkin. Director: Franklin J. Schaffner. Cast: Van Heflin, Luther Adler, Harry Townes, Charles Bronson, Cameron Prud'Homme.

THE TWILIGHT ZONE (CBS, 1959)*
(First-season shows produced by Buck Houghton,
except first episode)

October 2   "Where Is Everybody?" Producer: William Self. Director: Robert Stevens. Cast: Earl Holliman.

* Only those episodes that Serling wrote or adapted himself are listed herein.

October 9   "One for the Angels." Director: Robert Parrish. Cast: Ed Wynn, Murray Hamilton.

October 16   "Mr. Denton on Doomsday." Director: Allen Reisner. Cast: Dan Duryea, Martin Landau.

October 23   "The Sixteen-Millimeter Shrine." Director: Mitchell Leisen. Cast: Ida Lupino, Martin Balsam.

October 30   "Walking Distance." Director: Robert Stevens. Cast: Gig Young, Frank Overton.

November 6   "Escape Clause." Director: Mitchell Leisen. Cast: David Wayne, Thomas Gomez.

November 13 "The Lonely." Director: Jack Smight. Cast: Jack Warden, Jean Marsh.

November 20 "Time Enough at Last." Director: John Brahm. Based on a short story by Lynn Venable. Cast: Burgess Meredith.

December 4   "Judgment Night." Director: John Brahm. Cast: Nehemiah Persoff, Patrick Macnee.

December 11 "And When the Sky Was Opened." Director: Douglas Heyes. Based on the short story "Disappearing Act" by Richard Matheson. Cast: Rod Taylor, Jim Hutton.

December 25 "What You Need." Director: Alvin Ganzer. Based on a short story by Lewis Padgett. Cast: Ernest Truex, Steve Cochran.

1960

May 18   "In the Presence of Mine Enemies." *Playhouse 90,* CBS. Producer: Peter Kortner. Director: Fielder Cook. Cast: Charles Laughton, Arthur Kennedy, Susan Kohner, Oscar Homolka, George Macready, Sam Jaffe, Robert Redford.

THE TWILIGHT ZONE
(First season, continued)

January 1	"The Four of Us Are Dying." Director: John Brahm. Based on an unpublished short story by George Clayton Johnson. Cast: Harry Townes, Phillip Pine, Don Gordon, Ross Martin.
January 8	"Third from the Sun." Director: Richard L. Bare. Based on a short story by Richard Matheson. Cast: Joe Maross, Fritz Weaver.
January 15	"I Shot an Arrow into the Air." Director: Stuart Rosenberg. Based on an idea by Madelon Champion. Cast: Dewey Martin.
January 22	"The Hitch-Hiker." Director: Alvin Ganzer. Based on a radio play by Lucille Fletcher. Cast: Inger Stevens.
January 29	"The Fever." Director: Robert Florey. Cast: Everett Sloane, Vivi Janiss.
February 12	"The Purple Testament." Director: Richard L. Bare. Cast: William Reynolds, Dick York.
February 26	"Mirror Image." Director: John Brahm. Cast: Vera Miles, Martin Milner
March 4	"Monsters Are Due on Maple Street." Director: Ron Winston. Cast: Jack Weston, Claude Akins.
March 25	"People Are Alike All Over." Director: Mitchell Leisen. Based on the short story "Brothers Beyond the Void" by Paul Fairman. Cast: Roddy McDowall, Paul Comi.
April 1	"Execution." Director: David Orrick McDearmon. Based on an unpublished short story by George Clayton Johnson. Cast: Albert Salmi, Russell Johnson.
April 8	"The Big Tall Wish." Director: Ron Winston. Cast: Ivan Dixon, Steven Perry.

April 29   "Nightmare as a Child." Director: Alvin Ganzer. Cast: Janice Rule.

May 6   "A Stop at Willoughby." Director: Robert Parrish. Cast: James Daly.

May 20   "A Passage for Trumpet." Director: Don Medford. Cast: Jack Klugman, John Anderson.

June 3   "Mr. Bevis." Director: William Asher. Cast: Orson Bean, Henry Jones.

June 10   "The After Hours." Director: Douglas Heyes. Cast: Anne Francis.

June 17   "The Mighty Casey." Directors: Alvin Ganzer and Robert Parrish. Cast: Jack Warden, Robert Sorrells.

THE TWILIGHT ZONE (CBS)
(Second-season shows produced by Buck Houghton)

September 30   "*King Nine* Will Not Return." Director: Buzz Kulik. Cast: Robert Cummings.

October 7   "The Man in the Bottle." Director: Don Medford. Cast: Luther Adler, Vivi Janiss.

October 14   "Nervous Man in a Four-Dollar Room." Director: Douglas Heyes. Cast: Joe Mantell, William D. Gordon.

October 28   "A Thing about Machines." Director: David Orrick McDearmon. Cast: Richard Haydn, Barney Phillips.

November 11   "The Eye of the Beholder." Director: Douglas Heyes. Cast: Maxine Stuart, Donna Douglas, William D. Gordon.

December 2   "The Lateness of the Hour." Director: Jack Smight. Produced on videotape. Cast: Inger Stevens, John Hoyt.

December 16   "A Most Unusual Camera." Director: John Rich. Cast: Fred Clark, Jean Carson.

December 23   "Night of the Meek." Director: Jack Smight. Produced on videotape. Cast: Art Carney, John Fiedler.

1961

THE TWILIGHT ZONE
(Second season, continued)

January 6   "Dust." Director: Douglas Heyes. Cast: Thomas Gomez, John Larch.

January 13   "Back There." Director: David Orrick McDearmon. Cast: Russell Johnson.

January 20   "The Whole Truth." Director: James Sheldon. Produced on videotape. Cast: Jack Carson, Loring Smith.

February 10   "Twenty-two." Director: Jack Smight. Produced on videotape. Based on an anecdote in *Famous Ghost Stories*, edited by Bennett Cerf. Cast: Barbara Nichols, Arline Sax.

February 24   "The Odyssey of Flight 33." Director: Justus Addiss. Cast: John Anderson, Paul Comi.

March 3   "Mr. Dingle, the Strong." Director: John Brahm. Cast: Burgess Meredith, Don Rickles.

April 7   "A Hundred Yards over the Rim." Director: Buzz Kulik. Cast: Cliff Robertson, John Astin.

April 21   "The Rip Van Winkle Caper." Director: Justus Addiss. Cast: Oscar Beregi, Simon Oakland.

April 28   "The Silence." Director: Boris Sagal. Cast: Franchot Tone, Liam Sullivan.

May 12   "The Mind and the Matter." Director: Buzz Kulik. Cast: Shelley Berman.

May 26	"Will the Real Martian Please Stand Up?" Director: Montgomery Pittman. Cast: John Hoyt, Jack Elam, Barney Phillips.
June 2	"The Obsolete Man." Director: Elliot Silverstein. Cast: Burgess Meredith, Fritz Weaver.

THE TWILIGHT ZONE (CBS)
(Third-season shows produced by Buck Houghton)

September 22	"The Arrival." Director: Boris Sagal. Cast: Harold J. Stone, Fredd Wayne.
September 29	"The Shelter." Director: Lamont Johnson. Cast: Larry Gates, Jack Albertson.
October 6	"The Passerby." Director: Elliot Silverstein. Cast: Joanne Linville, James Gregory.
October 20	"The Mirror." Director: Don Medford. Cast: Peter Falk.
November 3	"It's a Good Life." Director: James Sheldon. Based on the short story "It's a Good Life" by Jerome Bixby. Cast: Billy Mumy, Cloris Leachman.
November 10	"Deaths-head Revisited." Director: Don Medford. Cast: Joseph Schildkraut, Oscar Beregi.
November 17	"The Midnight Sun." Director: Anton Leader. Cast: Lois Nettleton.
November 24	"Still Valley." Director: James Sheldon. Based on the short story "The Valley Was Still" by Manly Wade-Wellman. Cast: Gary Merrill, Vaughn Taylor.
December 22	"Five Characters in Search of an Exit." Director: Lamont Johnson. Based on the short story "The Depository" by Marvin Petal. Cast: William Windom, Murray Matheson.

December 29   "A Quality of Mercy." Director: Buzz Kulik. Based on an idea by Sam Rolfe. Cast: Dean Stockwell, Albert Salmi, Leonard Nimoy, Jerry Fujikawa.

1962

THE TWILIGHT ZONE
(Third season, continued)

January 12   "One More Pallbearer." Director: Lamont Johnson. Cast: Joseph Wiseman.

February 2   "Showdown with Rance McGrew." Director: Christian Nyby. Based on an idea by Frederick Louis Fox. Cast: Larry Blyden, Arch Johnson.

March 2   "To Serve Man." Director: Richard L. Bare. Based on a short story by Damon Knight. Cast: Lloyd Bochner.

March 30   "The Little People." Director: William Claxton. Cast: Joe Maross, Claude Akins.

April 6   "Four O'Clock." Director: Lamont Johnson. Based on a short story by Price Day. Cast: Theodore Bikel.

April 13   "Hocus-Pocus and Frisby." Director: Lamont Johnson. Based on an unpublished short story by Frederic Louis Fox. Cast: Andy Devine.

April 20   "The Trade-Ins." Director: Elliot Silverstein. Cast: Alma Platt, Joseph Schildkraut.

April 27   "The Gift." Director: Allen H. Miner. Cast: Geoffrey Horne, Edmund Vargas.

May 4   "The Dummy." Director: Abner Biberman. Based on an unpublished story by Lee Polk. Cast: Cliff Robertson, Frank Sutton.

May 25   "Cavender Is Coming." Director: Christian Nyby. Cast: Carol Burnett, Jesse White.

June 1   "The Changing of the Guard." Director: Robert Ellis Miller. Cast: Donald Pleasance.

1963

October 4   "A Killing at Sundial." *Bob Hope Presents the Chrysler Theater, NBC*. Executive Producer: Dick Berg. Director: Alex Segal. Cast: Stuart Whitman, Angie Dickinson, Joseph Callera, Robert Emhardt.

December 20   "It's Mental Work." *Bob Hope Presents the Chrysler Theater, NBC*. Based on a short story by John O'Hara. Executive Producer: Dick Berg.

THE TWILIGHT ZONE (CBS)
(Fourth-season one-hour shows produced by Herbert Hirschmann except where noted)

January 10   "The Thirty-Fathom Grave." Director: Perry Lafferty. Cast: Mike Kellin, Simon Oakland.

January 24   "He's Alive." Director: Stuart Rosenberg. Cast: Dennis Hopper, Ludwig Donath.

March 7   "No Time Like the Past." Director: Justus Addiss. Cast: Dana Andrews.

March 14   "The Parallel." Director: Alan Crosland. Producer: Bert Granet. Cast: Steve Forrest, Jacqueline Scott.

April 11   "Of Late I Think of Cliffordville." Director: David Lowell Rich. Producer: Bert Granet. Cast: Albert Salmi, Julie Newmar, John Anderson.

May 2   "On Thursday We Leave for Home." Director: Buzz Kulik. Producer: Bert Granet. Cast: James Whitmore, James Broderick.

May 23   "The Bard." Director: David Butler. Cast: Jack Weston, John Williams.

THE TWILIGHT ZONE (CBS)
(Fifth-season shows produced by Bert Granet except where noted)

September 27   "In Praise of Pip." Director: Joseph M. Newman. Cast: Jack Klugman, Billy Mumy.

October 18   "A Kind of Stopwatch." Director: John Rich. Based on an unpublished short story by Michael D. Rosenthal. Cast: Richard Erdman, Leon Belasco.

October 25   "The Last Night of a Jockey." Director: Joseph M. Newman. Producer: William Froug. Cast: Mickey Rooney.

November 8   "The Old Man in the Cave." Director: Alan Crosland, Jr. Based on the short story "The Old Man" by Henry Slesar. Cast: James Coburn, John Anderson.

November 15   "Uncle Simon." Director: Don Siegel. Cast: Cedric Hardwicke, Constance Ford.

November 29   "Probe Seven—Over and Out." Director: Ted Post. Producer: William Froug. Cast: Richard Basehart, Antoinette Bower.

December 6   "The Seventh Is Made Up of Phantoms." Director: Alan Crosland, Jr. Cast: Ron Foster, Warren Oates.

December 13   "A Short Drink from a Certain Fountain." Director: Bernard Girard. Based on an idea by Lou Holtz. Cast: Patrick O'Neal, Ruta Lee.

1964

March 27   "Slow Fade to Black." *Bob Hope Presents the Chrysler Theater, NBC.* Executive Producer: Dick Berg. Director: Ron Winston.

May 22   "The Command." *Bob Hope Presents the Chrysler Theater, NBC.* Adaptation from "The Strike." Executive Producer: Dick Berg. Director: Fielder Cook.

December 28   "A Carol for Another Christmas." *United Nations Special.* Producer-Director: Joseph L. Mankiewicz.

THE TWILIGHT ZONE (CBS)
(Fifth-season, continued: all shows produced by William Froug except where noted)

January 10   "The Long Morrow." Director: Robert Florey. Cast: Robert Lansing, Mariette Hartley.

March 20   "The Masks." Director: Ida Lupino. Producer: Bert Granet. Cast: Robert Keith, Virginia Gregg, Alan Sues.

March 27   "I Am the Night—Color Me Black." Director: Abner Biberman. Cast: Paul Fix, Michael Constantine, Ivan Dixon.

April 3   "Sounds and Silences." Director: Richard Donner. Cast: John McGiver.

April 17   "The Jeopardy Room." Director: Richard Donner. Cast: Martin Landau.

May 8   "Mr. Garrity and the Graves." Director: Ted Post. Based on an unpublished short story by Mike Korologos. Cast: John Dehner, J. Pat O'Malley.

May 15   "The Brain Center at Whipple's." Director: Richard Donner. Cast: Richard Deacon.

May 29   "The Fear." Director: Ted Post. Cast: Mark Richman, Hazel Court.

1965

January 22   "Exit from a Plane in Flight." *Bob Hope Presents the Chrysler Theater*, NBC. Executive Producer: Dick Berg.

THE LONER (CBS)
(Executive Producer: William Dozier. Producer: Andy White) (Starring Lloyd Bridges)

September 18   "An Echo of Bugles." Director: Alex March.

September 25   "The Vespers." Director: Leon Benson.

October 2   "The Lonely Calico Queen." Director: Allen Miner.

October 9   "The Kingdom of McComb." Director: Leon Benson.

October 16   "One of the Wounded." Director: Paul Henreid.

October 30   "Widow on the Evening Stage." Director: Joe Pevney.

November 6   "The House Rules at Mrs. Wayne's." Director: Allen Miner.

November 13   "The Sheriff of Fetterman's Crossing." Director: Don Taylor.

November 20   "The Homecoming of Lemuel Stove." Director: Joe Pevney.

November 27   "Westward the Shoemaker." Director: Joe Pevney.

December 4   "The Oath." Director: Alex March.

1966

THE LONER (CBS)
(continued)

January 15   "A Little Stroll to the End of the Line." Director: Norman Foster.

January 22	"The Trial in Paradise." Director: Allen Reisner.
February 5, 12	"The Mourners for Johnny Sharp." (two parts) Director: Joe Pevney.
April 29	"The Hate Syndrome." *Insight.* Syndicated. Religious program, representing modern-day morality lessons. Executive Producer/Host: Ellwood E. Keiser.
December 13	"The Doomsday Flight." *Project 120—World Premiere Theater, NBC.* Producer: Frank Price. Director: William A. Graham.

1968

September 12	"Certain Honorable Men." *On Stage, NBC.* Producer: Alan Landsburg. Director: Alex Segal. Cast: Peter Fonda, Van Heflin.

1969

September 22	Pilot episode, *The New People, ABC.* Producer: Aaron Spelling. Cast: Richard Kiley, Tiffany Bolling.
November 8	*Night Gallery. World Premiere Theater, NBC.* Producer: William Sackheim. "The Cemetery." Director: Boris Sagal. Cast: Roddy McDowall. "Eyes." Director: Steven Spielberg. Cast: Joan Crawford, Tom Bosley. "Escape Route." Director: Barry Shear. Cast: Richard Kiley, Sam Jaffe.

1970

February 6   "A Storm in Summer." *Hallmark Hall of Fame,* *NBC.* Producer: Alan Landsberg. Director: Buzz Kulik.

NIGHT GALLERY (NBC)
(First-season shows produced by Jack Laird: part of NBC's *FOUR-IN-ONE* series)

December 23   "Little Black Bag." Director: Jeannot Szwarc. Cast: Burgess Meredith.
"The Nature of the Enemy." Director: Allen Reisner. Cast: Joseph Campanella.
"The House." Director: John Astin. Based on a short story by Andre Maurois. Cast: Joanna Pettet, Steve Franken.

December 30   "Certain Shadows on the Wall." Director: Jeff Corey. Based on a short story by Mary E. Wilkins-Freeman. Cast: Louis Hayward, Agnes Moorehead.

1971

NIGHT GALLERY (NBC)
(First season, continued)

January 6   "Make Me Laugh." Director: Steven Spielberg. Cast: Godfrey Cambridge.
"Clean Kills and Other Stories." Director: Walter Doniger. Cast: Raymond Massey.

January 13   "Pamela's Voice." Director: Richard Benedict. Cast: Phyllis Diller.
"Lone Survivor." Director: Gene Levitt. Cast: John Colicos, Torin Thatcher.
"The Doll." Director: Rudi Dorn. Cast: John Williams.

January 20   "They're Tearing Down Tim Riley's Bar." Director: Don Taylor. Cast: William Windom, Bert Convy, Diane Baker.
"The Last Laurel." Director: Darryl Duke. Cast: Martin E. Brooks.

NIGHT GALLERY (NBC)
(Second-season shows produced by Jack Laird)

September 15   "The Boy Who Predicted Earthquakes." Director: John M. Badham. Cast: Michael Constanine, Clint Howard.

September 22   "A Death in the Family." Director: Jeannot Szwarc. Cast: E. G. Marshall.
"Class of '99." Director: Jeannot Szwarc. Cast: Brandon de Wilde, Vincent Price.

October 6   "A Fear of Spiders." Director: John Astin. Based on the short story "The Spider" by Elizabeth Walter. Cast: Kim Stanley.
"The Academy." Director: Jeff Corey. Based on a short story by David Ely. Cast: Pat Boone, Larry Linville.

November 3   "Midnight Never Ends." Director: Jeannot Szwarc. Cast: Susan Strasberg.

November 10   "The Diary." Director: William Hale. Cast: Patty Duke.

November 17   "Dr. Stringfellow's Rejuvenation." Director: Jerrold Freedman. Cast: Murray Hamilton, Forrest Tucker.

December 1   "The Dear Departed." Director: Jeff Corey. Based on a short story by Alice May-Schnirring. Cast: Steve Lawrence, Maureen Arthur, Harvey Lembeck.

December 8   "Cool Air." Director: Jeannot Szwarc. Based on a short story by H. P. Lovecraft. Cast: Barbara Rush, Henry Darrow.
"Camera Obscura." Director: John M. Badham. Based on a short story by Basil Copper. Cast: Ross Martin, Rene Auberjonois.

December 15   "The Messiah on Mott Street." Director: Don Taylor. Cast: Edward G. Robinson, Ricky Powell.

December 29   "The Different Ones." Director: John M. Lucas. Cast: Paul Koch, Jon Korkes.

1972

NIGHT GALLERY (NBC)
(Second season, continued)

January 5   "Green Fingers." Director: John Badham. Based on a short story by R. C. Cook. Cast: Cameron Mitchell, Elsa Lanchester.

January 12   "Lindesmann's Catch." Director: Jeff Corey. Cast: Stuart Whitman, Jack Aronson, Harry Townes.

January 19   "The Miracle at Camefeo." Director: Ralph Senensky. Cast: Harry Guardino, Ray Danton.

January 26   "The Waiting Room." Director: Jeannot Szwarc. Cast: Steve Forrest, Gilbert Roland, Buddy Ebsen, Larry Watson.

February 9   "Deliveries in the Rear." Director: Jeff Corey. Cast: Cornel Wilde, Rosemary Forsyth, Walter Burke, Peter Whitney.

February 23   "You Can't Get Help Like That Anymore." Director: Jeff Corey. Cast: Cloris Leachman, Broderick Crawford.

March 1   "The Caterpillar." Director: Jeannot Szwarc. Based on the short story "Boomerang" by Oscar Cook. Cast: Laurence Harvey, Joanna Pettet, Tom Helmore.

NIGHT GALLERY (NBC)
(Third season)

October 22   "Rare Objects." Director: Jeannot Szwarc. Cast: Mickey Rooney, Raymond Massey.

November 12   "You Can Come Up Now, Mrs. Millikan." Director: John Badham. Cast: Ozzie and Harriet Nelson, Roger Davis.

December 17   "Finnegan's Flight." Director: Gene Kearney. Cast: Burgess Meredith, Cameron Mitchell, Barry Sullivan.

1973

NIGHT GALLERY (NBC)
(Third season, continued)

January 14   "Something in the Woodwork." Director: Edmund M. Abrams. Cast: Geraldine Page, John McMurtry, Leif Erickson.

1976

August 26   "Sad and Lonely Sundays." *The Oath, ABC.* Producers: Aaron Spelling, Leonard Goldberg. Director: James Goldstone. Cast: Jack Albertson, Will Geer.

APPENDIX B:
FILMOGRAPHY

Patterns.   (United Artists, 1956)
  Produced by Michael Myerberg and Jed Harris.
  Screenplay by Rod Serling, based on his teleplay "Patterns" for
    Kraft Television Theatre.
  Directed by Fielder Cook.
  Stars: Van Heflin, Everett Sloane, Ed Begley, Beatrice Straight,
    Elizabeth Wilson.

The Rack.   (Metro-Goldwyn-Mayer, 1956)
  Produced by Arthur M. Loew, Jr.
  Screenplay by Stewart Stern.
  Story by Rod Serling, based on his teleplay.
  Directed by Arnold Laven.
  Stars: Paul Newman, Wendell Corey, Walter Pidgeon, Anne Fran-
    cis, Lee Marvin.

Saddle the Wind.   (Metro-Goldwyn-Mayer, 1957)
  Produced by Armand Deutsch.
  Screenplay by Rod Serling, based on the story by Thomas Thomp-
    son.
  Directed by Robert Parrish.
  Stars: John Cassavetes, Robert Taylor, Julie London, Donald
    Crisp, Royal Dano, Charles McGraw.

Incident in an Alley.   (United Artists, 1962)
  Produced by Robert E. Kent.
  Scenario by Harold Medford and Owen Harris.
  Based on a teleplay by Rod Serling.

Directed by Edward L. Cahn.
Stars: Chris Warfield, Erin O'Donnell, Harp McGuire.

Requiem for a Heavyweight.   (Paman Productions, 1962)
Released by Columbia Pictures.
Produced by David Susskind.
Screenplay by Rod Serling, based on his teleplay.
Directed by Ralph Nelson.
Stars: Anthony Quinn, Jackie Gleason, Mickey Rooney, Julie
    Harris, Nancy Cushman, Madame Spivy, Cassius Clay (Mu-
    hammad Ali).

The Yellow Canary.   (Cooga Mooga Film Productions, 1963)
Released by Twentieth Century-Fox.
Produced by Maury Dexter.
Screenplay by Rod Serling, based on the novel *Evil Come, Evil
    Go* by Whit Masterson.
Directed by Buzz Kulik.
Stars: Pat Boone, Barbara Eden, Steve Forrest, Jack Klugman,
    Jesse White, Milton Selzer, Harold Gould.

Seven Days in May.   (Seven Arts Production-Joel
    Productions, 1964)
Released by Paramount Pictures.
Produced by Edward Lewis.
Screenplay by Rod Serling, based on the novel by Fletcher Knebel
    and Charles W. Bailey II.
Directed by John Frankenheimer.
Stars: Kirk Douglas, Burt Lancaster, Fredric March, Ava Gardner,
    Edmond O'Brien, Martin Balsam, John Houseman.

Let Us Continue.   (United States Information Agency, 1964)
Produced by William Froug.
Written by Rod Serling.

Assault on a Queen.   (Seven Arts Productions-Sinatra Enterprises,
    1966)
Released by Paramount Pictures.
Produced by William Goetz.
Screenplay by Rod Serling.
Based on the novel by Jack Finney.
Directed by Jack Donohue.

Stars: Frank Sinatra, Virna Lisi, Tony Franciosa, Richard Conte, Reginald Denny.

Planet of the Apes.   (APJAC Productions, 1968)
Released by Twentieth Century-Fox.
Produced by Arthur P. Jacobs.
Screenplay by Michael Wilson and Rod Serling, based on the novel by Pierre Boulle.
Directed by Franklin J. Schaffner.
Stars: Charlton Heston, Kim Hunter, Roddy McDowall, Maurice Evans, James Whitmore, James Daly.

The Man.   (ABC Circle Films, 1972)
Released by Paramount Pictures.
Produced by Lee Rich.
Story and screenplay by Rod Serling, based on the novel by Irving Wallace.
Directed by Joseph Sargent.
Stars: James Earl Jones, Martin Balsam, Burgess Meredith, Lew Ayres, William Windom, Barbara Rush, Janet MacLachlan, Jack Benny.

APPENDIX C:
AWARDS

Rod Serling has been called the most honored writer in television history, and he probably is. Serling won dozens of awards and honors during his career, some major ones, numerous marginal ones; he cherished them all. Below are some of the encomia of which he was proudest.

EMMY:

1955: BEST ORIGINAL TELEPLAY WRITING
"Patterns," *Kraft Television Theater* (NBC)

1956: BEST TELEPLAY WRITING (ONE HOUR OR MORE)
"Requiem for a Heavyweight," *Playhouse 90* (CBS)

1957: BEST TELEPLAY WRITING (ONE HOUR OR MORE)
"The Comedian," *Playhouse 90* (CBS)

1960: OUTSTANDING WRITING ACHIEVEMENT IN DRAMA
The Twilight Zone (CBS)

1961: OUTSTANDING WRITING ACHIEVEMENT IN DRAMA
The Twilight Zone (CBS)

1963: OUTSTANDING WRITING ACHIEVEMENT IN DRAMA (ADAPTATION)
"It's Mental Work," *Bob Hope Presents the Chrysler Theater* (NBC)

GOLDEN GLOBE:
1962: BEST TELEVISION STAR, MALE.

253

HARCOURT-BRACE AWARD:
 1956: "Requiem for a Heavyweight," *Playhouse 90* (CBS)

GEORGE FOSTER PEABODY BROADCASTING AWARDS:
 1956: TELEVISION WRITING

LOOK MAGAZINE ANNUAL TELEVISION AWARDS:
 1959: Best Playwright
　　　"The Velvet Alley," *Playhouse 90* (CBS)

SYLVANIA:
 1955: BEST TELEPLAY WRITING
　　　"Patterns," *Kraft Television Theatre* (NBC)

 1956: BEST TELEPLAY WRITING
　　　"Requiem for a Heavyweight," *Playhouse 90* (CBS)

TELEVISION-RADIO WRITERS' ANNUAL AWARD:
 1956: "Requiem for a Heavyweight," *Playhouse 90* (CBS)

WRITERS GUILD OF AMERICA:
 1956: BEST ONE HOUR OR MORE TV DRAMA
　　　"Requiem for a Heavyweight," *Playhouse 90* (CBS)

 1958: BEST SCRIPT, MORE THAN SIXTY MINUTES
　　　"A Town Has Turned to Dust," *Playhouse 90* (CBS)

 1975: LAUREL AWARD

NOTES

PREFACE

1. Serling, speech before Library of Congress, June 30, 1968.
2. Museum of Broadcasting, *Rod Serling: Dimensions of Imagination* (New York: February 1982), 9. Catalog for exhibit.
3. *Connoisseur*, September 1989, 137.

PROLOGUE

1. *TV Guide*, June 3, 1972.

CHAPTER ONE

1. Marc Zicree, *The Twilight Zone Companion* (New York: Bantam Books, 1982), 42.
2. *Pipe Dream Features*, November 22, 1985, 5.
3. Ibid., 44.
4. *Beyond the Catskills. Jewish Life in Binghamton, New York: 1850–1975* (State University of New York, Binghamton: 1989), 11. Catalog for exhibit.
5. Louis Kosoff, interview with author.
6. Saydelle Agranovitch, interview with author.
7. *Binghamton Sun*, March 8, 1957.
8. Sybil Goldenberg, interview with author.
9. Lloyd Hartman, interview with author.
10. Maurice O'Brien, interview with author.

11. Ibid.
12. Norman Miller, interview with author.
13. *TV Guide*, June 3, 1972.

CHAPTER TWO

1. Norman Corwin, *13 by Corwin* (New York: Henry Holt, 1942), 56.
2. *Theater Arts*, March 1936.
3. Ibid.
4. *13 by Corwin*, 55.
5. Ibid., 67.
6. Ibid., 69.
7. Ibid., 76.
8. Norman Corwin, interview with author.
9. *Binghamton Sun*, May 30, 1955.

CHAPTER THREE

1. Zicree, 88.
2. Binghamton Central High School *Panorama*.
3. *Seventeen*, June 1957.
4. Vernon Hartung, interview with author.
5. Jack Warden, interview with author.
6. Swing, quoted in Major Edward M. Flanagan, *The Angels: A History of the 11th Airborne Division* (Washington, DC: Infantry Journal Press, 1948), 4.
7. Norman Miller, interview with author.
8. Ken Haan, interview with author.
9. Hartung interview.
10. Mike Dann, interview with author.
11. Haan interview.
12. Louis Kosoff interview.
13. Radio script, 11th Airborne Division.
14. Swing, quoted in Flanagan.
15. Frank Lewis, interview with author.
16. Serling, quoted in Joel Engel, *Rod Serling: The Dreams and*

Nightmares of Life in "The Twilight Zone" (Chicago: Contemporary Books, 1989), 47.
17. Ibid., 48.
18. Lewis interview.

CHAPTER FOUR

1. Engel, 67.
2. Miller interview.
3. *New York Daily News*, December 10, 1956.
4. Fred Rudolph, *American College and University* (New York: Oxford University, 1955), 87.
5. John Kittross, interview with author.
6. Don Scobel, interview with author.
7. *Antiochan*, March 1948.
8. Serling, quoted in *Emmy* magazine, February 1982.
9. Kittross interview.
10. Lillian Blake, interview with author.
11. Unpublished story by Don Scobel.
12. Carol Serling, quoted in Zicree, 6.
13. *Binghamton Press*, October 30, 1959.
14. Ann Goodman, interview with author.
15. Leona Serling, interview with author.
16. Scobel interview.
17. Barbara Agranoff, interview with author.
18. Theodore Bikel, interview with author.
19. Rudy Ruderman, interview with author.

CHAPTER FIVE

1. *Newsweek*, June 3, 1950.
2. In *Dr. Christian Show* broadcast, May 18, 1949.
3. Zicree, 6.
4. Sally Bedell Smith, *In All His Glory* (New York: Simon and Schuster, 1990), 267.
5. Ibid., 268.
6. Erik Barnouw, *Tube of Plenty* (New York: Oxford University Press, 1982), 155.

7. Carson Davidson, interview with author.
8. Mary Wood, interview with author.
9. Sara Lithgow, interview with author.
10. Charles Vaughan, interview with author.
11. Museum of Broadcasting, *Rod Serling: Dimensions of Imagination* (New York: February 1982), 18. Catalog for exhibit.
12. Rod Serling, *Patterns* (New York: Simon and Schuster, 1958).
13. Saul and Phyllis Marmer, interview with author.
14. *Dimensions*, 18.
15. Vaughan interview.
16. Gene Walz, interview with author.
17. Paul Bogart, interview with author.
18. Wood interview.
19. Jerome Hellman, interview with author.
20. *Writers' Digest*, December 1953.
21. Vaughan interview.
22. "No Gods to Serve," WKRC-TV (Cincinnati), December 22, 1952.
23. *Dimensions*, 18.
24. Ibid.
25. William Boddy, "The Vast Wasteland." Ph.D. dissertation.

CHAPTER SIX

1. Gore Vidal, interview with author.
2. Fielder Cook, interview with author.
3. Ethel Wynant, interview with author.
4. *Cincinnati Enquirer*, March 7, 1963.
5. Quoted in Barnouw, 158.
6. Ibid.
7. Ibid., 159.
8. Hellman interview.
9. Arthur Penn, interview with author.
10. Ibid.
11. Ibid.
12. Loring Mandel, interview with author.
13. Delbert Mann, interview with author.
14. George Roy Hill, interview with author.
15. Richard Kiley, interview with author.

16. Tad Mosel, interview with author.
17. From an interview on *The Golden Age of Television: Patterns*, Sonny Fox, producer, Public Broadcasting Service, 1982.
18. Kiley interview.
19. Vidal interview.
20. Mosel interview.
21. Ibid.
22. Buzz Kulik, interview with author.
23. Roddy McDowall, interview with author.
24. Vidal interview.
25. *The National Observer*, May 19, 1966.
26. Serling, *Patterns* 11.
27. Ibid., 12.
28. Felix Jackson, interview with author.
29. Vidal interview; Jackson interview.
30. *Cincinnati Post*, March 5, 1953.
31. Ibid.
32. *Writers' Digest*, December 1953.
33. Vidal interview.
34. *Writers' Digest*, December 1952.
35. Quoted in *Twilight Zone* magazine, April 1986.
36. *Writers' Digest*, December 1953.
37. Ibid.
38. *Writers' Yearbook*, December 1954.
39. *Cincinnati Enquirer*, March 21, 1954.
40. From "The Strike" by Rod Serling, in *Best Television Plays*, ed. Gore Vidal (New York: Ballantine, 1956), 9.

CHAPTER SEVEN

1. Sloan Wilson, *The Man in the Gray Flannel Suit* (New York: Simon and Schuster, 1955), 44.
2. *TV Guide: The First 25 Years*, ed. Sam J. Harris (New York: New American Library, 1966), 212.
3. *New York Times*, January 16, 1955.
4. Serling, *Patterns*, 29.
5. Ibid., 82.
6. *Dimensions*, 10.
7. Jackson interview.

8. *Cincinnati Post*, April 12, 1956.
9. Hellman interview.
10. Serling, *Patterns*, 13.
11. Hellman interview.
12. Barnouw, 155.
13. Ibid., 156.
14. Paddy Chayefsky, *Television Plays* (New York: Simon and Schuster, 1955), xiii.
15. *The Mike Wallace Show*, October 21, 1959.
16. Serling, "Patterns," 14.
17. *US Air Magazine*, November 1982.
18. Serling, "Patterns," 14.
19. *New York Times*, June 26, 1955.
20. Cook interview.
21. *Cincinnati Times-Star*, December 9, 1955.
22. Don Freeman, interview with author.
23. Hellman interview.
24. *Newsweek*, December 5, 1955.
25. Ibid.
26. Ibid.
27. George Githers, interview with author.
28. Ibid.
29. Ibid.
30. *Patterns*, 28.
31. Ibid., 24.
32. *The Mike Wallace Show*, October 1959, CBS.
33. *Cincinnati Times-Star*, April 26, 1956.

CHAPTER EIGHT

1. *New York Daily News*, April 6, 1956.
2. *New York Times*, October 12, 1956.
3. *New York Daily News*, October 12, 1956.
4. *New York Herald-Tribune*, October 12, 1956.
5. Del Reisman, interview.
6. *TV Guide: The First 25 Years* 213.
7. Martin Manulis, interview with author.
8. Dominick Dunne, interview with author.
9. Ibid.

10. Ibid.
11. Virginia Cox, interview with author.
12. *Seventeen*, June 1957.
13. Robert Parrish, interview with author.
14. Ibid.
15. Ibid.
16. Engel, 146.
17. Richard Grossman, interview with author.
18. *Vogue*, April 1957.
19. Marmer interview.
20. Ibid.
21. Ibid.
22. Ibid.
23. Mosel interview.
24. Bogart interview.
25. *New York World Telegram*, June 19, 1975.
26. *Television Age*, June 1957.
27. *New York Times*, April 15, 1956.
28. *Dimensions*, 9.
29. *New York Times Magazine*, November 24, 1957.
30. Hellman interview.

CHAPTER NINE

1. Hortense Powdermaker, *Hollywood: The Dream Factory*. (New York: Simon and Schuster, 1950), 83.
2. *Los Angeles Times*, April 7, 1958.
3. Kim Hunter, interview with author.
4. Cox interview.
5. Ibid.
6. Wynant interview.
7. Ibid.
8. From interview with John Frankenheimer on *The Golden Age of Television: The Comedian*, Sonny Fox, producer 1982.
9. *Cincinnati Post*. May 23, 1958.
10. *Time*, February 3, 1958.
11. *Cincinnati Post*, April 11, 1957.
12. Freeman interview.
13. *Cosmopolitan*, August 1958.

14. *Time*, February 11, 1959.
15. Marmer interview.
16. Freeman interview.
17. CBS press release, March 1959.
18. *Writers Guild Bulletin*, July 1959.
19. *New York World Telegram*, June 30, 1975.
20. Statement before Federal Communications Commission, January 5, 1960.
21. *New York Times*, January 9, 1959.
22. *Television Age*, December 25, 1961.
23. Joseph Persico, *Edward R. Murrow: An American Original* (New York: McGraw-Hill, 1989), 434.
24. Mandel interview.

CHAPTER TEN

1. Reprinted in Arlen Schumer, *Visions from the Twilight Zone* (San Francisco: Chronicle, 1991), 149.
2. *The Mike Wallace Show*, October 1, 1959, CBS.
3. Ibid.
4. Ibid.
5. Ibid.
6. Ibid.
7. Buzz Kulik, interview with author.
8. Bert Granet, interview with author.
9. Ibid.
10. CBS press release.
11. *New York Times*, November 25, 1958.
12. Ibid.
13. William Self, interview with author.
14. Earl Holliman, interview with author.
15. Jonathan Spota, interview with author.
16. Chester "Bud" Erion, interview with author.
17. Reisman interview.
18. Dick Berg, interview with Stephen Farber.
19. Reisman interview.
20. Martin Landau, interview with author.
21. Janice Rule, interview with author.
22. *Ithaca Journal*, September 5, 1974.

23. *The Mike Wallace Show*, October 1959, CBS.
24. *New York Times*, September 30, 1959.
25. *Binghamton Press*, December 13, 1959.
26. Ibid.
27. Owen Comora, interview with author.
28. *The Mike Wallace Show*, October 1959, CBS.
29. *Los Angeles Times*, October 3, 1959.
30. *New York Times*, October 4, 1959.
31. Buck Houghton, interview with author.
32. Claude Akins, interview with author.
33. Jack Warden, interview with author.
34. Richard Donner, interviewed in *Twilight Zone* magazine, July 1981.
35. Douglas Heyes, interview with author.
36. Ibid.
37. Kulik interview.
38. Quoted in *Emmy* magazine, October 1982.
39. Reprinted in *Twilight Zone* magazine, May 1981.
40. Ibid.
41. Zicree, 131.
42. Charles Beaumont, telegram to Dr. Frank Stanton, May 22, 1960.

CHAPTER ELEVEN

1. Zicree, 144.
2. Ibid., 31.
3. Ted Ashley, interview with author.
4. Ibid.
5. Ibid.
6. Zicree, 135.
7. Dr. Frank Stanton, interview with author.
8. Heyes interview.
9. Sydney Pollack, interview with author.
10. Vidal interview.
11. Reisman interview.
12. Mandel interview.
13. Kulik interview.
14. Dann interview.

15. Reisman interview.
16. Arlen Schumer, *Visions from the Twilight Zone* (San Francisco: Chronicle Books, 1991), 162.
17. Reisman interview.
18. Heyes interview.
19. Buck Houghton, interview with author.
20. Heyes interview.
21. Richard Matheson interviewed in *Twilight Zone* magazine, September 1981.
22. George Clayton Johnson, interview with author.
23. Ibid.
24. Houghton interview.
25. Johnson interview.
26. Ibid.
27. Ibid.
28. William Shatner, interview with author.
29. Ibid.
30. Reisman interview.
31. Ibid.
32. Ibid.
33. George T. Clemens, interview with author.
34. Ibid.
35. Cliff Robertson, interview with author.
36. Clemens interview.
37. Warden interview.
38. Zicree, 145.
39. Heyes interview.
40. Reprinted in *Twilight Zone* magazine, April 1989.
41. Zicree, 193.

CHAPTER TWELVE

1. *TV Guide*, June 30, 1962.
2. Zicree, 145.
3. *The Mike Wallace Show*, October 1959, CBS.
4. *TV Guide*, October 3, 1960.
5. Heyes interview.
6. Clemens interview.
7. Letter from Richard Matheson to author.

8. *Twilight Zone* magazine, September 1981.
9. Dann interview.
10. William Self interview.
11. Farber interview with Berg.
12. *Ithaca Journal*, July 7, 1962.
13. *TV Guide*, June 3, 1972.
14. Robert Wise, interview with author.
15. Ibid.
16. Mandel interview.
17. Alice Marble with Dale Leatherman, *Courting Danger* (New York: St. Martin's Press, 1991), 230.
18. *Los Angeles Times*, April 4, 1962.
19. David Levy, interview with author.
20. Pollack interview.
21. Ibid.
22. Rod Serling, *New Stories from the Twilight Zone* (New York: Bantam, 1962).
23. Carol Burnett, interview with author.
24. Ibid.
25. *TV Guide*, May 7, 1972.
26. *TV Guide*, April 21, 1962.
27. Zicree, 227.
28. Ibid., 229.
29. Ibid., 225.
30. Houghton interview.
31. Ibid.
32. *Dayton Daily News*, October 12, 1961.

CHAPTER THIRTEEN

1. *Los Angeles Times*, March 6, 1962.
2. CBS press release, October 1962.
3. *Cincinnati Enquirer*, December 2, 1962.
4. From the unpublished diary of Pearl Bentel, used with permission of Wendy Jeanne Murray Zoba.
5. *Dayton Daily News*, October 12, 1961.
6. *New York Journal-American*, October 18, 1962.
7. Broadcast of WBNS *Ten O'Clock Theater*, Columbus, Ohio, 1962.

8. *New York Times*, October 17, 1962.
9. *Los Angeles Times*, March 6, 1962.
10. *New York Times*, February 20, 1964.
11. Ibid.
12. Hartung interview.
13. Undated clipping, circa October 1964.
14. Zicree, 340.
15. Landau interview.
16. Houghton interview.
17. Malvin Wald, interview with author.
18. *Seventeen*, September 1966.
19. Film script, "Let Us Continue." United States Information Agency, Washington, D.C. 1964.
20. *Binghamton Press*, December 21, 1963.
21. Broadcast of "Slow Fade to Black," *Bob Hope Presents the Chrysler Theater*, March 27, 1964, NBC.
22. *Binghamton Press*, December 21, 1963.
23. Jeff Rovin, *TV Babylon* (New York: New American Library, 1984), 190.
24. *Winston-Salem Gazette*, April 2, 1964.

CHAPTER FOURTEEN

1. Farber interview with Berg.
2. Landau interview.
3. *New York Times*, November 11, 1964.
4. Walter Cronkite, interview with author.
5. Broadcast of 1965 Emmy Awards, September 12, 1965, ABC.
6. Mark Olshaker, interview with author.
7. *Frontier*, April 1982.
8. *New York Times*, November 2, 1964.
9. Pollack interview.
10. *New York Times*, July 28, 1966.
11. Reisman interview.
12. Wynant interview.
13. Pollack interview.
14. Ibid.
15. Kulik interview.
16. William Self interview.

17. Ibid.
18. *Life*, November 12, 1965.
19. *Philadelphia Bulletin*, September 12, 1965.
20. Dann interview.
21. Zicree, 433.
22. NBC press release, January 1968.
23. *New York Times*, September 13, 1968.
24. *Los Angeles Times*, March 27, 1969.
25. Kiley interview.
26. *Los Angeles Times*, June 25, 1967.
27. Ibid.
28. *Pipe Dream Features*, November 22, 1985.
29. *Washington Post*, June 30, 1968.
30. Foote, Cone, and Belding copy for television commercial.
31. Wise interview.
32. Buzz Berger, interview with author.

CHAPTER FIFTEEN

1. Stephen Farber, and Marc Green, *Outrageous Conduct: Art, Ego, and the Twilight Zone Case* (New York: William Morrow, 1989), 63.
2. Zicree, 434.
3. Olshaker interview.
4. Ibid.
5. Ibid.
6. Reisman interview.
7. *Ithaca Journal*, June 30, 1975.
8. Dr. Ed Hart, interview with author.
9. Goodman interview.
10. Benjamin Krepack, interview with author.
11. Ibid.
12. Craig Curtner, letter to author, June 5, 1990.
13. *Millimeter*, November 1975.
14. Berger interview.
15. *New Times*, September 1975.
16. Krepack interview.
17. *TV Guide*, June 3, 1972.
18. *Millimeter*, November 1975.

19. George Grunbok, interview with author.
20. Curtner letter.
21. Curtner interview.
22. Delbert Mann interview.
23. *Ithaca Journal*, June 30, 1975.
24. *New York World Telegram*, June 29, 1975.

EPILOGUE

1. Schumer, 161.
2. *Variety*, July 1, 1975.
3. Johnson interview.
4. Marc Scott Zicree, interview with author.
5. Stephen King, *Danse Macabre* (New York: Everest House, 1981), 280.

BIBLIOGRAPHY

ARCHIVES, VIDEOTAPES
AND MANUSCRIPTS

Fortunately, there is no dearth of Serling primary materials. The first—and longest—stop for any Serling scholar must of necessity be the State Historical Society of the University of Wisconsin's Madison campus, which has over eighty boxes of primary Serling material, including correspondence, produced and unproduced scripts and story ideas, and audiotapes.

The Museum of Television and Radio (formerly the Museum of Broadcasting) in New York contains a great deal of Serling's work on videotape, including rarely seen appearances on various talk shows. The museum's library facilities also provide much videography information.

The UCLA Research Library Department of Special Collections has thirty boxes of Serling's correspondence and work, much of it from the final ten years of his life. The Antiochiana Collection, located at the Antioch College Library, has a complete clippings collection as well as all of Serling's published works and crucial material on the history of Antioch itself. Finally, the Rod Serling Memorial Foundation, located in Binghamton, has extensive archives with a large collection of memorabilia, tapes, and photographs, which are available with the permission of the foundation.

BOOKS AND OTHER BACKGROUND MATERIAL

Arlen, Michael J. *The View from Highway One*. New York: Ballantine Books, 1976.

———. *The Camera Age: Essays on Television*. New York: Penguin Books, 1981.

Averson, Richard, and David Manning White, eds. *Electronic Drama: Television Plays of the 1960s*. Boston: Beacon Press, 1971.

Bailey, Charles W. III, and Fletcher Knebel. *Seven Days in May*. New York: Bantam Books, 1963.

Balanchine, George, Eugene Burdick, et al. *The Eighth Art*. New York: Holt, Rinehart, and Winston, 1962.

Bannerman, R. Leroy. *Norman Corwin and Radio: The Golden Years*. Birmingham: University of Alabama Press, 1986.

Barnouw, Erik. *The Television Writer*. New York: Hill and Wang, 1962.

———. *The History of Broadcasting in the United States. Volume One: A Tower in Babel*. New York: Oxford University Press, 1966.

———. *Volume Two: The Golden Web*. New York: Oxford University Press, 1968.

———. *Volume Three: The Image Empire*. New York: Oxford University Press, 1970.

———. *The Sponsor: Notes on a Modern Potentate*. New York: Oxford University Press, 1978.

Baughman, James L. *Television's Guardians: The FCC and the Politics of Programming, 1958–1967*. Knoxville: University of Tennessee Press, 1985.

Besen, Stanley M., et al. *Misregulating Television: Network Dominance and the FCC*. Chicago: University of Chicago Press, 1984.

Blair, Clay Jr. *MacArthur*. New York: Pocket Books, 1977.

———. *Ridgway's Paratroopers: The American Airborne in World War II*. Garden City, NY: Dial, 1985.

Boddy, William. "From the Golden Age to the Vast Wasteland: Television in the Fifties." Ph.D. diss., New York University, 1988.

Boroff, David, Jack Behar, et al. *TV as Art*. Chicago: National Council of Teachers of English, 1966.

Bibliography

Brenman, Gibson. *Clifford Odets, American Playwright: The Years from 1906 to 1940*. New York: Atheneum, 1982.

Brooks, Tim, and Earle Marsh. *The Complete Directory to Prime Time Network Shows: 1946–Present*. New York: Ballantine Books, 1981.

Brown, Les. *Television: The Business Behind the Box*. New York: Harvest, 1977.

Burgett, Donald R. *Curahee! Curahee! Curahee!* New York: Houghton, Mifflin, 1967.

Castleman, Harry, and Walter Podrazik. *Watching TV: Four Decades of American Television*. New York: McGraw-Hill, 1982.

Chayefsky, Paddy. *Television Plays*. New York: Simon and Schuster, 1955.

Clurman, Harold, ed. *Famous American Plays of the 1930s*. New York: Laurel Press, 1959.

Cook, Philip S., Douglas Gomery, and Lawrence W. Lichty. *American Media: The Wilson Quarterly Reader*. Washington, D.C.: The Wilson Center Press, 1989.

Corwin, Norman. *Thirteen by Corwin*. New York: Henry Holt, 1942.

Crosby, John. *Out of the Blue*. New York: Simon and Schuster, 1952.

Dardis, Tom. *Some Time in the Sun*. New York: Scribner's, 1976.

Denny, Reuel, Nathan Glazer, and David Riesman. *The Lonely Crowd: A Study of the Changing American Character*. New York: Doubleday, 1953.

Department of the Army, Office of the Chief of Military History. *The War in the Pacific*. Washington, D.C.: U.S. Government Printing Office, 1952.

Devlin, Gerard M. *Paratrooper!* New York: St. Martin's Press, 1979.

Downer, Alan S., ed. *American Drama and Its Critics*. Chicago: University of Chicago Press, 1965.

Engel, Joel. *Serling: The Dreams and Nightmares of Life in the Twilight Zone*. Chicago: Contemporary, 1989.

Ensign, Lynne Naylor, and Robyn Eileen Knapton. *The Complete Dictionary of Television and Film*. New York: Stein and Day, 1985.

Farber, Stephen, and Marc Green. *Outrageous Conduct: Art, Ego, and the Twilight Zone Case*. New York: William Morrow, 1988.

Fischer, Eric. *The Screen Arts*. New York: Sheed and Ward, 1969

Friedrich, Otto. *City of Nets: A Portrait of Hollywood in the 1940s*. New York: Perennial Press, 1987.

Gitlin, Todd. *Inside Prime Time*. New York: Pantheon, 1985.

————, ed. *Watching Television*. New York: Pantheon, 1986.

Goldman, Eric F. *The Crucial Decade and After: America, 1945–1960*. New York: Vintage, 1960.

Gordon, Patricia Neale, and Ned E. Hoopes. *Great Television Plays, Volume Two*. New York: Dell, 1975.

Green, Gerald. *The Last Angry Man*. New York: Scribner's, 1959.

Greene, Robert S. *Television Writing*. New York: Harper, 1952.

Halberstam, David. *The Powers That Be*. New York: Knopf, 1979.

Harris, Jay S. *TV Guide: The First 25 Years*. New York: New American Library, 1966.

Hawes, William. *American Television Drama: The Experimental Years*. Birmingham: University of Alabama Press, 1986.

Hewes, Henry. *Famous American Plays of the 1940s*. New York: Dell, 1964.

Houghton, Norris. *Seeds of Modern Drama*. New York: Dell, 1972.

Kaplan, E. Ann, ed. *Regarding Television: Critical Approaches—an Anthology*. Frederick, MD: American Film Institute/University Publications of America, 1983.

Kaufman, William I., ed. *The Best Television Plays, 1950–1951*. New York: Hasting House, 1952.

————. *The Best Television Plays, Volume Two*. New York: Merlin Press, 1952.

————. *The Best Television Plays, Volume Three*. New York: Merlin Press, 1954.

————. *How to Write and Direct for Television*. New York: Hasting House, 1955.

————. *The Best Television Plays of 1957*. New York: Harcourt Brace, 1957.

Kaufman, William I., and Robert S. Colodzin. *Your Career in Television*. New York: Merlin Press, 1950.

King, Stephen. *Danse Macabre*. New York: Everest House, 1979.

Kittross, John M., and Christopher H. Sterling. *Stay Tuned: A Concise History of Broadcasting*. Belmont, CA: Wadsworth, 1978.

Kiwanis Club of Binghamton. "A Picture Postcard History of New York's Broome County." Vestal, NY: Vestal Press, 1985.

Know Your Town: Yellow Springs, Ohio. Yellow Springs, OH: League of Women Voters, 1962.

Lyons, Eugene. *David Sarnoff.* New York: Harper and Row, 1966.

Lomask, Milton. *The Biographer's Craft.* New York: Perennial, 1986.

MacGowan, Kenneth. *Famous American Plays of the 1920s.* New York: Dell, 1959.

Mannes, Marya, ed. *The Relation of the Writer to Television.* Santa Barbara, CA: Center for the Study of Democratic Institutions, 1960.

Marill, Alvin H. *Movies Made for Television.* New York: Da Capo Press, 1980.

McNeil, Alex. *Total Television: A Comprehensive Guide to Programming from 1948 to 1980.* New York: Penguin, 1980.

Meyers, Jeffrey. *Hemingway: A Biography.* New York: Perennial, 1985.

Michael, Paul, and James Robert Parish. *The Emmy Awards: A Pictorial History.* New York: Crown, 1970.

Michael, Paul, ed. *The American Movies Reference Book: The Sound Era.* Englewood Cliffs, NJ: Prentice-Hall, 1970.

Minow, Newton. *Equal Time.* New York: Atheneum, 1964.

Monaco, James. *American Film Now: The People, the Power, the Money, the Movies.* New York: New American Library, 1984.

Mosel, Tad. *Other People's Houses.* New York: Simon and Schuster, 1956.

Museum of Broadcasting. *Rod Serling: Dimensions of Imagination.* New York: Museum of Broadcasting, 1984.

———. *Produced by . . . Herb Brodkin.* New York: Museum of Broadcasting, 1985.

Nash, Constance, and Virginia Oakey. *The Television Writer's Handbook.* New York: Barnes and Noble, 1978.

Newcomb, Horace, ed. *Television: The Critical View.* New York: Oxford University Press, 1987.

Norback, Craig T. and Peter G. *TV Guide Almanac.* New York: Ballantine Books, 1980.

O'Connor, John E. *American History/American Television: Interpreting the Video Past.* New York: Frederick Ungar, 1983.

O'Neill, William L. O. *American High, The Years of Confidence: 1945–1960.* New York: Free Press, 1986.

Opotowsky, Stan. *TV: The Big Picture.* New York: Dutton, 1961.

Osborne, John. *Look Back in Anger.* London: Faber & Faber, 1958.

Paper, Lewis J. *Empire: William Paley and the Making of CBS.* New York: St. Martin's Press, 1987.

Persico, Joseph E. *Edward R. Murrow: An American Original*. New York: McGraw-Hill, 1988.

Powdermaker, Hortense. *Hollywood: The Dream Factory*. 1950.

Rathbone, A. D. IV. *He's in the Paratroops Now!* New York: Robert M. McBride and Company, 1942.

Reach, James. *Patterns*, adapted from the television play by Rod Serling. New York: Samuel French, 1959.

Read, William H. *America's Mass Media Merchants*. Baltimore: Johns Hopkins University Press, 1976.

Rose, Reginald. *Six Television Plays*. New York: Simon and Schuster, 1956.

Rovin, Jeff. *TV Babylon*. New York: Signet, 1984.

Rudolph, Frederick. *The American College and University: A History*. New York: Vintage, 1962.

Schaffner, Franklin. *Worthington Miner*. Metuchen, NJ: Directors Guild of America Oral History/Scarecrow Press, 1985.

Schatz, Thomas. *The Genius of the System: Hollywood Filmmaking in the Studio Era*. New York: Pantheon, 1988.

Schulberg, Budd. *Writers in America: The Four Seasons of Success*. New York: Stein and Day, 1983.

Schumer, Arlen. *Visions from the Twilight Zone*. San Francisco: Chronicle Books, 1991.

Seldes, Gilbert. *The Great Audience*. New York: Viking Press, 1950.

———. *Writing for Television*. New York: Doubleday, 1952.

———. *The Public Arts*. New York: Simon and Schuster, 1956.

———. *The Seven Lively Arts*. New York: A. B. Barnes, 1962.

Serling, Rod. *Patterns: Four Television Plays with the Author's Personal Commentaries*. New York: Simon and Schuster, 1955.

———. *Stories from the Twilight Zone*. New York: Bantam, 1960.

———. *More Stories from the Twilight Zone*. New York: Bantam, 1961.

———. *New Stories from the Twilight Zone*. New York: Bantam, 1962.

———. *From the Twilight Zone* (Selection). New York: Doubleday, 1962.

———. *The Season to Be Wary*. New York: Random House, 1969.

———. *Rod Serling's Night Gallery*. New York: Bantam, 1971.

———. *Rod Serling's Night Gallery 2*. New York: Bantam, 1972.

Shale, Richard, ed. *Academy Awards*. New York: Frederick Ungar, 1978.

Siepmann, Charles A. *Radio's Second Chance*. Boston: Little, Brown, 1946.

———. *Radio, Television, and Society*. New York: Oxford University Press, 1950.

Simonson, Solomon. *Crisis in Television*. New York: Living Books, 1966.

Sklar, Robert. *Prime-Time America: Life on and Behind the Television Screen*. New York: Oxford University Press, 1980.

Smith, Sally Bedell. *In All His Glory: The Life of William S. Paley—the Legendary Tycoon and His Brilliant Circle*. New York: Simon and Schuster, 1991.

Sperber, A. M. *Murrow: His Life and Times*. New York: Freundlich Books, 1986.

Spoto, Donald. *The Dark Side of Genius: The Life of Alfred Hitchcock*. New York: Ballantine Books, 1983.

Stuart, Frederick. *The Effects of Television on the Motion-Picture and Radio Industries*. New York: Arno Press, 1979.

Swanberg, W. A. *Citizen Hearst*. New York: Ballantine, 1971.

Tuchman, Barbara. *Practicing History: Selected Essays*. New York: Ballantine, 1981.

Verna, Tony. *Live TV: An Inside Look at Directing and Producing*. Boston: Focal Press, 1987.

Whyte, William Foote. *Street Corner Society*. Chicago: University of Chicago Press, 1955.

Wicking, Christopher, and Vahimagi, Tise. *The American Vein: Directors and Directions in Television*. New York: E. P. Dutton, 1979.

Wilson, Sloan. *The Man in the Gray Flannel Suit*. New York: Simon and Schuster, 1955.

Zicree, Marc Scott. *The Twilight Zone Companion*. New York: Bantam, 1982.

Zinsser, William, ed. *Extraordinary Lives: The Art and Craft of American Biography*. New York: American Heritage, 1986.

INDEX

Index

Index